Praise for *Obstetrics for*

Rachel Macfarlane's book is exactly what we all need right now. The perfect antidote to COVID-19 gloom, it's a stirring call to arms in the fight against education inequality. Macfarlane counters the defeatist acceptance that the education system will inevitably fail some students and, through a series of case studies, shows how it is possible to ensure that *every* student receives a great education. Accessible, practical and inspiring, *Obstetrics for Schools* is a great read for anyone who cares about education.

Lucy Heller, Chief Executive, ARK

I love this book! If we can improve the process of childbirth so dramatically, we must apply similar fail-safes to the next 18 years of every young person's life, especially their time at school. In *Obstetrics for Schools* Rachel Macfarlane brings her formidable intellect and experience as a successful head teacher to show us how a certain kind of expansive education can solve the postcode lottery of our birth. The book is packed full of practical strategies to help you decide what will work for you and your learners. Anyone working in a school will want to have this terrific guidebook beside them.

Bill Lucas, educational reformer, researcher and award-winning author

This book is rare in providing both a compelling vision for education and a range of practical ideas to help achieve it. It is also perfectly timed for the post-COVID world, showing both the humanity we need to readjust and the practical wisdom we need to rethink.

Driven by a passion for ensuring the most disadvantaged succeed in life, Rachel Macfarlane uses her experience as a great head teacher to show how each of the barriers standing in the way of young people can be dismantled. Drawing on excellent practice from her own schools and those she has worked with, she provides fresh insights into both leadership and classroom practice. She transcends the artificial divisions between traditionalists and progressives, instead focusing on the importance of young people achieving great results and also becoming powerful lifelong learners.

If you are looking for a fresh take on social mobility, and if you believe that a better society comes from unlocking the potential of each and every child, then *Obstetrics for Schools* will give you inspiration and hope. The work is never easy, but the rewards, as Macfarlane shows, are immense. This elegantly written book will give renewed impetus to those seeking a more expansive vision for education.

Peter Hyman, Co-Director, Big Education, and co-founder
and first head teacher of School 21

In this timely book, Rachel Macfarlane poses a blunt question: why do we tolerate inequality in education? Drawing on a wide range of case studies across every phase of education, Macfarlane shows how a can-do spirit of optimism, combined with the careful application of research findings, can help schools to improve every child's life chances.

Whilst *Obstetrics for Schools* is a visionary book, it is also firmly grounded in reality. In particular, Macfarlane draws substantially on her own track record as an exceptional head teacher and system leader. The many case studies show how ideals can be put into action in a wide range of different schools and contexts, and they also act as a testament to Macfarlane's commitment to collaborative school improvement.

If you think it's intolerable that a child's success in school is largely predicted by how well off their parents are, then you must read this book. It didn't just heat up my outrage; it gave me practical examples of how I might become a better school leader, too. It also gave me courage.

Dr Julian Grenier, Head Teacher, Sheringham Nursery School and Children's Centre, Director, East London Research School

Obstetrics for Schools takes a bleak account of poverty, disadvantage and underachievement and – using real-life case studies and data – shows that it doesn't have to be like this. If ever there were a time to recalibrate our education system around equity, it's now. If ever there were a book to help us to do it, it's this one.

Geoff Barton, General Secretary, Association of School and College Leaders

Written with passion, care and a deep understanding of the issues, *Obstetrics for Schools* gets under the skin of what schools and school leaders can do to address inequity in education. Full of practical ideas, down-to-earth strategies and authentic case studies, it doesn't just point the way to eliminating failure and combatting disadvantage amongst young people – it shows us the way too. Macfarlane also offers a refreshing departure from so much academic writing that too often considers and analyses the problems but leaves us floundering for practical solutions.

Obstetrics for Schools is a triumph, and so timely too. I love it and will be recommending it everywhere I go.

Steve Munby, Visiting Professor, Centre for Educational Leadership, UCL

Obstetrics for Schools is a fantastic and important contribution to the growing evidence and research base about the challenges that leaders in the education sector face. Rachel Macfarlane rightly acknowledges that this will be our main focus in the years ahead – not simply because of the post-pandemic context but because it is morally and strategically the right thing to do. Furthermore, she draws upon her own leadership experience, as well as that of others, to consider carefully the priorities we should be seeking to address.

This book gets to the heart of what is right, and morally just. If we want our young people to grow into adulthood as successful learners, ready to move to the next stage of their journey, we need to address the core issues today. We can currently see an avalanche of opinion pieces and publications on the imperative of doing more for disadvantaged children – but if you only have time to explore a few thoughtful publications, make this book one of them.

Sir David Carter, Executive Director of System Leadership, Ambition Institute

Obstetrics for Schools is a wonderful book. Through sharing vignettes and reflections from her own leadership experience, Rachel Macfarlane powerfully illustrates that high expectations for all is the most essential mindset for teachers and school leaders. The book also provides practical grounded examples throughout, with prompt questions designed to challenge and encourage the reader, and presents stories about the profound impact of seemingly small positive actions which illustrate the power that schools have either to diminish or to enable. There were many times as I was reading the book when I wanted to punch the air and exclaim 'Yes!' – and so many occasions when the author's experiences resonated with my own as a school leader.

I recommend *Obstetrics for Schools* to all teachers, school leaders and governors who are committed to truly making a difference within their community.

Dame Alison Peacock, Chief Executive, Chartered College of Teaching

Obstetrics for Schools is a powerful call to arms to eradicate inequity in the education system. Tackling disadvantage is a hugely complex and challenging task, but Rachel Macfarlane has confronted the brutal facts and communicates her faith that something can be done. Informed by evidence and grounded in the reality of schools, the book covers topics ranging from the importance of relationships with students and parental engagement to metacognition and the power of oracy. It is also packed with a wide range of exemplar case studies that bring the book alive, inspiring hope and belief in what is possible. If ever there were a book for our time, this is it: a powerful reminder of the life-changing difference the teaching profession can make.

Andy Buck, founder of Leadership Matters and creator of the BASIC coaching method

Obstetrics for Schools is firmly focused on the difference schools can make, and how best to support children from disadvantaged backgrounds to achieve their potential. Whilst recognising the significant broader challenges contributing to the socio-economic gap for attainment, Rachel Macfarlane draws on her deep professional experience as a teacher and leader in education to show how schools can and do make a difference in raising the attainment and supporting the life chances of disadvantaged pupils. Teachers and school leaders will find a range of practical strategies and case studies exemplifying successful practices for narrowing the gap. Moreover, they will be galvanised by Macfarlane's encouragement and determination that infuse the book, and by the inspiring examples of positive change.

Becky Francis, Chief Executive, the Education Endowment Foundation

Every school leader and teacher reading *Obstetrics for Schools* will find a wealth of strategies and case studies illustrating the various ways by which the education and life chances of disadvantaged learners can be improved. Rachel Macfarlane draws on her own successful school leadership experience and provides a wide range of practical examples and research findings to construct a powerful case that every learner, however disadvantaged, can succeed. This book will make a real difference in the schools where its lessons are applied.

Sir John Dunford, author of *The School Leadership Journey*
and former National Pupil Premium Champion

It is a disgrace that we can accept that a third of our children will fail at school. Such a rate of attrition, and such inequity, is no longer tolerated in childbirth, and it should not be tolerated in schools. Medicine has developed robust procedures to make sure this doesn't happen – but where are the equivalents in education? Thankfully, they are right here, in Rachel Macfarlane's brilliant *Obstetrics for Schools*. Wise, passionate, compassionate and, above all, practical, this book is an intimate guide to reducing the poverty gap in education. Every head teacher, administrator and minister of education should read it and be judged on their responses to it. If this doesn't happen, it will only show that we as a society still don't really care, and that intellectual and ethical torpor still rule the roost.

Guy Claxton, author of *The Learning Power Approach:
Teaching Learners to Teach Themselves*

I love this book. It is pragmatic, comprehensive, intelligent, challenging and evidence informed. It is also rooted in the experiences of a school and system leader with a brilliant track record. Any opportunity to work with Rachel Macfarlane is a rich, enlightening and positive experience, and her knowledge, expertise and values are interweaved throughout *Obstetrics for Schools* – from building relationships with families to the importance of getting it right with classroom interactions.

The book makes uncomfortable reading at times, and rightly so. In its current state, our education system practically guarantees that a third of our pupils leave school without qualifications in English and maths. To counter this, Macfarlane provides a framework that sets out to ensure that all pupils can achieve – including those that experience the diving bell of disadvantage. It is a book for the moment. I would argue that we will never have a better chance than now to adopt the pupil-led approach to addressing underachievement advocated by Macfarlane. The provision-led approach driven by labels or accountability measures has failed too many.

Obstetrics for Schools is a brilliant book for support staff, pastoral teams, teachers, leaders, governors, system leaders and policy makers.

Marc Rowland, Pupil Premium and Vulnerable Learners Adviser,
Unity Schools Partnership

Rachel Macfarlane

Obstetrics for Schools

A guide to eliminating failure and ensuring the safe delivery of all learners

Crown House Publishing Limited
www.crownhouse.co.uk

First published by
Crown House Publishing Limited
Crown Buildings, Bancyfelin, Carmarthen, Wales, SA33 5ND, UK
www.crownhouse.co.uk

and

Crown House Publishing Company LLC
PO Box 2223, Williston, VT 05495, USA
www.crownhousepublishing.com

Cover illustration © David Bull, 2021

First published 2021.

Quotes from Ofsted and Department for Education documents used in this publication have been approved under an Open Government Licence. Please see http://www.nationalarchives.gov.uk/doc/open-government-licence/version/3.

Page 14, figure © Dan Nicholls, 2020. From 'Urgent action required – addressing disadvantage', *Dan Nicholls* [blog] (5 April) Available at: https://dannicholls1.wordpress.com/2020/04/05/urgent-action-required-addressing-disadvantage. Page 38, extract © Teacher Tapp, 2020. From questions posed on the Teacher Tap app. Available at: https://teachertapp.co.uk. Page 82, extract © Becky Allen, 2020. From 'Parental load theory', *Becky Allen: Musings on Education Policy* [blog] (29 April). Available at: https://rebeccaallen.co.uk/2020/04/29/parental-load-theory. Page 118, extract © Guy Claxton, 2020. From 'Knowledge and skills: how you can achieve both in your school', *SecEd* (30 June). Available at: https://www.sec-ed.co.uk/best-practice/knowledge-and-skills-how-you-can-achieve-both-in-your-school-guy-claxton-education. Page 129, extract © Peter Hyman, 2020. From 'Helping every child find their voice'. In. R. Blatchford (ed.), *The Forgotten Third: Do a Third Have to Fail for Two Thirds to Pass?* (Woodbridge: John Catt Educational), pp. 115–122. Page 183, extract © Julian Grenier, 2020. From 'What makes the biggest difference to a child's success in early learning?' *The Education Exchange*. Available at: https://theeducation.exchange/what-makes-the-biggest-difference-to-a-childs-success-in-early-learning/. Page 226, figure © Jonathan Sharples, Bianca Albers, Stephen Fraser and Stuart Kime, 2018. From *Putting Evidence to Work: A School's Guide to Implementation – Guidance Report.* Available at: https://educationendowmentfoundation.org.uk/public/files/Publications/Implementation/EEF_Implementation_Guidance_Report_2019.pdf reproduced with permission.

British Library Cataloguing-in-Publication Data

A catalogue entry for this book is available from the British Library.

Print ISBN 978-178583540-7
Mobi ISBN 978-178583564-3
ePub ISBN 978-178583565-0
ePDF ISBN 978-178583566-7

LCCN 2021933039

Printed and bound in the UK by
TJ Books, Padstow, Cornwall

For my parents: my role models.

Foreword

'A guide to eliminating failure and ensuring the safe delivery of all learners' runs the beguiling subtitle of this compelling book. Let's set this proper ambition for *all learners*, firstly, in an international context and, secondly, within a UK historical perspective.

International context

The Organisation for Economic Co-operation and Development (OECD) has run its Programme for International Student Assessment (PISA) tests since 2000. They measure the ability of 15-year-olds to apply their skills and knowledge to real-life problem solving in reading, maths and science. The rankings are based on samples of pupils in each country, with about 600,000 pupils having taken this most recent round of tests (Schleicher 2019). In the latest league table – based on results for the tests taken in 2018 – China, Singapore, Macau and Hong Kong continue to lead maths and reading rankings. In science the same countries dominate, with Estonia rising to join the top table. Canada and Finland are up there too, as they have been for a number of years.

As to the UK, it has climbed the rankings since the 2015 tests. It has gone from:

- 22nd in reading to 14th.
- 15th in science to 14th.
- 27th in maths to 18th. (Reported in Coughlan 2019)

These UK figures are based on a sample of about 14,000 pupils in 460 schools. If government and opposition politicians were commenting on these results, claims and counterclaims would doubtless be made for the impact of phonics and mastery maths, academies and increased funding in classrooms. A more sober analysis lies with Andreas Schleicher, the OECD's education director, who said there were 'positive signals' from the UK's results which showed 'modest improvements'. He went on to say that at the current rate of progress it would take a 'very long time' for the UK to catch up with the highest achieving countries (quoted in Coughlan 2019).

So what is the UK not doing that the 'top table' are? I recently met a group of undergraduates who are studying education at the University of Reading. Many come from the countries which feature at the top of the PISA league. They argue strongly that culture trumps systems, that the esteem in which teachers are held in their societies is *the* determining factor alongside the value placed on education by parents. Tutoring outside school also plays a part, they suggested. These undergraduates spoke eloquently about the expectations which *all* teachers have that all children will succeed.

Dig a little deeper into how the 'top table' countries organise things, and examinations at age 16 are a feature of the past, considering that the vast majority of young people are in education or training until the age of at least 18. Not to mention trusting teachers to assess their own students, externally verified. Ask folk in Canada or Finland about the balance between school accountability and school support and they find the Ofsted model an alien force.

The UK will not feature in the top PISA ranks in the coming decades unless there is a seismic shift in how our society values education and teachers – and in how the profession works with government to challenge the accepted orthodoxy that failure for a third is baked into our system. The Chinese, Japanese, French, Indian and Libyan undergraduates I spoke to cannot believe we do this. Why would you? Why do we?

UK perspective

In 1963, John Newsom and his colleagues presented to the government of the time a beautifully crafted, 300-page report entitled *Half Our Future* (Central Advisory Council for Education 1963). The landmark report painted a picture of success and positive self-esteem for 50 per cent of the nation's 15-year-olds. It went on to identify that the other 50 per cent languished with an unsuitable curriculum resulting in poor or no qualifications. The report's various recommendations led to the raising of the school leaving age in 1973. Six decades on and that 50 per cent identified by John Newsom has become *the forgotten third*. When we talk about social justice and 'levelling up', it is these young people who most need our attention.

In 2019 I chaired an independent commission set up by the Association of School and College Leaders (ASCL).[1] Every August in this country we celebrate as a time-honoured ritual the achievements of our higher attaining students. Local newspapers

---

1   For more information, see our report (Association of School and College Leaders 2019).

picture them jumping for joy. But there's another story. Every year there are many, many thousands of 16-year-olds who fall short of a grade 4 pass in English and maths – and this after 12 years of compulsory schooling. Their chances of progression in further study, future careers and, ultimately, in life are diminished.

What is perhaps not widely understood is that this rate of attrition, this forgotten third, happens year in and year out because it is built into our exam system. In the poignant words of one student: 'it seems a third of us have to fail for two-thirds to pass'.

Grimly surreal as it may seem to the uninitiated, this level of collateral damage is an accepted part of the process for determining the distribution of GCSE grades. In other words, we judge the success of our education system by the number of young people who *don't* gain that pass. Few other high-performing jurisdictions would think that sensible or morally acceptable.

The long tail of underachievement casts a shadow over the UK education system today just as it did in 1963. It is not a necessity but a political choice. System change is needed – and quickly. Indeed, examination reform may come – and sooner than we imagine in an era of disruption in which the extraordinary becomes the common-place, at a faster and faster rate.

Obstetrics for Schools is rooted in another historical perspective, namely that the infant mortality accepted in the Victorian era has been almost eliminated today. Why, the author asks, can the same not be true in education? Why can't *all learners* succeed? In the same way that today's physicians have harnessed the best science and their considerable skills to bring forth safely just about every newborn, why can't this generation of skilled teachers – steeped as they are in strong research as never before – deliver comparably good educational achievements for children and young people?

Rachel Macfarlane's radical, evidence-led narrative contests that with the highest of expectations – and different ways of doing – the current school system *can* deliver top outcomes for almost all students. She may be right. History is against her. The future may be with her.

Roy Blatchford, CBE

Acknowledgements

I would like to thank all the inspirational educators and students with whom and from whom I have learnt in the last five decades. Particular thanks must go to my colleagues at Walthamstow School for Girls, Isaac Newton Academy and Herts for Learning, as well as to all others whose stories feature in this book.

I am grateful to Jo Spencer and Mireille MacRaild for their most helpful feedback on sections of the text and to Roy Blatchford for his compelling foreword.

Thank you to Louise Penny and all at Crown House Publishing for their support, high standards and professionalism.

Thank you to David Swain for his patience during the writing of this book.

But, most importantly, a huge thank you to Eric Macfarlane, whose encouragement, wisdom and candid feedback on each chapter was invaluable and appreciated more than I can express.

Contents

Introduction

Imagine if all children were on an equal playing field. Imagine children waking up believing that their dreams could come true. Imagine what that belief could do for the future of this country.

Marcus Rashford, MBE[1]

This book is about righting wrongs. It takes a look at the deficiencies in learners' outcomes in the UK education system and at the inequity of education provision. The former is evidenced by the shocking percentages of learners who fail to leave school with grades commensurate with adequate acquisition of literacy and numeracy skills, and the latter by the significant over-representation of disadvantaged learners in the third of children who 'fail' at school. This book examines a number of factors that contribute to the current state of affairs. Each chapter focuses on a key potential barrier and offers various strategies related to that aspect of provision, aimed at addressing the educational 'fatality rate' and ensuring success for all. The book is aimed at teachers and leaders in all phases, from early years to sixth form, and at those working in both mainstream and special education.

Many of the chapters contain case studies – glimpses into how particular schools are addressing a challenge and eliminating a barrier to success. The case studies are in the words of leaders at the schools featured. In a few places, I include case studies of specific learners. Here I have protected identities by changing names; however, the stories are completely true. The autobiographical stories I tell are as accurate as my memory allows, but in places I have changed the names of those involved for the same reason.

Each chapter contains some questions, and sometimes suggested activities, for the reader. I very much hope that these will be useful for the purpose of general reflection and application to your own setting and will not come across as patronising. If you don't like them, feel free to skip over them!

---

1   See https://twitter.com/marcusrashford/status/1328446896176844806?lang=en.

I often refer to practice that my colleagues and I introduced at my previous schools, and particularly at Isaac Newton Academy (INA), the all-through school I set up in 2011 and led until 2018. I also include some examples of INA tools as appendices at the end of the book. These are offered as ideas and illustrations; I am not suggesting that I have all the answers or that the schools that I led had totally cracked the problem of fatalities in the education system. My aim is not to tell you what to do or how to do it. It is important that each school feels accountable for its disadvantaged and vulnerable learners and devises and takes responsibility for its own actions. There are many different roads to success, and it is vital that schools adopt systems and practices that work for them, in their context and with their cohorts.

It might be helpful to clarify at the outset some points related to definitions and terminology. During this book I shall make references to 'low-income families', 'disadvantaged learners', 'children eligible for free school meals (FSM)' and 'those eligible for pupil premium (PP) funding'. At times I will use eligibility for PP funding as a measure of disadvantage, although it is, of course, an imperfect proxy. It is important to guard against an assumption that it is only those eligible for PP funding who experience economic poverty. Hobbs and Vignoles (2010) found that a large proportion of FSM-eligible children (between 50% and 75%) were not in the lowest-income households. This is partly because the very act of receiving means-tested benefits and tax credits, which entitle a child to FSM, raises the household income above that of the 'working poor'. As educators, we recognise that a proportion of families over and above those eligible for PP funding also experience economic hardship. Likewise, we must remember that financial constraints do not constitute the only form of poverty. Thomas Rogers (2016), writing in the *TES*, argued:

The problem is, I think, that the most significant 'poverty' in the UK today is emotional poverty, mind-set poverty, aspiration poverty, in essence; 'values poverty'.

We know that educational disadvantage can result from many more factors than economic hardship: a special educational need or disability (SEND), a first language other than English, a dysfunctional or fractured family life, being a young carer, or exposure to abuse or neglect. When referring to educational disadvantage, I am taking a wide definition of the causes, and the strategies I recommend in this book to overcome disadvantage and ensure high attainment are effective for learners with a wide range of needs and none.

I also write a lot about parents. When I refer to 'parents', it is in the knowledge that many learners live with carers rather than parents – so, in effect, I mean parents, carers and other responsible adults.

At this point, I should also clarify an important point about the purpose of education and the role of examinations. In this book, I shall focus a lot on strategies to assist all learners in achieving examination success. You might assume from this that I see the role of educators as being to equip learners with the knowledge necessary to succeed in public exams, but that is only partially correct. There is far more to a good education.

If asked to define what I see as the purpose of education, I would say that it is about preparing learners in a holistic way to be ready to lead rich, rewarding and fulfilling lives as thoroughly good people: to thrive in modern society, to enjoy loving relationships, to contribute in a positive and tangible way to the local or wider community, to be happy and healthy, and to identify and enjoy pursuits in which they are 'in their element' – to coin the phrase used by the late, great Ken Robinson in *The Element* (2008). So a good education is about developing learners' character and influencing their behaviour every bit as much as it is about teaching knowledge and skills for exam success. As we will explore in Chapter 6, it is about building learning power, so that learners are self-regulating and autonomous and will continue to learn for life. Great educators care about their legacy beyond results day, just as medical professionals judge infant mortality rates not just on survival at the birth itself but on the baby thriving into their early years and beyond.

However, none of this detracts from the fact that, in our current society, examination success and assessment systems are inextricably linked to enjoying the kind of life that I have just described. There are many who feel (and I count myself as one amongst them) that our education system has not got the balance right between methods and types of assessment by which to determine whether learners have received a good education – that we do not measure all the learning that matters and that some of what we assess is of little practical use as preparation for leading a good life. Yet it is the system in which we operate, and it has a profound impact on life chances.

We could debate whether the Year 6 SATs and GCSE English and maths exams test the skills that are really essential to thrive at secondary school and in the wider world. Nonetheless, if we apply the 'what would I want for my own child?' test, I suspect that we would all wish for our daughters and sons to achieve the early years (EY) benchmark standard greater level of development (GLD), the Year 6 age-related expectations (ARE), a standard pass at GCSE, and so on, as a basic indicator of their preparedness for their next stage in life. Likewise, we would all want our children to have a genuine choice as to whether they progress on to university or higher education.

As Neil Harrison and Richard Waller (2019) point out, 'the unavoidable reality is that by far the strongest predictor for participation in higher education is attainment in school.' They assert that many working-class young people fail to progress to higher education not 'because they lack ambition, but because the accumulation of disadvantage throughout their childhood becomes embodied in their qualifications.' It is imperative that we eliminate our examination fatalities in order that we improve the life choices and chances of those left behind, who are disproportionately from disadvantaged groups even before they are made additionally vulnerable by their school record.

So what has motivated me and, perhaps more importantly, what qualifies me to write on this matter? In my 30 years as a teacher and school leader, I was always motivated by two overriding desires: firstly, to support students to get the best learning outcomes and be equipped with the skills to prepare them for life beyond school, and, secondly, to level the playing field and tackle the disadvantage gap through my role as an educator. Like most practitioners, as a history teacher and then head of department – long before the days of performance league tables and subject/class residuals in schools – I would pore over my classes' exam results, breaking down percentages, looking at value added, striving for my and my team's results to be the best in the school. In the 2000s and 2010s, when I was a head teacher, I always retained a teaching commitment and took the opportunity – when possible – to have at least one exam class each year so that I was held to account for supporting learners to achieve great outcomes, along with everyone else. And, like all head teachers, I would wait impatiently on results days to compare my school's outcomes by each measure against our school's previous best, against the scores of neighbouring competitors and, importantly, against those of top-performing schools nationally.

The scores achieved by the highest attaining students were always crucially important to me, as a class teacher, middle leader and a head. I have long believed that striving for academic excellence in a comprehensive setting is vital. I was proud that, in 2017, 32% of the GCSE grades at INA were 9–7 and that that was surpassed in 2018, when the figure was 35%. But equally important was supporting students who had historically been lower attainers to reach a level whereby they could safely graduate and progress to the next stage of their education, career and life: a C grade or, latterly, a 4/5 at GCSE, for example. At INA, with cohorts which were very much at the national average in terms of attainment on entry, and with a third of learners eligible for PP funding, we always aimed for 100% pass rates at GLD, phonics screenings, SATs and GCSEs, almost always setting targets of over 90% and believing them to be eminently achievable. Crucially, we strove to ensure that progress made and outcomes achieved by disadvantaged learners were as strong as their more advantaged peers'.

In my time at the school, we never quite hit a 100% pass rate in external assessments, but we got very near on occasions. In 2017, the GCSE results of the first exam cohort placed the school comfortably within the top 1% in the country for progress. We didn't achieve complete parity in the attainment and progress scores of PP and non-PP learners, but the gaps were very small and students eligible for PP funding significantly outperformed their PP peers nationally. In 2018, Ofsted (2018: 3) recognised that disadvantaged learners 'make exceptional progress across the curriculum' at the school. So, in my career as a teacher and leader, I didn't manage to reach the goal of 0% fatalities within the cohorts in my care, but my staff and I got close at times; close enough for me to believe that the dream could be a reality and to think that some of the strategies we adopted are worth sharing.

Many of the ideas offered in the following chapters, however, come from schools that I have not led or worked in. In my 16 years as a head, I was fortunate to collaborate with and learn from leaders of literally hundreds of other mainstream and special, nursery, primary, secondary and all-through schools. From 2009 to 2018 I led a project for the London Leadership Strategy called Going for Great (G4G). This involved working with cohorts of leaders from outstanding schools across the capital (117 schools in total) and supporting them in sharing great practice and writing about initiatives that had led to their high performance. The work culminated in nine volumes of great practice case studies.

In my current role, as a director of education services in Hertfordshire, I am privileged to see outstanding practice in a wide range of schools and settings across the county. In 2018 I set up a programme – called Great Expectations – which facilitates networking between leaders of participating schools to share great practice in terms of closing progress and attainment gaps and raising attainment for all. The aim of the programme is to bring leaders of some of the most successful schools in Hertfordshire – across all phases and sectors – together to:

- Explore the key features and qualities of schools that have a strong ethos and culture of high performance, the highest expectations of – and aspirations for – all and a no-excuses culture.
- Research strategies and review literature focused on schools that have effectively closed attainment and progress gaps between disadvantaged students and their more advantaged peers.
- Share exceptional practice and ensure that strong schools are contributing to system leadership in Hertfordshire.

Thus I continue to observe a range of strategies that work in reducing fatality rates – strategies that, if adopted consistently across the country, would radically reduce our national fatality rate and level the inequalities between the disadvantaged and their more advantaged peers. Many of these approaches are shared in this book.

Chapter 1

The problem laid bare

The best anti-poverty program is a world-class education.

Barack Obama[1]

We need to remember that societies are strong when they care for the weak. They are rich when they care for the poor. And they are invulnerable when they care for the vulnerable.

Rabbi Sacks[2]

Let's jump straight in and take a look at some sobering facts and statistics which illustrate the problem we face:

- 'By age five, children from low-income backgrounds are, on average, 15 months behind their better-off peers.' (Gadsby 2017: 12)

- 'Children from wealthier backgrounds are approximately 20 percentage points more likely to meet the expected standards at 11 than those from low-income families.' (Gadsby 2017: 14)

- In 2019, only 45% of disadvantaged pupils in England achieved passes at levels 9 to 4 in English and maths, compared with 72% of non-disadvantaged pupils. (Starkey-Midha 2020: 4)

- The disadvantage gap has now begun to widen across all three phases of education – the early years, primary school and secondary school. (Hutchinson et al. 2020: 11)

- 'The gap for the most persistently disadvantaged pupils, already twice the size of the gap for the least persistently poor pupils, has increased in every year but one since 2014.' (Hutchinson et al. 2020: 32)

1 See https://twitter.com/barackobama/status/8305989038?lang=en.
2 https://rabbisacks.org/the-politics-of-hope/.

- 'Since 2011, the gap between pupils from black and White British backgrounds has increased in the order of 60–70 per cent. Meanwhile, the gap for pupils who arrive late into the English state school system with English as an Additional Language (EAL) has widened by 11 per cent.' (Hutchinson et al. 2020: 32)

- For SEND pupils, progress in closing the gap for both school support and education, health and care plan (EHCP) pupils has slowed since 2015, 'and reversed for pupils with the greatest needs.' (Hutchinson et al. 2020: 32)

- 'By Year 13 (age 17), nearly one in three young people eligible for free school meals are not participating in education, compared to only one in seven not eligible.' (Gadsby 2017: 20)

- '24% of pupils eligible for free school meals attend higher education, compared to 42% of non-free school meal pupils.' (Gadsby 2017: 24)

- Low-income undergraduates are less likely to stay on a university course. 'Each year, one in 12 university freshers from a low-income background drops out, some 2,000 students in total.' (Gadsby 2017: 26)

- 'Students from higher income families earn around 25% more than those from low-income families. [...] three and a half years after graduation [...] privately educated graduates earn £4,500 more than their state school counterparts. Their salaries also increase more quickly.' (Gadsby 2017: 28)

- 'Without five good GCSEs, a young person loses out on an average of £100,000 in earnings over their lifetime.' (Starkey-Midha 2020: 3)

- 'Every graduate Prime Minister since 1945 has been an Oxford alumnus.' (Gadsby 2017: 34)

- The cost of poor social mobility to the UK economy per year by 2050 is estimated to be 14 billion. (Gadsby 2017: 10)

- 'If you're born poor, you will die on average 9 years earlier than others.' (Prime Minister's Office and May 2016)

These figures speak for themselves. They convey the moral imperative for educators to take action.

In summary, we know that, compared with 'other OECD countries, children in the UK are more likely to achieve along socio-economically predictable lines; well-to-do children tend to achieve higher outcomes than children raised in poverty' (Goodall 2017a: 4). Disadvantaged children are over-represented in the tail of low attainment in our schools. In July 2019, the annual report by the Education Policy Institute (EPI) warned that disadvantaged pupils finish school 18 months behind their more advantaged peers (Hutchinson et al. 2019: 10). A year later, the 2020 report announced the sobering news that the gap had expanded to 18.1 months, and 22.7 months for the persistently disadvantaged (those eligible for FSM for 80% or more of their school life) (Hutchinson et al. 2020: 35). Top-attainers in England perform at a similar standard to high-achievers in some of the most successful developed nations in the world, but what distinguishes the UK is a long tail of low attainment, highly correlated with family income and background.

So, as we have seen from the statistics quoted, young people from disadvantaged backgrounds are less likely to progress into higher education. They have lower average earnings, poorer health and a shorter life expectancy than their more affluent peers. The Social Mobility and Child Poverty Commission's State of the Nation report (2014: 64) highlighted that children from disadvantaged backgrounds are twice as likely to not be in education, employment or training (NEET) and at higher risk of ending up in poverty as adults.

Why the reference to obstetrics in this book's title?

You may well have been asking yourself this question. Well, it's because, although I have opened this book with some rather bleak statistics, if we look at the history of obstetrics and changes in infant mortality rates, we find a story of hope and some important lessons from which we, in education, can learn.

In 1800 the global child mortality rate was 43%. With a combination of the discovery of antiseptics, advances in surgery, vaccines against and cures for infectious diseases, improvements to maternity and infant care and better general health and diet, this had reduced to 22% by 1950. It dropped to just 4.5% by 2015 (Roser et al. 2013). In most parts of the world, the death of a baby during childbirth or as an infant is now a rare tragedy, rather than a commonplace feature of society. There are, of course, still significant variations around the world: infant mortality stands at 11% in Afghanistan at the time of writing, whereas it is just 0.4% in the UK.[3] However, the overall advance is both striking and uplifting.

Like infant mortality rates around the globe, educational outcomes vary considerably from region to region and even between schools in the same locality. In some settings in England, including many which are non-selective, almost all students reach

---

3   See https://worldpopulationreview.com/country-rankings/infant-mortality-rate-by-country.

the standards of literacy and numeracy required to gain a grade 4 or better at GCSE (or the equivalent), whilst in others the majority of students leave school without the level of maths and English qualification required for progression into higher education or gainful employment. This, of course, reduces their earning potential, their chances of enjoying a rich and rewarding career and life, and even their life expectancy.

This variation is unacceptable, as is the overall approximately 30% 'failure' rate. What is more, it is no more an inevitability, I suggest, than the high infant mortality rates witnessed at the start of the 19th century. Barring a few exceptions (for example, students with cognitive impairments and certain learning disabilities), all students educated in UK schools should be capable of attaining the level of skills and competence required to gain a grade 4 in English and maths by the age of 16 in our currently norm-referenced assessment system.

Our job as educators is to strive to create the best conditions for learning – an environment in which all students can, and almost every student does, succeed, safely delivered into the world as a healthy and resilient learner. Like a well-functioning hospital obstetrics ward, our schools should, and can, be environments in which failures are reduced to occasional exceptions. In this book we will explore the conditions required for this to happen.

Why am I writing this book now?

Well, it appears that, far from being on course to incrementally reduce and close the disadvantage gap, we are in danger of leaving it jammed wide open. Whilst there were some encouraging signs of the disadvantage gap closing at the beginning of the 2010s, the EPI's 2019 report found that the reduction of disadvantage gaps in education seemed to have been slowing down markedly in recent years, with progress in gap-narrowing at Key Stage 4 looking to have ground to a complete halt (Hutchinson et al. 2019: 10–11). In its 2020 report, the EPI brought us the news that:

The disadvantage gap has stopped closing over the last five years and there are several indications that it has begun to widen. […] This is a concerning indication that inequalities have stopped reducing and have started to widen. (Hutchinson et al. 2020: 9, 11)

The report presents stark data regarding increased numbers of learners coming from persistently disadvantaged families, where the attainment gap is greatest (23 months at age 16) (Hutchinson et al. 2020: 17). The data regarding other vulnerable groups is equally concerning. The 2020 EPI report also showed a significant widening of the gap over the last decade for pupils from Black backgrounds and for 'late arriving EAL pupils' (Hutchinson et al. 2020: 20). Stubborn inequities persist for vulnerable groups too: the gap between the attainment of looked after children and their peers is 29 months and for those with a child protection plan it is 26 months (Hutchinson et al. 2020: 24).

And then COVID-19 struck in early 2020. England's schools closed to all but a small number of children as the nation struggled to contain the coronavirus outbreak. It was apparent within days that home learning was going to be a vastly different experience from family to family. Where children from more affluent backgrounds would likely have their own room, desk, stationery, books, computer, internet access, a home printer and an outdoor learning environment, many of the disadvantaged children in England were living in conditions much less conducive to home learning, with limited resources (traditional and digital). Where well-educated parents could assist with learning tasks and middle-class parents could afford a tutor to support their children, those from poorer backgrounds were more likely to have parents who had to go out to work and who were not as able to assist with school tasks. Many schools were not furnished with 'intelligence' as to which of their students lacked the necessary resources to learn. In normal times, schools are engineers of social mobility, but in lockdown this was going to be much harder. As Mariella Wilson (2020) predicted in April:

What is clear is that the learning and, therefore, the attainment gap – between those who are disadvantaged and those who are not – that has worried the profession and the government for over a decade, is set to grow exponentially. As our lockdown looks set to be extended, the impact of missed schooling will have long-lasting effects.

On 13 May 2020, Vicki Stewart, the deputy director of the Department for Education (DfE) PP and school food division, told a Westminster Education Forum event that the pandemic and the resulting partial school closures would 'almost certainly' have 'a very significant impact' on the attainment gap: 'The predictions are stark – up to a 75 per cent widening' (quoted in Whittaker and Booth 2020).

As this book goes to press, the first anniversary of the start of the 2020 lockdown measures looms and these prophecies appear depressingly accurate. Whether we are considering access to digital technology, attendance rates in schools or the impact of the virus on communities, the divisions in our already unequal society have been painfully visible and ever-growing during the pandemic.

Let's start with the inequity in terms of the sectors of society most affected by COVID-19. In February 2021, the BBC reported that nearly six out of every 10 people who died with coronavirus in England between January and November 2020 (30,296 out of 50,888) were disabled (*BBC News* 2021). The Office for National Statistics (2021b) reported that:

Looking at people with a medically diagnosed learning disability, the risk of death involving COVID-19 was 3.7 times greater for both men and women compared with people who did not have a learning disability.

The significantly increased infection and mortality rates for people from black, Asian and minority ethnic (BAME) backgrounds has been well-documented and much debated. A report by Public Health England (2020: 6) into disparities in the risk and outcomes of COVID-19 stated that:

people of Bangladeshi ethnicity had around twice the risk of death than people of White British ethnicity. People of Chinese, Indian, Pakistani, Other Asian, Black Caribbean and Other Black ethnicity had between 10 and 50% higher risk of death when compared to White British.

It has also been the case that mortality rates from COVID-19 have been significantly higher in areas of socio-economic disadvantage. The Office for National Statistics (2020b) reported that between 1 March and 30 June 2020 in England:

the age-standardised mortality rate for deaths involving COVID-19 in the most deprived areas [...] was 139.6 deaths per 100,000 people; this was more than double the mortality rate in the least deprived areas (63.4 deaths per 100,000 population). The most deprived areas in Wales had a mortality rate for deaths involving COVID-19 of 119.1 deaths per 100,000 people between March to June 2020, nearly twice as high as in the least deprived areas (63.5 deaths per 100,000 people).

This can partly be explained by more crowded living arrangements, a greater likelihood of adults needing to leave home to work and having no option but to use public transport. Our disadvantaged and vulnerable learners are more likely to have been directly impacted by the virus and, sadly, to have experienced a bereavement from COVID.

The increased prevalence of the virus in more disadvantaged parts of the nation has also had a significant impact on school attendance rates. During the autumn and early winter of 2020, the education of thousands of learners was disrupted by positive cases amongst students and staff leading to isolation from school. Fewer vulnerable learners were in school than their more advantaged peers.

DfE figures released for the period up to 15 October 2020 showed that pupil attendance was at around 89%: 92% in primary, 86% in secondary but only 81% in special schools and 59% in alternative provision. And in mainstream schools, the attendance rate of pupils with an EHCP stood at just 84%, as did that of children in need. The autumn term 2020 attendance rates revealed considerable regional variation (Department for Education 2020a). James Carr (2020) reported in *Schools Week* on 22 October that 11 local authorities had secondary attendance below 75%, with Liverpool at 67%, Calderdale at 64% and Knowsley at 61% (all areas of significant economic deprivation). Carr gave the example of The Prescott School in Liverpool, where 69% of the students had missed some school in the first half of the autumn term for COVID-related reasons and Year 10s had had to study at home for four of the seven weeks. The experience of a Key Stage 4 learner preparing for GCSEs at a school like this bore no comparison to that of students in a part of the country with low infection rates and no disruption to education provision. Freddie Whittaker (2020) reported in *Schools Week* that, 'as of November 26, secondary attendance ranged from 37 per cent in Sandwell to 92 per cent in Southend.'

Then, in December 2020, a new and more virulent strain of coronavirus emerged, leading to a rapid rise in cases in schools in London and the South-East. Data on school attendance in the final weeks of the autumn term, when eventually released by the government in January 2021, showed a shocking picture in the capital. James Carr (2021), writing in *Schools Week* on 14 January, revealed that in the London Borough of Havering only 24% of secondary-aged learners were in school in the last week before the Christmas holidays; in Redbridge the figure was 17% and in Thurrock just 14%.

The correlation between attendance and pupil progress is well understood. In a blog entitled 'Urgent action required', Dan Nicholls (2020) presents a graph illustrating the link between attendance and progress in the secondary academies in his multi-academy trust (MAT), the Cabot Learning Federation. It identifies the Progress 8 score typically achieved by disadvantaged learners (light grey) whose attendance falls below 90%, and those whose attendance is between 90 and 95%, and their non-disadvantaged counterparts (dark grey). The bars show not only the effect of absence from school on performance but also the disproportionate impact that absence has on disadvantaged learners, reducing Progress 8 by a further 0.36 (one third of a GCSE grade) compared to non-disadvantaged children with less than 90% attendance.

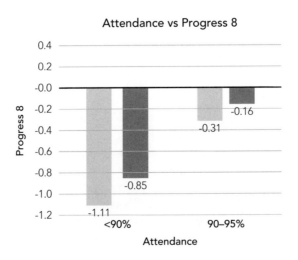

Source: Nicholls (2020)

Reflecting on the emerging picture of variable school attendance rates, Nicholls said:

as with the pandemic, the impact is never felt equally across society; the asymmetry will deepen, the disadvantaged (and others) will fall further, losing their foothold in education.

And so we come to the digital divide. The variable experiences of children from working- versus middle-class backgrounds, attending schools in affluent versus deprived areas and studying at state versus independent schools began to reveal themselves just a couple of weeks into the first lockdown and have not levelled in the succeeding months. Research from the Sutton Trust showed that, by the start of April 2020, 23% of pupils were participating in online lessons (live or recorded) each day, but that pupils from middle-class homes were much more likely to have taken part

(30% compared to 16% of working-class pupils). At private schools, 51% of primary and 57% of secondary students had accessed daily online lessons. 37% of schools situated in the most affluent areas had an online platform for the receipt of work, compared to just 23% of schools serving the most deprived catchments (Cullinane and Montacute 2020: 1).

Aware of the implications of a digital divide, the government promised computers to disadvantaged learners. However, it quickly transpired that, initially, only certain groups were eligible for the free devices: those who had a social worker, were in care or in Year 10. Supply problems ensued and many of the devices delivered came with attendant password access issues. The results of an Office for National Statistics (2020a) survey – covering 12,000 families and published in July 2020 – revealed that 50% of parents reported that their child had struggled to continue with home education during lockdown. For households with one parent, 21% said that this was due to the lack of a device that would enable them to access remote learning.

In recognition of the deleterious effect of the pandemic – and resultant school closures – on learners' educational development, in June 2020 the government announced a £650 million catch-up fund for schools and a £350 million National Tuition Programme (NTP). But in late July it became apparent that the tutors on the NTP would only start to be deployed in November 2020 and the scheme would not be fully operational until spring of 2021. Furthermore, the allocation of the £650 million (amounting to £80 per pupil) in catch-up funding was criticised for failing to target the most needy and most adversely affected by lockdown. David Laws, executive chairman of the EPI, asserted in July 2020 that the cash is: 'badly targeted and is unlikely to prevent a widening of the learning gap between children from poor backgrounds and other pupils' (quoted in Dickens 2020c).

He went on to say:

It is concerning that the government has missed an opportunity to target extra funding to where it is most urgently needed. At a time when social mobility was already in danger of stalling, and with COVID significantly worsening the learning outlook for poor children, (this) decision could prove to be a costly mistake. (Quoted in Dickens 2020c)

Arguments rumbled about both the government's laptops for the disadvantaged scheme and the NTP. John Dickens (2020a) reported in *Schools Week* on 23 October that the government had delivered over 105,000 laptops since the start of September but, at the same time, had cut schools' allocations by up to 80% of what they had been expecting. This came at a moment when the government introduced the legal duty for schools to provide immediate remote learning in the case of self-isolation or localised lockdown. However, Ofcom estimated that 'up to 1.78 million pupils still had no access to a laptop, desktop or tablet at home' (as quoted by Siobhain McDonagh in questions to Secretary of State for Education Gavin Williamson in the House of Commons (Hansard 2020)). As regards to the NTP, *Schools Week*'s John Dickens (2020b) reported on 16 October 2020 that 140 million (40%) of the fund remained unspent and only 150 of the 1,000 academic mentors promised would be in schools by the end of the year.

Ten months into the coronavirus pandemic, at the start of 2021, the digital divide was still a major worry. The Sutton Trust's briefing on the digital divide in schools in England stated that:

- *Just 10% of teachers overall report that all their students have adequate access to a device for remote learning. A similar proportion say that all of their pupils have access to the internet.*
- *There are substantial differences between the state and private sector, with just 5% of teachers in state schools reporting that all their students have a device, compared to 54% at private schools.* (Sutton Trust 2021)

Sir Peter Lampl, founder and chairman of the Sutton Trust, was quoted as saying:

As our new research shows, the picture has barely changed. Despite the heroic efforts of teachers, many pupils still face being left behind because of digital poverty. The government has made some positive steps but they must go further and faster to ensure that every child has the resources they need to learn while schools remain closed. (Quoted in Sutton Trust 2021)

In 'Different lockdown, same problems?', Erica Holt-White (2021) writes:

Before the pandemic, Ofcom estimated that up to 1.78 million children in the UK were living in a household without access to a laptop, desktop or tablet. [...] So far, only 560,000 devices have been delivered to schools in England.

The toll of the pandemic has been disproportionately heavy on our most vulnerable young people, who have experienced higher levels of bereavement, loss of employment in the family, disruption to key support systems – such as social workers or youth groups – and extended periods of remote learning in conditions which are not conducive to study. So, now more than ever, disadvantaged learners and those vulnerable to poor outcomes need the spotlight shone on them and their needs. We face an unprecedented challenge in closing the disadvantage gap and eliminating educational failure, but with this challenge comes the opportunity to view the landscape through fresh eyes and to commit to doing things differently, to ensure that our disadvantaged schoolchildren do not pay the price of the coronavirus pandemic. As Milton Friedman (1982: ix) said, 'Only a crisis – actual or perceived – produces real change.'

We have a crisis all right. So let's examine some of the cornerstones required to support all learners to succeed and to eliminate education fatalities.

Chapter 2

The elephant in the room

Whether you think you can or you think you can't, you're right.

Attributed to Henry Ford[1]

Perpetual optimism is a force multiplier. The ripple effect of a leader's optimism is awesome.

General Colin Powell (Quoted in DeFraites 1999: 3)

The chapters of this book and the strategies they propose are not hierarchical. Yet the ground covered in this chapter is a kind of 'base camp'. It considers the essential foundations that are required for any of the other approaches to stand a chance of succeeding. There are some hard-hitting messages and some big challenges for you in the following pages, whether you are reading this book as a school leader, a teacher, an operational staff member or a parent. But I figure that if Chapter 1 hooked you in, you are probably the kind of person who likes to be set a challenge and strives to meet audacious and compelling goals.

Limiting assumptions and fixed mindsets

Let's return to the analogy of childbirth and infant mortality first presented in the introduction. Imagine that you are about to have a baby. You go to your local hospital for your final check-up before being admitted to the maternity ward for the delivery. You casually enquire as to the department's success rate, and it transpires that the current target for successful deliveries that the obstetrics team is working to meet is 75% per annum. Well, of course, this just wouldn't happen! Could you imagine the fallout? The world's media would descend on the hospital within minutes and the obstetrics department would likely be closed with immediate effect for thorough investigation. Whilst a small number of fatalities is sadly inevitable, across most of the world it would now be considered shocking for medical staff to accept such a

---

1   See https://quoteinvestigator.com/2015/02/03/you-can/.

significant infant mortality rate. I would imagine that there is not a hospital in the country with a target much below 100%. How could anything else be acceptable in this day and age?

Yet there is an expectation, and acceptance, of 'baked in' educational failure for around a third of 16-year-olds in the UK each year (with a higher percentage in the most disadvantaged areas), which was clearly shown in the algorithm constructed by Ofqual to calculate GCSE grades in the summer of 2020, when learners had not been able to sit public exams. Quite rightly, the flaws in a formula that penalised high-attaining learners who happened to be studying at schools and colleges with historically mediocre outcomes were exposed in the national arena, leading to a government U-turn and the awarding of grades based on centres' assessments.

Despite this, we all know of schools, departments, phases and classes where targets are set, agreed and worked towards that are far short of 100% success. A primary teacher might have a performance development target of '80% of the Year 6 class to reach ARE in reading, writing and maths next summer' or a secondary head teacher might be set a target by their governing or trust board of '70% of Year 11s to gain five or more standard pass grades at GCSE, including English and maths'. In neither of these cases would this be likely to cause a murmur of surprise, let alone media interest.

Why? Well, partly because such targets might well signify an improvement on previous/current performance for the teacher or school. It is worth noting that the latter target would represent performance above the current national average. The sad truth is that we have become accustomed to a situation in which around a third of our primary pupils transition to secondary school without being fully 'secondary ready' in terms of their core subject skills, and a third of our 16-year-olds graduate from school without having acquired the standard level of literacy and numeracy required to progress into many careers and professions.

Let's take another everyday example of target-setting practice in school. Chantelle Blackmore enters Year 7 and the senior leaders look at her Key Stage 2 SATs results – supplied by the feeder primary school – and the scores from a cognitive ability test (CAT) that she sat in the first week of secondary school. They use that data to predict her GCSE outcomes five years later and to generate target grades for her subjects. These target grades are communicated to each of her subject teachers, who record them on the front cover of her exercise books, explaining their significance to

Chantelle and her classmates. At a 'settling in' parents' evening a few weeks later, they meet Chantelle's parents and have a conversation along the following lines:

Teacher: Hello Mr and Mrs Blackmore. Lovely to meet you for the first time. Well I'm really enjoying getting to know Chantelle, although we've only had four geography lessons so far. She's settling in well.

Parent: We've been following her work so far in her exercise book and it looks really interesting. Can you explain to us what the number on the cover means, please?

Teacher: Ah, well, we have looked at her results from the Year 6 SATs and she took a CAT in September. And from that information we set target grades for GCSE. That 3 is Chantelle's target grade. That's what she is on course to achieve if she takes GCSE geography.

Absurd, isn't it?! But credible? Sadly, yes. I have seen practice like this in too many schools to believe that this is a rare exception.

It is not only the current norm in terms of educational outcomes which accounts for the fact that parents like the Blackmores experience conversations like this. It has a lot to do with belief about what is acceptable and possible. In other words, it has to do with our expectations and our mindset. Logically, if a school sets a target for 70% of their learners to reach the national threshold for success, subject leaders, heads and governors/trustees must presumably all agree that this is the maximum possible – or the most it is reasonable to expect.

Now if the target-setting process was happening a few months before the terminal exams and the past education experience of the cohort had been severely disrupted, agreeing conservative performance targets might well be pragmatic. But what if, year after year, the school's targets were pegged at around 70%? Let's go back to Chantelle. How do we explain Chantelle being set a target grade of a 3 (technically a 'fail') in GCSE geography by staff who do not know her or her family, five years before she would even sit the exam – assuming she chose the subject for GCSE three years later? What does that say about the culture of the school and the staff's beliefs about what it is possible to achieve with an 11-year-old learner in five years?

How have we found ourselves in a situation in which we readily accept success targets of well below 100% in schools, whilst agreeing that equivalent practice would be unacceptable on the part of those setting targets for safe deliveries in hospital obstetrics departments? It must come down to what is agreed as acceptable and perceived as possible. Our first challenge, if we want to improve education delivery rates, is to change perceptions and raise expectations.

Just how much of a limiting factor is staff belief in learners? I believe it can be quite a significant barrier, but one that school leaders are often unaware of, reluctant to admit to, or uncomfortable to discuss. Hence the title of this chapter – 'the elephant in the room'.

On what do I base this view? Well, over a 30-year teaching career I worked in seven schools. All were successful, and either 'good' or 'outstanding' in Ofsted's terms. I worked with inspirational colleagues in each school, but I also heard individuals saying things like the following:

'What can you expect of kids like these?'

'He just isn't any good at history.'

'They're not musical.'

'He's never going to pass the phonics screening test.'

'She wouldn't cope with triple award science.'

'She's just a typical PP kid.'

'I'm not expecting anyone in set 6 to get a pass grade.'

'My low-ability kids …'

'There's only one high-ability student in that class.'

I'd suggest that each of the above phrases belies a fixed mindset attitude and a frailty of belief in the potential of certain individuals or groups to achieve at a high level.

I once attended a union conference at which the Ofsted expert said, in a presentation to a room packed with head teachers, 'Well, of course, it's never going to be possible to close the attainment gap completely between PP pupils and the rest.' Chaos did not ensue; there wasn't even a murmur of dissent in the audience.

At INA the senior leaders and I handpicked every member of staff, weeding out anyone without a growth mindset. Yet still there were times when each one of us found it hard to keep the faith! So I am sceptical whenever a head teacher tells me that they have absolutely no issue in their school with their staff's limiting assumptions. As books like Pragya Agarwal's *Sway* (2020) show us, we all have unconscious biases. In a typical staffroom, some of these will be related to gender, some to class, some to ethnicity, some to disability and some to family background.

A culture of growth mindset and high expectations of all

Schools that achieve the best progress and attainment outcomes for their learners have developed an ethos of high expectations for all and a shared culture of belief in the potential of every student to achieve great outcomes, with the right conditions, support and tuition. The word 'shared' is key here. We are talking about school leaders, teachers, teaching assistants, operational staff, parents, governors and learners all having the mindset that high performance is something that every learner can enjoy; not just those who have historically been high-attainers or those who come from affluent, or professional, or stable, or English-speaking (or all of the above) families. Where every adult in a school has a true growth mindset – believing unwaveringly in the potential of all learners to achieve amazing outcomes – the pace of progress can be striking, and the momentum generated by the cultivation of students' self-belief and self-esteem infectious. This is what Powell is referring to in the quote at the start of this chapter.

Let's unpick that a bit. Colin Powell talks about the ripple effect of a *leader's* optimism. A high-performance school culture starts with the head. It has to be led from the top to be fully effective and all-pervading. We have all seen examples of an individual teacher or team leader achieving amazing outcomes if they have an optimistic outlook and successfully create a culture of belief in their class or team. But there is no doubt that, for a whole school community to demonstrate a firm and unwavering high-expectations culture, the head needs to be the driver, passionately role modelling their belief and ensuring that a growth mindset underpins every decision and action.

A great school leader refuses to settle for goals that leave behind any learners, whatever their personal circumstances or starting points. Like a great leader of an expedition, they measure success in terms of everyone reaching the destination. It may be that some get to the finish line later than others and require more assistance along the way, but there is an assumption that success is an entitlement for all.

Great school leaders paint a picture of collective success that is so enticing that no one associated with the institution can fail to want to be part of the journey to achieve the vision. They give cautious colleagues a sense of belief that they can make great things happen and the confidence to dream big and exciting dreams. The story they tell of a community in which there are no fatalities is so compelling that it inspires all the staff; it galvanises them to pursue this better future.

Leaders of high-performing schools make a commitment to strive towards bold and audacious goals and then work to create the conditions in their school whereby teachers and students who might struggle elsewhere can perform to a high standard. Stephen Denning talks of this in *The Secret Language of Leadership* (2007: 77):

Once a commitment is made, the goal will seem larger, bolder and more exciting. Leaders need to fix on it like a laser beam. They need to see it intensely, even obsessively. They feel it, they hear it, they taste it. They smell it. It becomes part of them, their very identity, because it is something they are committed to make happen.

They set exacting standards for themselves and others and communicate the highest expectations, but then work relentlessly to support staff and learners to achieve them. This way, colleagues are happy to sign up to the bold goals, and to play their part in the big picture, secure in the knowledge that their leader is in it with them. The leader 'has their back' and will move heaven and earth to create the ideal conditions for realising the targets. If they hit the goal, incredible! If they fall slightly short, they will know that they tried their hardest and achieved great heights.

When staff set audacious goals and chase big dreams, they are much more likely to see their vision become a reality. Some schools refuse to set a target below ARE or GCSE 4 grade for any pupil, regardless of the subject, the learner's current attainment or their education history. Their staff know that the brain is like a plant, capable of ongoing growth given the right conditions. They don't underestimate the challenge – the time, hard work and practice that will be required to get a low prior attainer to succeed – but they refuse to believe that it is not possible, to miss any opportunity or lose any time in chasing their goal. Let's replay that conversation between Mr and Mrs Blackmore and Chantelle's geography teacher, but place them in such a school:

Teacher: Hello Mr and Mrs Blackmore. Lovely to meet you for the first time. Well I'm really enjoying getting to know Chantelle, although we've only had four geography lessons so far. She's settling in well.

Parent: We've been following her work so far in her exercise book and it looks really interesting. Can you tell us how well she is doing and what kind of grade we can expect her to achieve at GCSE?

Teacher: Ah, well, I have taken a look at her results from the Year 6 SATs and from a CAT she took in September. That data gives me some indication as to the skills she has developed and the knowledge she has gained already. That will help me to tailor my teaching to support her to progress quickly, but it doesn't tell me about her potential. What is key is how focused she is on her studies over the next five years, how hard she practises the skills we help her to develop. And you have a key role to play in facilitating her home learning too. At our school we strive to support every student to achieve GCSE success. At the moment, Chantelle is a bit behind some of her peers in her reading and writing. That could be down to a number of factors. Our job is to identify the reasons and work to overcome any barrier we discover. But the fact that Chantelle has a starting point that is lower than we might expect does not mean that she cannot achieve a good GCSE grade. She has more ground to cover than some of her classmates, but we have seen lots of previous students achieve top grades from where Chantelle is now and she has five years to get there. Let's talk about what support you think Chantelle might benefit from and how we can work productively together.

So, to create a culture of high performance for all, the leader has to demonstrate the steely determination and courageous leadership referred to by Denning. But, equally importantly, they have to be able to take *all* staff – teaching and operational – with them. If only some of their staff have an unswerving belief in the potential of every learner, the vision will – at best – be partially realised. And certain learners will get left behind. They will sense that not all their teachers have the same belief in them and their capacity to succeed. This will impact on their self-esteem and, without self-esteem, their progress will be stunted. Likewise, if parents and carers are not onside with a growth mindset, they can unintentionally undermine the great work taking place at school. Smart schools recognise the crucial role that parents can play in affecting high performance (as well as the damage they can do if not onside).

That might clarify *what* needs to be done, but it doesn't address *how* to raise the expectations of everyone in the school community. The remainder of this chapter explores a number of key ways to create a high-performance culture, in which everyone shares a belief in the potential of all learners.

The leader's role modelling

In schools with an ethos of high performance for all, everything that the leaders say – to staff, parents and pupils – demonstrates their conviction that each one of the learners can achieve at impressive levels. Every decision they make is designed to help translate this belief into a reality, and each action they take is showing others how to step closer to realising the goal. The leader must miss no opportunity to communicate the key message.

As a head teacher, I endeavoured to weave messages about the power of growth mindset, the staff body's belief in all our pupils and the importance of focus, practice and determination into every assembly, awards event, vote of thanks at the end of concerts and sporting fixtures, staff continuing professional development (CPD) event, parent workshop and newsletter – always seeking a fresh angle or a new take on the same theme. Every leader will employ their own particular way of doing this – their style reflecting both their context and their personality. At open evenings for parents of prospective Reception pupils, for example, my 'script' of notes and prompts included statements like the following:

We are a growth mindset school. That means that we believe in the almost limitless capacity for everyone to achieve great things. We don't believe that some students are bright and that others aren't. We don't believe that babies come out of the womb with a certain amount of intelligence. We don't think that it is written in the stars that some people will be great sportsmen or women, or musicians or scientists. We don't believe in the idea that someone can be a 'natural' linguist or artist. We believe that what we become, what we achieve, the skills we acquire and the knowledge we develop is down to the right learning conditions – great teaching, great facilities, hard work, application, coaching, support and resilience. We know that the brain is not of a fixed size. It can grow and grow if we feed it in the right ways. Our job is to grow great brains! If your child joins this school, we will be setting out on a 14-year journey together, through Reception, primary, secondary and sixth form. Our goal will be to equip your children *with the knowledge, learning power and character necessary for success at university and beyond*. That means we will be supporting them to achieve top grades at GCSE and A level. It doesn't mean that we are saying that university is the only route or the best pathway after school; there are lots of other exciting career and apprenticeship routes at 18. But it does mean that we are serious about supporting all our students to get the qualifications necessary for all options, including university, to be open to them. Do we believe that is realistic? Of course we do! Do we think it will be easy? Not at all! We will all need to work really hard together to achieve this goal – the staff, you as parents, and your sons and daughters.

The message was primarily for prospective parents, but it was also for the staff, by means of reinforcement of our collective commitment to leave no stone unturned in pursuit of the very best for every child.

> ### Reflection
> What events and occasions at your school are used as opportunities to communicate a 'high aspirations for all' message?
> Are there any missed opportunities?
> Do you have an agreed 'script'? If not, would it be useful to create one?

The italicised section of my script is from INA's mission statement. It was deliberately aspirational and challenging. We displayed it prominently on noticeboards, in student organisers, at the top of each policy document, on the website, etc. as a constant reminder of what we were about and what we were aspiring to achieve. By declaring it publicly we were inviting others to hold us to account. My role as principal was to ensure that this was our lode star, and that we used it to guide each key decision, referring to it each time we reset our strategic direction or had to make a crucial choice regarding our priorities.

Heads of schools with high aspirations for all have to ensure that every structure and procedure will provide opportunities for, and facilitate the progress of, all learners. Such decisions might involve pupil groupings (of which more later), staff deployment, curriculum pathways, course content and course options.

Curriculum pathways, course content and course options

Let's illustrate this with a couple of small but significant examples.

I once came across a school that set Year 7 English classes according to students' attainment scores in Key Stage 2 SATs and tailored the programme of study for each group. The 'top' sets studied *Oliver Twist*, whilst the 'bottom' sets read *Charlotte's Web*. Now, each text has its own merits, but the fact that the content of the curriculum was so different for each group would have made it very difficult for a learner to move from a lower set to a higher one and understand the more advanced learning. They would have had no exposure to Dickens, making their next encounter with him, via *A Christmas Carol* in Year 9, all the more challenging. It was as if it had not occurred to those designing the curriculum that the aim might be to give all learners access to the same rich canon of literature, ensuring that it was made accessible for their various starting points, but with the aspiration that all students would be capable of A level standard literary appreciation at some point.

In a similar vein, I have long thought that the options that schools offer to their learners at GCSE reveal much about the leaders' mindset. It is still very commonplace that, in schools that consider themselves to be comprehensive, triple award science is only offered to those in the higher attaining sets at the end of Key Stage 3. What does this say about the school's belief in the potential of students to make accelerated progress during Key Stage 4? Or the rights of a lower attaining student who loves science to study it in more depth for more hours each week than would be afforded by a double award course?

Leaders of schools with high expectations of all are sensitive to such issues and ensure that systems are in place for relentless tracking and monitoring of access and uptake – by gender, ethnicity, SEND and eligibility for PP funding.

Reflection

Do the curriculum pathways, course content and programmes of study at your school allow for easy movement between sets?

Do all learners have access to study any subject of their choice? If not, why not, and how is the messaging around course options managed?

Language and labels

I've stressed that everything that leaders say must demonstrate their conviction that each one of their learners can achieve at impressive levels – this is absolutely crucial. When I visit schools or address groups of leaders I often ask whether they have a language policy. I very rarely come across a school that does. And yet if I were to be asked which of the hundred or so policies that my colleagues and I wrote when setting up INA was the most crucial, the language for learning policy would without doubt be in the top five. In writing it, we were heavily influenced by the work of Carol Dweck (2006), Ellen Langer (1989) and Martin Seligman (1991). They taught us that the quality and climate of teaching and learning are shaped hugely by the language used by staff; how adults talk about learning and demonstrate their own learning habits have a very powerful effect on young learners.

Dweck (2006: 173) says:

Every word and action can send a message. It tells students how to think about themselves. It can be a fixed-mindset message that says: 'You have permanent traits and I am judging them.' Or it can be a growth-mindset message that says: 'You are a developing person and I am interested in your development.' It is remarkable how sensitive children are to these messages.

The language we use to talk about education and learning deeply affects how individuals, even as young as early years pupils, see themselves as learners.

Ellen Langer, professor of psychology at Harvard University, has shown that small shifts in a teacher's language can induce marked shifts in the learning habits that students develop. Even something as simple as changing 'is' to 'could', or talking about 'learning' rather than 'work', makes a difference. If a teacher says that something definitely 'is' the case, students will take it literally and try to remember the 'fact'. If the teacher says of the same thing that it 'could be' the case, students become more engaged, more thoughtful, more imaginative and more critical. That 'could be' invites learners to learn more actively and inquisitively. Students will question and solve problems more readily if knowledge is presented to them as being provisional. Langer found that when she probed their understanding with more creative and open-ended questions, 'could be' students far outperformed their 'is' peers.

Martin Seligman discovered that toxic words like 'never' and 'always' can be damaging to learners in certain circumstances. If a student says, 'I can never understand this type of problem' or 'Maths is always too hard for me', this displays a lack of optimism and grit. Likewise, if a teacher says, 'You are always distracted' or 'You never complete your homework', it implies a lack of faith in the student to grow as a learner. The word 'work' has a similarly toxic effect. 'High performance for all' schools tend to talk about 'learning' rather than 'work', as changing such terminology has a positive effect on how learners perceive tasks.

The INA language for learning policy, designed for staff but published on the website for parents and students to see, covered language of praise, language of aspiration, language of honour, respect and inclusion, but it started with growth mindset. Here is an extract:

Growth mindset language

The language of ability and labelling students as high- or low-ability, top set or bottom set, or gifted or talented goes against the concept of growth mindset as developed by Carol Dweck. At INA we talk in terms of prior attainment and current performance rather than ability, in the belief that everyone can improve on their scores and has the potential to grow their mind and that human qualities (including intellectual skills) can be cultivated by effort and application. So setted groups range from the class with the highest current attainment to that with the lowest current attainment.

As staff we believe in students' potential to grow their intelligence and we speak the language of growth mindset. We ask 'How can I teach this concept to this student?' rather than 'Can I teach this concept to this student?' We ask 'How will they learn this best?' rather than 'Can they learn this?'

At INA we avoid language that labels certain students or groups. So we talk about 'students with SEND' rather than 'SEND students' and 'pupils with EAL' rather than 'EAL pupils'.

As staff we emphasise in our language and behaviour that making mistakes is a natural and important part of the learning process: learning from mistakes is what learning is all about! It is important that as adults we talk about our learning mistakes and how we put them right.

Evidence shows that the students of adults who preach and practise a growth mindset perform considerably better than those taught by adults who believe in fixed intelligence. The fixed mindset limits achievement.

Schools that expect high performance from everyone tend to be very language conscious. They train and support their staff to use language of aspiration and inclusion. They have a 'common language', often expressed in a policy, and they will induct each new member of staff in it. Their staff know that every label, word and action sends a message and tells students what the adults think of them and how they should think of themselves. They appreciate that it is easy enough for students to label themselves or each other without adults adding to the damage! They are sensitive to the fact that, once established, labels are hard to erase and can have a crushing impact on progress and attainment. They understand that it is important that everyone uses growth mindset language all the time. They challenge every little slip, without blame or chastisement, but relentlessly.

If I were to give just one piece of advice to school leaders about adapting language to change the messaging around expectations, it would be to suggest that they ban the use of the word 'ability' in describing individuals or groups of learners: 'low ability', 'high ability', 'more able' and 'less able' have no place here. And I would eradicate the word in all its uses across the school: able pupils' policy, ability awards, book recommendations for highly able readers, catch-up for low-ability learners and so on. By replacing the word 'ability' with 'attainment', the message conveyed changes dramatically. Describing a student as low attaining in maths is an objective and helpful description, highlighting the need for additional support or intervention. To call the same learner 'low-ability' is judgemental and dangerous. It implies that they are not capable of catching their peers up or attaining as highly. It is the language of consignment. It condones low expectations and excuses failure.

I challenged members of a senior leadership team recently about their 'able, gifted and talented pupils' policy', which I had read on the school website. I asked them how they determined which students were able, how they described the learners who were not labelled 'able, gifted and talented' and whether they had analysed the effect of the policy on the motivation, progress, attainment and self-esteem of both sets of learners. The leaders very quickly decided amongst themselves to scrap the policy, change the language and focus instead on pursuing an ethos of high attainment for all. By the time I left the school the link to the policy had come down from the website. The harder task, of course, will be to eradicate the use of the language of ability (and the beliefs associated with it) from the school community.

Reflection

How aware are your colleagues of the language they use?

Do you have an agreed language policy?

If not, what might you include in one?

In what contexts, and by whom, is the word 'ability' used in your school? What impact might banning its use have?

Grouping learners

Talking of labels, let's consider pupil groupings.

I attended a small village primary school in the 1970s. In my Year 5 class, we were grouped across six tables, each named after a different animal. The table groupings were based on 'ability'. The 'top-ability' table was, of course, the lions. I can still see the children on the lions table now; I remember each of their names. We sat in our animal configuration groups for maths, literacy, topic work, everything, all year. Nothing that anyone on the giraffe or antelope table did was going to turn them into a lion. There was only space for four lions in that classroom – the teacher had probably decided that it would be too dangerous to have more! My friend Joanne and I were on the tiger table. It was the second to top ability group, as we were only too aware, gazing in envy at the lions. Tigers are pretty impressive beasts but, as I saw it, if my teacher didn't see me as a lion I might as well behave like a monkey, and increasingly I did. I can't remember what animal the 'lowest ability' table was named after, but those children might as well have been called amoebas for all the chance they had of being seen as capable of metamorphosing into lions.

In many schools, the 'ability' groupings established when each cohort first joins the school are set pretty firm for successive years. In her book *The Elephant in the Classroom*, Jo Boaler (2009: 116) reports that 88% of children placed in ability groups at age four remain in the same groupings until they leave school and reflects that:

For schools to decide what children can do, for the rest of their school career, when they are four years old – or any other primary school age – is nothing short of criminal.

Mixed groups enable children to develop socially and avoid the psychological damage and feelings of inadequacy that setting can reinforce. With boys, those eligible for PP funding, and children from BAME backgrounds often being disproportionately represented in 'low-ability' groups, setting compounds a historical cycle of poor performance amongst boys, ethnic minorities and children from low socio-economic backgrounds. Hallam and Parsons (2013) found a strong correlation between being placed in a 'top set' and having an autumn birthday or coming from a family where the parents were homeowners. Thus we create structural disadvantage in our schools. Daniel Sobel cautions that the incidence of children being placed into the 'wrong set' based on one test is high, warning that 'surrounding a disadvantaged child exclusively with peers who are themselves disadvantaged will often have negative effects' (2018: 14). Peers matter in the classroom, not just teachers.

Leaders need to track the make-up of sets carefully and ensure that no group is over- or under-represented. However, this is not to say that setting students by attainment is always to be avoided. It can be the best way to accelerate progress for all learners, especially if sets with lower-attaining learners are assigned the most experienced, qualified and effective teachers in the school.

Growth mindset schools put considerable thought into the optimal student group-ings as this is central to achieving their ambitious goals. They understand that their grouping arrangements need to be honestly and carefully explained to learners and their parents and carers. They might use attainment setting, but they are careful to explain that it is just that – attainment, not ability, setting. It is based on what pupils know and can do *now*, not on what their teacher thinks they are capable of or will learn. The staff have judged that by grouping learners for a time or activity with peers who are at the same stage, they will progress more speedily and can be supported more effectively. Without this open and honest dialogue, there is a real danger that children and their parents believe that they have been set according to how 'able' they are perceived to be. Learners need to know that moving to a higher attaining group is within their power through hard work and improved performance. They need to see this happening, and being celebrated, all the time.

At INA, we always endeavoured to ensure that a healthy mix of criteria was used to determine student groupings, not just academic performance. In any given year, stu-dents would study some lessons in mixed classes and others in setted groups. We started with the question 'What grouping arrangement will best enable us to meet our aims?' We considered whether students were most likely to acquire knowledge and understanding and make the quickest progress in classes in which there is fine setting, loose setting or mixed prior performance grouping. We thought about which type of grouping was most likely to lead to the best outcomes for students, which type of grouping was most likely to support their skills development, and which was most supportive of our ethos and values. We reviewed group arrangements at the end of each term and moved students around if their relative performance level had changed or if, for other educational reasons, a move was deemed desirable. Optimal grouping arrangements were reviewed and reconsidered on an annual basis, with reference to student progress and attainment data. As in most schools, primary classes and secondary tutor groups were created to ensure a complete mix in terms of prior attainment, gender, socio-economic background, ethnicity, SEND, EAL and month of birth.

The INA student grouping policy, which was written to assist middle leaders and teachers when arranging learners into and within classes, also stressed that:

All teachers and learning assistants will have and communicate the highest expectations of the potential of all students, whatever their current performance level and regardless of which set or group they are currently in.

All lessons, regardless of whether they are being planned for a mixed or setted group, will be planned in the knowledge that there is a spread of prior attainment within the group. Every class will require differentiated learning objectives, resources and learning activities to meet the full range of needs within it.

Reflection

How does your school's grouping policy complement your drive for high attainment for all?

How regularly is the composition of sets reviewed?

Are disadvantaged learners or other groups over-represented in any particular sets? Who monitors this?

Selecting, developing and challenging staff

As I said earlier, ensuring that all staff have a growth mindset is key to developing a high performance for all culture. At INA the senior staff and I had a huge advantage in that we recruited all the staff ourselves and could therefore carefully vet applicants' attitudes and character traits during the interview process. Recruiting for a large and growing all-through school, which needed around 40 new staff per year on top of any vacancies that arose, meant that we conducted literally thousands of interviews. We came to appreciate that appointing candidates with the right character was far more important than selecting on the basis of experience or expertise. Like most schools, we had a generic recruitment pack containing details about the school, which we customised for each vacancy with information about the post, the job description and person specification. The generic section of the recruitment pack was peppered with Dweck quotes, references to growth mindset and the school's mission statement. It sent a clear message that we wanted our students to be taught by staff who genuinely believed that every child had the potential to get top grades – qualifications that would make progression to university and exciting careers possible – and that such pathways were open to them. If prospective applicants were invited to interview, we probed further with our questions to see whether they shared this conviction.

We might ask a candidate for a phase leader or head of subject post: 'What target would you set Year 6 for ARE?' or 'What target would you set your department for 9–4 grades at GCSE?' We would ask all teachers questions like: 'What can you tell us about your track record of raising attainment?', 'How did you build students' self-belief in your last role?' or 'How have you worked with parents to ensure that they are supporting their child and working with the school to gain the best possible outcomes?'

We also talked at interview about the concept of growth mindset, explaining what it meant to us and why words like 'ability' and 'gifted' were banned at INA – because there is no such thing as fixed intelligence, highly able or low ability, just currently high-attaining or low-attaining pupils. We would check that they shared our view that inherent talent has minimal impact on eventual performance – that what leads to great performance is desire, self-belief, hard work, great teaching, good resources and purposeful practice. This routine, without doubt, enabled us to amicably part ways with some interesting candidates who just would not have been right for INA, nor – I suspect – have been happy at the school. In addition, it was useful at times, if a staff member was not demonstrating growth mindset behaviour, to gently remind them of the discussions we had had at interview.

Reflection

Is having a growth mindset a selection criterion when recruiting staff at your school?

Do you ask any questions at interview to assess whether candidates believe in the potential of virtually all learners to achieve at very high levels? If not, what might you ask?

Of course, most leaders inherit their staff body, rather than hand-picking a team of colleagues (although, over time, opportunities to make new appointments will arise). In this scenario, leaders seeking to establish a culture of high expectations need to determine which members of staff already share their unswerving belief in the potential of all learners, and which might have conscious or unconscious biases that could limit some learners' progress.

When I was at secondary school, I had a history teacher who clearly had high expectations of and big ambitions for me. I knew how highly she thought of my potential as a historian because she asked me challenging questions in class, she marked my book thoroughly, she never let me get away with giving her second best and she always pushed me that little bit further. And I loved it; I loved the subject because of her skilled, dynamic and high-quality teaching. I wanted to work really hard for her, to please her and to show her that her faith in me was well founded. I suspect the fact that I studied history at university had a lot to do with her. That isn't, of course, an unusual response to a teacher who demonstrates high expectations and challenges students to perform just beyond their current capabilities; it's the natural response. We know that all students, whatever their current level of performance, respond positively to this type of skilled teaching and belief in their potential.

However, Mrs Scott didn't treat everyone the way she treated me. In her class, I sat next to my best friend, Joanne of tiger table fame. Joanne would most likely have been eligible for PP funding had it existed in the 1970s. She was from a family in which there was little emphasis on education and no expectation that she would go on to university. She played outside in the evenings rather than doing homework. She was never pushed academically, despite the fact that she was a quick learner and capable in every subject. (In fact, back on tiger table she had often helped me with my maths and English.) At secondary school she had a boyfriend whom she dressed to impress, with heavy makeup and a skirt of a length that I would never have been allowed to leave the house wearing.

I knew that Mrs Scott judged Joanne by what she saw and pitched her expectations accordingly. The questions that were directed to me in class were never asked of Joanne, although she was every bit as capable of answering them. The comments that were directed at her were normally about what she was wearing, and delivered with thinly veiled disdain. Bored, and sensing that she was overlooked, Joanne resorted to dreaming and doodling in history lessons and submitted slapdash homework. Mrs Scott's views of her then sank even further. It confirmed that she had been right to write Joanne off as one of those children who was never going to get a good O level grade. Joanne was never encouraged to perform at a higher level, or to take history, or any other subject for that matter, at A level. She left school at 16, and was married and pregnant soon after. She eventually returned to studying and realised her intellectual potential, but that was many years later.

As much as Mrs Scott was a great teacher for me, I never wanted a Mrs Scott on my staff and neither would any leader striving to create a school with an inclusive high-performance culture. How prevalent are the Mrs Scotts in schools today? I suspect more than we might care to admit! Leaders need to be equipped with strategies for detecting potential biases or fixed mindsets amongst staff. This might be as simple as walking the school frequently, popping into lessons to watch the classroom dynamic, listening for the language that is being used, checking comments in exercise books, observing staff discussions with care and seeking feedback (using well-chosen questions) from learners and parents. If and when leaders pick up possible signs of a fixed mindset – staff praising achievement rather than effort, making pejorative comments, voicing stereotypical views, excluding certain groups of students from opportunities, sending the same learners out of class – they need to resolve to address them swiftly, never overlooking a lapse, always picking issues up and politely but firmly challenging them. They need to train others to have the skill, confidence and resolve to do the same.

You will probably be familiar with the Pygmalion effect – the idea that others' expectations of us affect our performance. Simply by giving someone a label, we predicate our inherent bias. This was powerfully illustrated by Robert Rosenthal, professor of psychology at the University of California, who supported the hypothesis that reality can be positively or negatively influenced by the expectations of others (the observer-expectancy effect).

He conducted a study with Lenore Jacobson (1968) in which all students in a single Californian elementary school were given an IQ test. The scores were not disclosed to the children or their teachers, but the teachers were given the names of around 20% of the cohort and told that these children were predicted to be 'intellectual bloomers', doing better than expected in comparison to their classmates. In actual fact, Rosenthal had selected the names at random. At the end of the study, the students retook the same IQ test. All the cohorts in both the experimental and control groups showed a mean gain in IQ. However, what was striking were the statistically significant gains made by the 'intellectual bloomers' in the younger cohorts. This led to the conclusion that teacher expectations, particularly for the youngest children, can influence student achievement. Rosenthal believed that even the teacher's attitude or mood could positively affect the students, if they believe that they are 'bloomers'. As Angus McBeath (2003: 12) reflects:

We are truly beholden to teachers because teachers determine, in many instances, who will live in poverty and who will live with some measure of prosperity.

Leaders who are aspirational for all their learners need to have their antennae poised to detect not only staff members who may have lower expectations of children from certain demographics, but also those who fail to see disadvantage and barriers to high performance. I was shocked to read the Teacher Tapp responses to a question posed on 4 April 2020: 'What strategies is your school using to support the disadvantaged to learn at home?' The results of the poll, to which 7,466 teachers responded, are shown below:

- Providing laptops/devices 25%
- Enabling internet access (e.g. supplying a dongle) 6%
- Providing online training 4%
- Providing general advice 52%
- Contacting parents re: advice 37%
- Providing extra lessons for PP 16%
- None 22%
- Not relevant 11%

Who are these teachers who believe that there are literally *no* disadvantaged learners in their school? How shocking is it that 750 respondents appeared to be saying that seeking strategies to support disadvantaged learners with remote learning was not a relevant activity for schools?

Growth mindset training

Aspirational leaders ensure that it is not only they who are motivating their staff with growth mindset addresses, but that their team is exposed to a variety of persuasive voices espousing the same message. I was extremely fortunate in being able to persuade Matthew Syed, former British table tennis champion and author of *Bounce* (2010), to spend an evening with my founding staff before INA opened. It was one of the most powerful pieces of training we ever conducted and set the foundation perfectly in terms of school culture. However, there are a wide array of exciting, inspirational and dynamic speakers on the theme of growth mindset who could be used to win hearts and minds and provide the energy to drive your flywheel.

Some leaders use well-chosen TED Talks, blogs or readings as a stimulus to generate discussion in staff meetings. This is a great way to gather momentum and also to weed out sceptics. Perhaps the most powerful messages of all come from members of the school community itself – teachers and operational staff talking about key moments in their life when a significant adult either built up their self-esteem and showed faith in them, changing their destiny for the better, or displayed a fixed mindset and consequently closed opportunities to them.

Leaders need to work relentlessly to ensure that all staff are espousing and role modelling an aspirational mindset. Here are a few suggestions of activities designed to strengthen growth mindset culture:

- When recruiting, ask growth mindset questions of candidates – for example, 'Tell us about a time when you witnessed a disadvantaged learner being the victim of limited assumptions or unconscious bias. How did it make you feel? What did you do about it? How has it changed you?'

- Use some of the statements I listed on page 22 in a staff training activity. You could pair staff and ask them to take turns to role play: A reads a statement, B responds as though A had come into the staffroom and made the statement to colleagues, then B reads a statement and A responds, and so on. The respondent in each case has to try to convince their partner to adopt a growth mindset attitude.

- Scan through your school policies and documentation looking for the words 'ability' and 'able'. Check in each case that it is not indicating a fixed mindset and limiting assumptions. Change your language if it is!

- Set up a swear box for any member of staff to contribute to if they use the word 'ability' or 'able' in a fixed mindset context. You could use the proceeds to fund resources for disadvantaged learners.

- Set a challenge for staff and/or learners to find and submit blatant examples of fixed mindset in the media. You could set up a student panel to judge submissions and choose the 'winner'.

Through well-considered recruitment activities, ongoing staff training and coaching (about which more will follow in Chapter 5), the development of a common language of high expectations, and a culture of everyone (including operational staff) signing up to play their part, a high-performance environment is created.

Reflection

Has your school devoted any staff training and learning time to growth mindset?

Who could you utilise as a speaker and what activities might you arrange to challenge limiting assumptions?

Convincing students

Confucius is believed to have said, 'Every child is capable of learning anything, depending on the way it is presented to them and the effort they put into learning it.'

We know that there is strong evidence of a link between high expectations, staff belief in all pupils' potential, aspirations for higher education and consequent attainment and progress. We know the impact of using peers to encourage, to show how to practise, to tell stories of failure and recovery, and to give others the confidence to think differently and dream bigger. Aspirational leaders grow a school of staff – not just teachers – who strive to develop every child's self-esteem. They constantly shine a light on and showcase stories – from history, from the media and from the school – of amoebas becoming lions through hard work, purposeful practice, determination and resilience.

Case study: Johal's story

Johal entered secondary school with a statement (as EHCPs were called in 2011) for cognitive delay and very low English, maths and science scores (national curriculum level 3). He was placed in class sets for the lowest attainers, but he and his parents were told that no one was judging his 'ability' or potential, just placing him in the group in which he was most likely to make the quickest progress. His teachers set about developing his subject knowledge and skills; all staff worked on building his self-esteem and supporting his personal development. Johal's tutor knew from the home visit that the head teacher had conducted when Johal was in Year 6 that he loved, and was very good at, origami. In fact she had an origami butterfly that Johal had made on her noticeboard. He was invited to set up an origami club for his peers, supported by a member of staff – the first student-led enrichment activity in the school! Johal quickly made friends and his confidence grew. Through hard work, and supported by a close relationship between his teachers and parents, Johal's literacy and numeracy skills developed and he moved up an attainment group for maths. This was announced in assembly. Johal continued to progress and move up groups and in Year 9 he addressed the Year 7s and 8s in assembly as proof that determination, focus, lots of practice and self-belief can lead to impressive improvement. Johal achieved 7 GCSE passes in Year 11 (4s and 5s, with 5s for English and maths), took an A level in RE and a BTEC in business, and is now studying for a business degree at Westminster University.

In schools that are aspirational for all, staff have informal coaching conversations with learners all the time, helping them to see the progress they have made, acknowledging and praising their effort, guiding and encouraging them as they take their next steps, sharing stories of others' success in reaching their goals from similar starting points, and discussing their own learning journeys. We will return to this in Chapter 3, when we take a look at building impactful relationships.

Carol Dweck's research, referenced in her book *Mindset*, demonstrates the impact of the language used by teachers – when they acknowledge and praise students and in their marking and feedback – on learners' self-belief and levels of motivation. Growth mindset teachers are aware that the right kind of praise can be motivational and affirming but the wrong kind can have negative effects. For example, making a big fuss of a student who gives the correct answer to a question can suggest that the teacher is surprised by their knowledge! They understand that:

The wrong kind of praise leads kids down the path of entitlement, dependence and fragility. The right kind of praise can lead them down the path of hard work and greater hardiness. With the right kind of feedback even adults (!) can be motivated to choose challenging tasks and confront their mistakes. (Dweck 2006: 137)

Growth mindset practitioners know that if students are told 'That's a really good score. You are really smart at this', 'You're really talented', or 'You're a natural', they love it and it gives them a boost – but only for a moment. The minute they hit a snag, their confidence goes and so does their motivation. Such praise reinforces a fixed mindset and leads to all the negative fragilities of fixed mindset learners. In contrast, if students get feedback acknowledging their effort and their improved scores – 'You really studied for that test and look at how it is reflected in your improved grade', or 'You tested yourself and prepared thoroughly and see how it paid off', or 'I like the way you tried some new strategies until you finally understood that' – this makes them far more willing to push themselves further and take on new learning challenges.

As Doug Lemov states in *Teach Like A Champion* (2010: 37): 'Great teachers praise students for their effort but never confuse effort with mastery.' They use simple, positive language to acknowledge what the student has achieved but show their expectation that they can go even further: 'I like what you have done. Can you take it further?' or 'You're almost there but there's a bit more ...' or 'I like most of that.'

Finally, it's important to remember that over-praising a run-of-the-mill response sends confusing messages about the expected standards. Praise can be diluted by overuse. The best teachers keep their most effusive praise for truly exceptional responses: 'That was a really insightful answer.'

> ## Reflection
>
> How do you build learners' self-esteem and self-belief?
>
> How do you ensure that teachers recognise and celebrate effort and progress rather than attainment in their marking, feedback and dialogue with learners?
>
> How do you profile and celebrate stories of hard work and grit, in which learners have progressed from low starting points to achieve great outcomes?

Convincing parents

All aspirational leaders will be working away at influencing the beliefs of their staff and their learners. Sometimes, in amongst all the other priorities, extending the high performance for all message to parents and carers can be overlooked. But we leave out this crucial group of influencers, with whom many learners spend far more time than in school, at our peril.

Every school will have a different way of explaining their educational rationale to parents – why they use the language they do, why they group learners as they do, why they organise the curriculum as they do, why they feed back to learners as they do. Each school will have a sense of the optimal way to seek to ensure that parents' behaviour, language and role modelling complements that of the staff. At INA we held regular interactive workshops for parents, at which leaders and learners would explain and explore the school's beliefs and approaches.

Case study: INA growth mindset parent workshops

We would start with the killer question: 'Do you believe that some people are born more intelligent or talented than others?' To this the answer was invariably 'no'. (Who would want to think that their child was born less intelligent than their neighbour's?!)

We then went on to explain that we did not believe that:

- Some people are born clever and others aren't.
- Some people are born with gifts and others aren't.
- Some people can achieve and others can't.
- Some people are born naturally great at music, sport, art, languages, etc.

Instead, we believe that:

- Everyone can grow their brain, like a muscle.
- Everyone has the potential to become really good at what they put their mind to.
- Everyone can become more intelligent.

We explained the rationale behind banning words like 'ability' and 'gifted'.

We asked parents and carers to think about something they had become really good at – for example, making samosas, dressmaking, singing or public speaking – and how they had come to be accomplished at this skill. This led nicely into identifying what leads to great performance:

- Lots of focused practice.
- Embracing and learning from mistakes and failures.
- Great teaching and coaching.
- Great resources.
- Someone to believe in you and acknowledge your effort.
- Self-belief.

We explained how we were developing growth mindset at the school by:

- Only appointing staff who believe in growth mindset.
- Discussing growth mindset with students.
- Communicating our belief in every student.
- Using growth mindset language.

- Role modelling being learners ourselves and talking about how important mistakes are in the learning process.
- Stressing the power of practice and teaching students how to practise.
- Marking and feeding back in a growth mindset way.

We asked parents and carers to support us in developing growth mindset:

- Through the language they use.
- By not allowing their child to believe that they are not good at something (by use of the word 'yet').
- By not letting siblings or others put down their aspirations.
- By stressing the power of hard work.
- Through praising effort, not achievement.
- Through praising the job, not the person.
- Through supporting with practice.
- By discussing learning and challenges with their child.

We finished by reminding everyone that growth mindset learners:

- Aren't afraid of not coming first.
- Know that they can get better and how to improve their performance.
- Don't worry about how others view them.
- Have inner confidence that they will keep improving their performance in the right conditions.
- Are more likely to succeed in exams.
- Are more likely to be effective lifelong learners.
- Are more likely to be happy in life.

Audiences often engaged in lively debate and reflection at such evenings. They never left unclear about our mission or unconvinced about our rationale. On one memorable occasion, a recommended reading list resulted, and a group of converts was formed that provided invaluable support at subsequent events.

Reflection

How have you worked to communicate your core beliefs about high expectations of all learners to parents and carers?

How have you supported them in role modelling a growth mindset?

Might a variation of the growth mindset workshop described in the case study have impact at your school?

Closing thought

This chapter has considered what leaders can do to establish a culture of high performance for all and how to spread an infectious belief in the potential of every learner, so that no staff member, parent or student is immune to the culture. As Matthew Syed says in *Bounce* (2010: 128):

Perhaps the key task of any institution is to encourage a growth mindset. When that kind of philosophy becomes embedded in a culture, the consequences can be dramatic.

Chapter 3

Building strong relationships with students

I've learned that people will forget what you said, people will forget what you did, but people will never forget how you made them feel.

Often attributed to Maya Angelou[1]

Kids don't learn from people they don't like.

Rita Pierson (2013)

We can all recount stories of the staff who taught us at school. The chances are that, in amongst them, will be one or two who seemed not to like children at all. But when we recall our favourite teachers, they are usually the ones with whom we formed a strong bond, those individuals who went the extra mile and took the time to get to know us personally. We may not remember all our interactions with them or exactly what they said to build our confidence or self-esteem but, as Maya Angelou expresses in the quote above, we remember vividly how they made us feel and the self-belief they generated in us.

In schools that are serious about maximising all learners' chances to achieve, leaders appreciate that, before great learning can happen, great relationships need to be formed. Their primary focus is on creating a climate in which every adult takes (and demonstrates) a genuine interest in the pupils. They seek to appoint educators (teachers and operational staff) who love to be with children, and they diplomatically part ways with those who don't.

---

1   https://quoteinvestigator.com/2014/04/06/they-feel/.

The importance of relationships

Research by John Hattie, in his analysis of the thousands of meta-studies that made up *Visible Learning* (2008), suggests that the quality of the relationships that teachers have with their students is crucial for learning. By making learning visible, the most effective teachers are demonstrating to their students that they care and that they are aware of the impact they can have. Along with competence, dynamism and immediacy, Hattie identifies trust as a key element of a teacher's credibility. He talks of the importance of teachers being genuine, sincere and honest with their students, demonstrating that they care about their progress and learning, being fair and consistent and taking an interest in their lives outside of school. In *Visible Learning for Teachers*, Hattie (2012: 26) goes on to talk about the importance of 'developing a climate of trust between teacher and student.' He says that 'The picture of expert teachers, then, is one of involvement and respect for the students, of a willingness to be receptive to what the students need' (Hattie 2012: 27).

When we were planning for the opening of INA, we designed a staff expectations policy which laid out the non-negotiables in terms of the beliefs, behaviours and characteristics that were required from school employees. In one section it stated:

To take responsibility for developing students' emotional wellbeing as well as nurturing their academic potential: never behaving in a derogatory, intimidatory, abusive or sarcastic manner towards any member of the school community.

We would discuss this policy with candidates at interview in order to satisfy ourselves that we were appointing educators who genuinely loved working with young people and would treat them with honour and respect. We often asked prospective members of the operational team – for example, finance officer, receptionist – 'Why do you particularly want to carry out this role in a school?' On occasions, it would be necessary to take a member of staff back to the policy if their behaviour had fallen short for any reason. I never had cause to lose a member of staff due to concerns about their desire to work with young people, but I would not have hesitated to do so if necessary.

> ## Reflection
>
> Does your school have a staff expectations policy? If you were to write one, what would you put in it?

One way in which INA was perhaps atypical was that all staff had a number of activities built into their roles that might not traditionally be seen in other schools. They were there to facilitate and encourage the forging of strong staff–student relationships. Every job description had the following requirements in it:

To get to know the academy's students and to take an interest in their lives beyond school through regular informal dialogue around school, joining them for lunch in the school dining hall daily and accompanying them on school trips and visits.

To attend key whole-school events in the annual school calendar, such as open evenings and awards ceremonies.

To attend school assemblies each week.

To deliver or contribute to at least one enrichment session for students each week during term time.

I was striving to create a community in which every child was properly known by the staff. An environment in which their loves, passions, out-of-school experiences, dreams, frustrations and fears were understood by adults who were significant to them. I wanted to create time and opportunities for rich and rewarding conversations to take place and strong relationships to develop. These requirements in the job description were designed to facilitate this. My motivation was threefold. Firstly, I was convinced that, for all pupils, learning would be facilitated by strong relationships with staff and the trust that came with it. Secondly, I believed that open and honest relationships would enable pupils to communicate their learning needs and teachers to personalise their support more effectively. Thirdly, for learners who did not get impactful support and encouragement from adults outside school, I wanted to ensure that adults in school could perform the role played by the parents of their more fortunate peers. Some of the pupils in need of a 'surrogate' were eligible for PP funding, but many were not; we all know that learners eligible for PP funding are as different from each other as they are from those who do not fall into that classification.

When Tim Brighouse came to address the staff at INA in 2013, he talked of the 'Kes Factor'. In the film *Kes*, based on Barry Hines' powerful novel *A Kestrel for a Knave* (1968), Billy Casper, a working-class boy with a bleak home life in a northern mining town, finds and trains a kestrel. When he is invited by his schoolteacher to talk on a subject about which he is knowledgeable, he speaks in front of his class with passion, confidence and articulacy about training his kestrel, to the amazement of everyone. Brighouse stresses the imperative for discovering the Kes Factor for all 'harder to reach' learners and the power of doing so in terms of hooking them into learning, raising aspirations and unblocking barriers to progress and attainment.

Inspired by Brighouse, I wanted my school to be characterised by staff communicating with students as they welcomed them at the gate at the start of the day, when they conducted their break duty and supervised the lunch queue – chatting to students about what they watched on TV the night before, what they had done at the weekend, where their football team was in the league, their views on topical and political issues, what clubs and enrichment activities they were attending that term, and so on. I wanted to see tutor group noticeboards with displays about what tutees were reading and their book reviews, pictures of newborn siblings and much-loved grandparents. I wanted to see adults confident to show their human side (sharing their own learning journeys and challenges), being approachable (sharing details from their personal – but not private – lives, such as their favourite sports team, interests and hobbies) and demonstrating their fallibility (discussing mistakes made and lessons learnt).

I wanted to see family-style dining, with adults and students eating and chatting together, pondering philosophical questions and reviewing their days so far. If a member of staff had had a run-in with a particular student, I would sometimes suggest that they engineered the opportunity to sit with them at lunch to get to know them better and strengthen their relationship outside of the classroom. I wanted pupils to see teachers and operational staff in the audience at concerts, sporting events and awards celebrations, sharing in the joy of their achievements and successes. The practice of every member of staff giving an hour of their time each week to run or support an enrichment activity was a powerful way of demonstrating to learners and their families the staff's commitment to the pupils and their investment in the community. It also enabled children and adults to bond in a less formal setting and was a great leveller between teachers and operational staff in terms of adults as educators.

The role of leaders in developing relationships

There are several ways in which I have seen leaders develop a school culture which fosters and prioritises great relationships between staff and learners. The first, most obvious and perhaps most powerful way is through role modelling the behaviour expected from colleagues. The best leaders work hard to get to know the names of as many learners as possible, acknowledge them with a cheery smile and a greeting when they pass them in the corridor. They never miss an opportunity to make a comment that shows personal knowledge of the pupil – 'Good to see you back after your accident' – or ask a question that shows genuine interest – 'I know you're interested in studying medicine. What did you think of that visiting GP's talk in assembly?' They are well known for their warmth, openness, approachability and care. They never publicly shout or humiliate. They never overlook a learner, and they go out of their way to make time to engage with groups and individuals, in the playground, in the lunch queue, when they visit lessons, at the school gate, and anywhere else they might encounter them.

Secondly, they notice which members of staff are great at building and developing relationships and find opportunities to showcase their behaviours, publicly recognising and thanking them. This could be via a 'shout out' during staff briefings, inviting students to thank staff for showing random acts of kindness or awarding a box of chocolates to colleagues for going 'above and beyond' in their actions. By so doing, they are signalling to the rest of the staff that 'this is what is valued around here'.

Thirdly, they notice which staff don't find it quite so easy to form relationships with learners and, working with their line managers, ensure that support is put in place to help them develop these vital skills. At INA we took note of those members of staff who seemed ill at ease dining with students they didn't know. We provided ideas of conversation themes – such as, 'If you could have a superpower, which would you choose?' – and circulated ideas from *The Little Book of Thunks* (Gilbert 2007) as questions to pose to start a philosophical conversation. We encouraged them to sit on a table with a staff member who was more at ease in conversation with learners, to observe the strategies and techniques they used.

Lastly, such leaders intervene to support staff whose relationships with certain learners, or groups of learners, are negative or even toxic. They provide training and coaching as appropriate, they make their expectations clear, they set targets where necessary, and they move colleagues on if they are really not the right fit for the school.

Reflection

How do your staff demonstrate their commitment to the learners?

Do you look for vulnerable learners' Kes Factor? How? What do you do with this knowledge?

Do you have any members of staff who find it hard to build and sustain relationships with learners? What support and intervention is in place to help them and with what impact?

Staff champions

You may have come across the charismatic American educationalist Rita Pierson, sadly now departed, via her compelling TED Talk (2013). In it she argues that:

Every child deserves a champion – an adult who will never give up on them, who understands the power of connections and insists that they become the best that they can possibly be.

Addressing teachers around the world, she says, 'We're educators. We're born to make a difference.' The difference Pierson refers to is not only facilitating students' learning, but also being a positive force in their lives. She calls on teachers to build relationships with their students, no matter how challenging that may be. Her TED Talk was part of the inspiration for an interesting initiative at one Hertfordshire secondary school.

Case study: Tring School

The 'every child deserves a champion' initiative, introduced 18 months ago, was motivated by a desire to improve staff understanding of the barriers to learning for students from disadvantaged backgrounds. Tring School is committed to ensuring that all students have equity of access to an enriching and inclusive educational experience. The school's vision is that all students will become 'successful learners, confident individuals and responsible citizens'. To achieve this, staff work in partnership with students and families to maximise their educational experience.

Leaders believed that all students deserved a 'champion', who would demonstrate an interest in their educational and social growth to unlock their talent and realise their potential. For the large majority of students, this investment and support is provided in the home. However, this is not the case for all students and, where there is a gap, a member of school staff adopts the role of champion as a 'PP advocate'. Leaders at Tring School made a commitment that every child eligible for PP funding would be provided with an advocate on entry to the school, who would stay with them on their educational journey. Staff were asked to opt out, rather than opt in, and 98.6% of staff became PP advocates. Staff made a commitment to be 'irrationally crazy' about their assigned student. Staff were able to identify a student with whom they felt they had a good relationship and the assistant head for PP then matched students with advocates. In order to manage the roll-out, advocates were appointed in waves, starting with students who were identified as being most in need. Students meet their advocate every other week for a conferencing session of up to 30 minutes. The focus of the early sessions is on building the relationship and really getting to know the student.

It was felt that the staff required a much deeper understanding of individual students' experiences and needed to have access to confidential information about their backgrounds to enable them to understand their needs. The Tring School student passport was introduced. It linked class lists, registers and the school's information management system. The passport contains information regarding SEND, attendance, improvement plans, pastoral interventions and any use of inclusion provision. A tab allows the PP advocate to record up to three things that the student feels it is important that all staff know about them and three positive statements that they want to be true about themselves. This provides information to all staff quickly, ensures that key data is shared to support learning in the classroom, and helps teachers support disadvantaged learners in the pursuit of their three key goals.

The results have been impressive: 18 months into the initiative, 83% of staff feel that they are more confident in engaging with and supporting vulnerable students and working with their families; 57% think that it has changed how they think about students and their home situations. In a pilot group, 94% of staff said that it was now significantly easier to access information relating to students' needs and that, in some situations, information about disadvantaged students had led to them being able to handle a situation differently and more effectively. After a relatively short period of time, 30% of students with advocates had improved their attendance; 25% had made significant academic progress; 67% felt that the work with their advocate had helped them to understand how they can do better, either in or out of school; and 33% said that they feel more able to talk about their feelings.

Sally Ambrose and Lucy Williams

Reflection

Do you have any learners who might benefit from a champion or advocate?

How might you determine who they are and who might be matched with them?

Staff who are fully knowledgeable about their learners

In September 1989, as an NQT about to start my first teaching post, I was sent a list of the children in my tutor group: 24 Year 7s. I was furnished with their first and last names and details of any who had a specific form of SEND or a medical condition. That was it. Over the next three years I gradually gleaned snippets of information about them and, once a year, met with the parents of some of them for a five-minute appointment, if I happened to teach them history. I can clearly remember my awkwardness when distributing letters or messages to be passed on to parents, conscious that for some of my tutees I did not know whether they lived with their mother and father, with only one parent, with extended family or with a carer. I would say, 'Take this home to give to your mum or dad', hoping that this instruction applied to them. I knew nothing about where my tutees lived or how conducive their home environments were to independent learning. The role of the tutor did not extend to facilitating out-of-school learning.

Fast forward to September 2012, when I assembled the founding staff of my new school, INA, for the first day of a three-week training and induction period. Much of this time was devoted to getting to know the community and our first cohort of students, in order to support them as well as possible as learners, in and out of school. The staff were given statistics about the housing, education, employment and leisure opportunities in the locality. They were appraised of the school's intelligence regarding crime-, drug- and gang-related activity in the area. All the information gathered in the transition process (which we will explore in more detail in Chapter 4) was passed on. It was important to me, as it was to the leaders at Tring School, that my tutors were equipped with a wealth of rich data on which to build strong and impactful relationships with their tutees. In short, we were supporting them to become fully knowledgeable about their learners.

Schools that are serious about knowing about learners' lives outside of school invest training and development time in that endeavour. They know that this is necessary to ensure that the staff understand the experiences of those whose backgrounds are likely very different to their own. Let's go back to Tring School for an example.

Case study continued: Tring School

Many Tring staff come from an academic background, where education is valued and deemed hugely important to people's futures. Staff were being asked to understand the challenges that some students arrive at the classroom with, which are far removed from their own experiences. Although empathy is a strength of all colleagues at Tring School, it was deemed important to invest in training for all staff and for them to be exposed to some of the realities and challenges that a minority of Tring students face and, furthermore, to understand how adverse childhood experiences (ACEs) can impact on young people throughout their lives. In an attempt to provide a greater understanding and appreciation of some students' challenges, staff participated in a whole-school trial of John Timpson's Attachment Training, which addressed the impact of trauma and ACEs. This proved to be a positive step in enabling staff to reflect on student reactions in the classroom and raised the need for staff to seek first to understand rather than to be understood. The whole school community engaged in training around attachment theory and spent time learning about the very early connections and relationships that young people create, the importance of these and the trauma that can occur for our young people when these bonds are not formed or maintained. Consequently, the school has adapted its behaviour policy and classroom climates have been altering. There has been a culture shift: punitive sanctions are avoided and replaced with restorative justice. All interactions with adults from the start of the day centre on support and nurture, whilst maintaining high expectations of all students.

Sally Ambrose and Lucy Williams

Reflection

In your school, how well equipped are tutors (secondary) and/or class teachers (primary) with key information about the learners in their care?

Lockdown experiences

One of the striking inequities during the lockdown periods of spring/summer 2020 and winter/spring 2021 was the experience that different learners had in terms of contact with their teachers. From tracking conducted across the county in which I work, it was clear that, during the initial period of lockdown, some schools prioritised maintaining regular and personalised communication with children, via telephone calls, Zoom or Microsoft Teams meetings, online videos, cards and letters, and deliveries of books and activities. But learners from other schools languished for weeks on end without one-to-one contact. By the third national lockdown, the government made its expectations of regular contact with each learner much more explicit, but the digital divide continued to make this a challenge in many cases.

I have a niece and a nephew at the same stage in their education: both halfway through their first undergraduate year when the pandemic struck. Rosie is reading English literature and American studies at a top Russell Group university and Patrick is taking a degree in acting and musical theatre at one of the leading drama schools in London. Their learning experiences during the first period of lockdown couldn't have been more different. Patrick has seven tutors: a course leader, an acting tutor, two voice teachers, a tutor for text analysis, a physical theatre teacher and a tutor who leads weekly workshops with his class of 18. Pre-lockdown he had classes from 9am until 6pm most days. From March 2020 until July 2020, when all students were at home due to the pandemic, he had six hours of classes each day, from 1pm until 7pm. The hours were set to accommodate the location of all the class members, three of whom were in different time zones (one on the East Coast of the USA, one on the West Coast, and another in Argentina). In addition to his classes, Patrick had regular one-to-one sessions with each of his tutors, who always checked on his wellbeing and home circumstances. Although he did not need additional support (Patrick is a well-adjusted boy from a stable, middle-class family, with ideal home learning conditions), a friend of his, whose mother was in hospital, found the one-to-ones and other forms of support invaluable.

In contrast, as soon as Rosie arrived home in March 2020 she went to work full-time at the local Waitrose. Her university made it clear that, although online lectures would continue, attendance would not be compulsory and end of year exams would, likewise, be optional. As a school student she had been eligible for PP funding, and her parents continue to face economic challenges, so the opportunity to earn some extra cash to see her through her remaining years at university was an attractive one. She worked at the store for 35–40 hours each week from March through to September 2020 and chose not to attend lectures, do the reading or sit the exams. Other than one essay, she did no university work at all in that period. She received regular generic emails from the university, with details of who to contact if she had any problems, but no personalised one-to-one support from a tutor or supervisor.

It strikes me that the difference between Rosie's and Patrick's experiences is in no small part explained by the different attitudes held, and approaches taken, by their universities to building quality relationships with learners. Rosie has an academic adviser with whom she can book one-to-one sessions. She did meet her in the first six months of her course, but not frequently enough to build up a relationship. The adviser emailed her group during lockdown, but never contacted Rosie personally. In contrast, Patrick's course leader knows him well. She knows that he has a brother and a sister, where he went to school, with whom and where he lives and the family dynamic. Patrick says, 'You can email or text her whenever.' Of his acting tutor, Patrick reflects:

I have at least two one-to-ones scheduled with her each term, but I can book a session with her whenever I want – in the evening or at the weekend. I have had extra sessions with her for up to an hour. Once she couldn't make a class but she wanted to catch up the hours with us so she asked if we could do it on a Saturday instead. We all really like her. She pushes us and tests us. But she is really patient. She is good at pushing you beyond what you think are your limits. I feel she knows me really well and I have got to know her well too. It's so obvious that she loves the plays we study.

She really cares about what we are working on and she wants us to feel the same way. She takes us out of our comfort zone. She challenges us and it is uncomfortable, but we trust her. She knows what she is doing and she cares about her students. Even if she is brutal, she's really good!

Listening to Patrick, I was reminded of what a huge advantage it is for those learners who are fortunate enough to have an educator like his acting tutor, and reflected on how much Rosie would have benefited from the equivalent relationship.

Reflection

Reflecting on the lockdown experiences of students in your school, are they more similar to Rosie's or to Patrick's?

What advice have you given to staff regarding how to maintain and foster relationships with students when teaching and learning take place remotely?

Have you sought feedback from students about which staff are especially good at maintaining relationships when learning is taking place remotely? If not, how might you do this and what might you ask them?

I suspect that the schools and universities that had forged, nurtured and sustained quality relationships between staff and students prior to lockdown would have maintained them most successfully during the pandemic.

In the special school sector, providing a high-quality education during lockdown, as well as care and support in a COVID-secure environment, was particularly challenging and depended on well-established relationships with learners and their families. This is illustrated by the following case study from a special school for primary aged children with social, emotional and mental health (SEMH) needs in Hemel Hempstead.

Case study: Haywood Grove School

In normal times our children experience a significantly heavy stress load and so we knew that many would find tolerating the additional change, disruption and uncertainty brought about by COVID-19 particularly difficult to bear. We anticipated that their relationships with their parents, carers and siblings may also be impacted due to the additional pressures and tensions faced by families. We therefore set about developing ways of working with them that would help to alleviate some of these additional pressures.

In the first instance, we talked to our parents and carers individually, establishing the needs, concerns and vulnerabilities that existed within their households. We surveyed their opinions and sought information through the use of a question-naire, in order that we could provide sensitive responses to personal circumstances and deliver bespoke intervention. We developed a vulnerability indicator for children and families and used this as a framework for monitoring and responding to ongoing and changing support needs, including those of a safeguarding nature.

Some families wanted full-time provision during lockdown and others were reluc-tant to return their child to school and so, as we opened more widely, we were determined to see as many children as possible in the space of a week. We wrote to parents and carers, providing information about the extensive risk assessments undertaken – of individual children, of the environment and of the activities we would offer – in addition to providing each child with a bespoke timetable, blend-ing face-to-face in-school and remote learning where possible. We worked in a fast and improvised way, developing a remote curriculum that, as far as possible, replicated our in-school offer. We surveyed our families to get a sense of what they might want and need, offering telephone calls, video calls, letters and post-cards home, communication through our home–school link books and email, the provision of work packs, learning gifts in the post, virtual play/games, play ther-apy sessions and group video calls. As we fell into a natural rhythm, we continued to identify what else might be needed and to improve our offer. This meant that we delivered resources to family homes, undertook socially distanced garden visits, provided laptops and dongles for those without equipment or internet and made individually accessible videos for those with more complex and/or sensory needs who were less able to access our more traditional methods of communica-tion. We found ways of bringing children who would otherwise have had to use public transport into school safely.

This situation has given us the chance to get to know each other better and to get to know the children more fully on an individual basis. Never has there been a time when we can better prove that attending to social and emotional needs is crucial to providing a foundation for fostering creativity, innovation and talent in all members of the community. We have been pushed to give more ownership and trust to our colleagues and in turn have discovered gifts and capabilities that we didn't know were there. The warmth and unconditional positive regard shown to the children and each other have been remarkable.

Catherine Smith

Equally important was the planning that schools undertook to rebuild relationships post-lockdown, as they welcomed back learners from all year groups in September 2020. Barry and Matthew Carpenter's influential blog on the 'recovery curriculum', posted in the spring of 2020, reminded educators that some children would be suffering from the loss of social interaction and that it might take time for them not to feel threatened by the nearness of others. They said:

We can't expect our students to return joyfully, and many of the relationships that were thriving may need to be invested in and restored. [...] Our quest, our mission as educators, should be to journey with that child through a process of re-engagement, which leads them back to their rightful status as a fully engaged, authentic learner.

Time and time again, in conversations with dozens of school leaders throughout the autumn of 2020, I heard articulated a recognition of just how important the rebuilding and sustaining of strong relationships was.

Closing thought

In *A Manifesto for Excellence in Schools*, Rob Carpenter talks about 'teachers who create climates for learning that strengthen confidence and motivation amongst learners', where 'fear of failure is replaced by mutual appreciation, collaboration between pupils and investment in each other's triumphs and disasters.' He asserts that 'In essence, it is the climate and culture created in classrooms that determines outcomes for young people' (Carpenter 2018: 65). I couldn't agree more.

The impact of such teachers is greatest on the most disadvantaged learners and those who are not fortunate enough to get such encouragement and motivation from adults outside of the school community. I end this chapter with an extract from an email exchange I had recently with a colleague, who was retiring after a very successful career as a primary teacher, head teacher and, latterly, senior school effectiveness adviser:

My belief in the power of education to make a difference to the life chances of any child has been my driving force. I grew up in poverty. We had no heating, no bathroom, no hot water and only an outside loo. The first time I had any of these facilities was when we were moved to a council house when I was 15. My mum couldn't read or write, and was an alcoholic. I worked every weekend from when I was 12 and, when I got to 16, I was made to get a full-time job in a motorway service station.

My teachers took me under their wing. Firstly, my teacher in Year 3, who took a shine to me because she ran the school choir and I could sing. It was the first time that I had ever felt believed in at school. At secondary school, my teachers arranged my timetable so that I could study for three A levels as well as go to work. I worked at the motorway service station doing long shifts on Fridays through to Mondays, and had my school lessons on Tuesdays, Wednesdays and Thursdays. I knew that I wanted to teach but my teachers were determined that I should go to university and get a degree, not go straight into teacher training.

Part of my mum's family cut me off when I went to university as they saw it as a betrayal of my roots. A couple of my cousins have been in and out of jail for dealing in drugs and stolen cars. I must share a large amount of genetic material with them, but our outcomes have been so very different as a result of environment. I had teachers that believed in me and an education that gave me options. This didn't happen for them.

Norah Tattersall

Chapter 4

Impactful parental engagement

Those who exert the first influence upon the mind, have the greatest power.

Horace Mann (1872: 10)

The purpose of a school is to help a family educate a child.

Don Edgar (Quoted in Donahoo 2013)

In some international education systems the role of teachers and school leaders is seen as largely concerned with what takes place during the school day and contained within the school's physical boundary. Indeed, the same is true in some UK schools, with teachers arguing that they should concern themselves solely with delivering first-class lessons in their subject and imparting the key knowledge of the formal curriculum, rather than liaising with parents and involving themselves with learners' lives outside of school. Whilst they might well set homework tasks, especially for older students, they would see it as the role of parents, assisted by a range of external agencies, to take responsibility for children's wellbeing and wider 'education' outside of the school building and out of hours. However, I suspect that there are fewer proponents of this view now than at the start of 2020, when the coronavirus struck.

Since 2007, when the early years foundation stage (EYFS) statutory framework was introduced (Department for Education 2017), there has been a legal requirement for early years providers to identify a 'key person' on the staff body for each child, to liaise with their parents or carers. The expectations of that key person are laid out clearly. Settings and schools are required to inform parents/carers of the name of the key person, and explain their role when the child joins. The key person must help ensure that every child's learning and care is tailored to meet their individual needs. They must seek to engage and support parents/carers in guiding their child's development at home. They should also help families engage with specialist support if appropriate. Sadly, there is no such requirement in the later phases of education.

Returning to our medical analogy, the best healthcare workers will devote time to building relationships with expectant parents and will prioritise those who most need their support. They will guide and educate without making assumptions, rushing to conclusions or patronising. They will listen to, respond to, work with and empower – just like the best teachers. Many students who are eligible for PP funding have highly educated and supportive parents and homes full of books, but some experience less 'education' outside of school than their more advantaged peers. So smart school leaders devote time to training their staff on how to build and maintain positive and productive relationships with all parents, but, additionally and importantly, how to identify those who would most benefit from extra, nuanced support. They encourage their staff to persist in forging links with those who are hardest to reach or most challenging to work with. Their staff demonstrate that they value their learners' parents, welcome their feedback (even when it is challenging) and act on it. They support and offer guidance on co-educating. They assist financially without allowing stigmatisation or seeking gratitude. They work in effective partnership to remove barriers and enable learners to soar.

The challenge of engaging parents

When the organisation I work for, Herts for Learning, conducted research with head teachers in 2013 for a report entitled *Pupil Premium in Hertfordshire: Use and Impact* (2014), school leaders identified lack of parental engagement as the greatest challenge they faced in raising the attainment of disadvantaged learners. In 2018, I explored this situation in finer detail with leaders of the 28 Hertfordshire schools engaged in the Great Expectations programme (mentioned in the introduction to this book) that year. I wanted to understand the nature of the barriers faced by children where parental engagement was considered to be an issue. In some cases this was to do with low parental aspirations, or poor attitudes to education over several generations, whilst in other cases it related to limited engagement with school, a lack of parenting skills or parents having insufficient time to support learning. Schools that are serious about creating a high-performance culture recognise the need to work with parents and carers, and address the specific engagement issues that apply in their particular context. They start out by articulating what it is they are intending to achieve. They ask the question: 'What would great parental engagement look like?'

At INA we did this through a parental engagement policy, from which the extract below is taken:

Creating and sustaining effective relationships with every parent/carer is our priority. We particularly endeavour to engage those parents/carers who are hard to reach, in order to support a more active and personal level of participation in their child's learning.

We engage effectively with parents through the following six key activities:

- *Building relationships.*
- *Communicating effectively.*
- *Reporting progress regularly.*
- *Helping parents to support their child's learning.*
- *Involving parents in decision making.*
- *Extending links beyond the school day.*

In this chapter we will explore each of these aspects and consider a variety of strategies to develop parental engagement.

Building relationships

Smart schools prioritise getting to know pupils and their families and building positive relationships with them prior to the child joining the school. At primary, home visits (usually conducted by two members of staff in the late afternoon or early evening) are relatively commonplace, but less so at secondary, which baffles me. As the head of an all-through school, I saw the immense benefit of home visits for both 4- and 11-year-olds, to meet their families, to discuss the pupils' educational histories, strengths, challenges, fears and dreams, and to communicate the school's vision, expectations and the belief in the importance of a strong and productive home–school partnership.

In the literally hundreds of home visits I conducted whilst at INA, I met siblings and grandparents, and pet rabbits and parrots; I saw holiday snaps, certificates and medals, bookshelves and hobby collections; I chatted about dietary and medical requirements, religious observance and cultural practices. I shared our growth mind-set philosophy and high expectations (of ourselves, of students, and of parents). I was trusted with confidences around family separations, losses and traumas. I was invited to sample favourite dishes, share meals and take tea with families. It was so much more powerful as a means of getting to know a pupil and their family than simply relying on their nursery or primary class teacher's feedback, or just talking to the pupil in school. The simple investment of 30–45 minutes to visit the home was a powerful way of demonstrating interest in the family and the importance of the home–school partnership. It set the relationship off on a strong footing and built what Stephen Covey (2006) calls 'the speed of trust'. In his book of the same name, Covey argues that things happen more quickly and efficiently, and time is saved, when people really trust each other. In other words, 45 minutes spent establishing a positive relationship and getting a family onside and believing in the credibility and integrity of the school staff from the outset is likely to save hours of time spent on queries, difficult conversations, wrangles or even complaints in future months or years should staff need to discipline a child or call home with a tough message.

The home visit is a sign of the school's commitment to the child and a manifestation of the staff's determination to do their best for them. In my seven years of overseeing home visits (180 per year for Year 7s and 90 per year for Reception) I could count on one hand the number of families who were suspicious of the initiative or reluctant to invite staff into their home. In these situations we held the visit at a local café or in school. But most families felt honoured to host a visit from a senior leader, class teacher, form tutor or member of the operational team. They were delightful occasions and I encouraged as many staff as possible to conduct them. New recruits would shadow more experienced colleagues and then lead their own visits. Often the student being visited would be waiting at the door or behind the curtain, keeping watch for the visitors. I recall one occasion when a youngster was standing at the end of the road and, as I came around the bend, he ran towards his home shouting 'She's coming!' loudly enough for all the residents of the street to hear.

Reflection

At your school, how do you demonstrate to parents your commitment to their child?

What actions do you take to build up a 'speed of trust' with families to enhance your relationship with them?

Seeking to understand

Following home visits, staff can ascertain levels of parental support, engagement and capacity, economic hardship, cultural capital and the interventions and differentiation that will have most impact. It is a means of what Rita Pierson called 'seeking to understand'. Although in most cases the home visits conducted at INA highlighted the support that families would provide, on a few occasions they alerted staff to children who were going to be heavily dependent on school staff to take on some of the roles traditionally fulfilled by parents. Sometimes they were those eligible for PP funding and sometimes not.

I can clearly remember a visit I made to the home of a Year 6 girl one Saturday morning, at the appointed time, to find her there alone. I knew from the primary school records that this girl had recently lost her mother and the appointment had been made for me to meet with her and her father. When I asked where her dad was, she told me that he was out with his new girlfriend. I asked whether they had filled in the pre-visit documentation that we had posted. They hadn't – in fact, she couldn't find it. I went ahead with the meeting with just the girl, whom I quickly discovered was articulate, quick witted and delightful. However, I also discovered that her father's new girlfriend was expecting their baby and that his daughter was being badly overlooked, left alone to deal with her grief. As a result of the encounter, I was able to prepare the staff to take extra care of this student and to champion her throughout her years with us. She and I never discussed that first meeting after she joined the school, but it gave us a bond. She took her GCSEs a term after I left INA. When I went back for the cohort's presentation evening, to celebrate with students and their parents, I was delighted to see her (without her father) and to have the opportunity to share in her joy at gaining the grades she required for her chosen post-16 courses.

On occasions, the home visit enabled support to be fast-tracked, accelerating the learner's progress upon joining the school, as the following example illustrates.

Case study: Dipu's story

Dipu was the last student to be allocated a place in the founding Year 7 cohort of INA, late in July, after the end of term. When I conducted his home visit, I met with him, his parents and his younger brother in a flat above a chip shop in Ilford. They were Bengalis, who had just arrived from Italy and spoke virtually no English.

Through pidgin English (theirs) and Italian (mine), I was able to ascertain that Dipu knew no one and had no summer plans, but that he loved drawing (he showed me his artwork) and football (idolising Zlatan Ibrahimović). I went back to school and scoured through the home visit notes of the other 179 students joining the school in September and found another Italian-speaking Bangladeshi boy, Moynul, who was also crazy about football. I called up his mum and asked if her son could meet up with Dipu during the holidays, teach him some English and introduce him to his mates at the local park so that Dipu could hit the ground running in September. When I went back to visit in late August, there were two pairs of boys' slippers outside the front door of the flat – Dipu's and Moynul's. They had become firm friends, meeting up most days over the holidays to play football. Dipu now spoke basic English and was feeling excited about starting school in the UK. His parents had also become friends with Moynul's mum and dad and were more settled in the community. Dipu went on to achieve 10 GCSE passes, having not spoken any English five years earlier.

Smart schools use the hard and soft data collected during home visits to determine pupil groupings and to inform tutors and teachers of additional support needs and barriers to be overcome. From the INA home visits, we compiled a database of 'qualitative information': with whom the students lived; whether they had older siblings who could perhaps offer support with independent learning; whether they had a quiet space in which to study and access to a computer, printer and Wi-Fi; their hopes, aspirations and anxieties; their favourite subjects and those that they found harder; their interests and hobbies; their reading habits (or lack of); whether they had a full and active life outside of school or a paucity of cultural capital; whether the adults in their life seemed to be time-rich or lacking the capacity to devote attention to their child's wider education. All of this was passed on to the tutors, along with attendance and attainment information from feeder primary schools. These tutors were equipped with a wealth of rich data on which to build strong and impactful relationships with their tutees, not to mention their parents who, by virtue of the home visits programme, were already convinced of the school's commitment to working with them. Home visits allow arrangements to be put in place prior to the first day of school to give each and every learner the best start to their education.

When society went into lockdown in March 2020, statistics quickly emerged of the number of families without the resources to access the, often impressive, digital learning provided by their child's school. The Children's Commissioner's report of 22 April 2020 asserted that, prior to the coronavirus pandemic, more than 125,000 children were housed in temporary accommodation and 90,000 families in England were estimated to be sofa-surfing. Roughly 60,000 children in the UK, the report continued, had no Wi-Fi, whilst 700,000 did not have a laptop, desktop or tablet in their home. Many more children were having to share a device with siblings and parents who were trying to work from home (Children's Commissioner 2020: 2).

In some schools, teachers seemed oblivious to the potential lack of learning resources in homes. Online lessons required children to use scissors, coloured pencils, glue, card, string and beads, with little awareness that such materials were not readily accessible in many homes. In other schools we witnessed leaders scrabbling around to determine who lacked a computer, which families did not have a printer and which homes were without internet. Schools that already had this intelligence from home visits were a crucial step ahead. Unwilling to wait for the UK government's promised laptops (many of which did not arrive for months), lots of school leaders loaned equipment and supplied internet dongles in the early days of the first national lockdown, but inevitably there was a time delay, during which learners from poorer families were disadvantaged. Schools that had audited access to digital learning during a home visit, prior to the learner joining the school, put themselves in a position to access solutions well before the pandemic.

In a world that may well have to get used to living with viral pandemics and their impact on education institutions, it is more important than ever that school staff understand the home learning environment of each of their learners and put interventions in place to support those who will struggle to learn independently at home (on which more will follow in Chapter 6). Indeed, schools should be considering the practicalities well in advance of any necessity to home-educate. Leaders should be encouraged to use funding allocated for disadvantaged learners to purchase resources for the home – desks, stationery, lamps, laptops and Wi-Fi devices.

Reflection

How do you gain an insight into your students' home learning environments?

How accurate and comprehensive is the picture you produce? How could it be improved?

In *Narrowing the Attainment Gap*, Daniel Sobel (2018: 82) talks about how we know that parents have invaluable insights to offer about their children and their learning. Yet many parents are distrustful of the education system, sometimes as a result of negative experiences during their own schooling or perhaps due to fears that school staff will judge them critically. This can lead them to conceal details of their inability to assist with out-of-school learning, lack of learning resources or cramped or chaotic home conditions. Parents are more likely to give honest and open responses to questions about the logistics of home learning when in dialogue face-to-face with staff members in their home. They might just tick 'yes' to a survey question asking whether there is a computer at home, when the reality might be that there is only one and it is used throughout the day by a parent for work. A positive home visit, which starts to form a relationship of mutual trust and respect, can be a vital first step in eroding negative attitudes towards the school and the system, and can start an honest conversation about the assistance that the school can provide. The key, of course, is to ensure that once the foundations for a strong parental partnership have been laid, they are built on and strengthened.

Communicating effectively, reporting progress regularly and involving parents in decision making

Some parents and carers can find communicating with their child's school very challenging, for a myriad of reasons. Practically, making contact is not always easy. Some school phones ring unanswered or are only staffed for a few hours per day. Others use impersonal automated messages, hold callers in queues for ages or provide a baffling array of options for parents who may not know the person with whom they need to speak. Some schools can be overzealous in projecting the message that parents should not come into school without an appointment, giving the impression that they are not welcome or are a bit of a pain. Others are inflexible with appointment times, meaning parents can struggle to come in around work and caring commitments.

Parents whose own experience of school was negative can be reluctant to engage. Painful memories of poor relationships with their own teachers can affect their perception of staff at their child's school. Parents who struggled academically and were not supported by staff in their school days may be defensive and put off asking questions about their child's progress or provision. Others may be overly deferential, influenced by cultural perceptions of teachers being high status; they wouldn't dream of contacting school and 'making a fuss'. Others are pressured by painfully self-conscious adolescents who don't want their parents anywhere near school and convince them that no one else's parents communicate with the staff. If the school communicates with home infrequently and fails to welcome parents into the building, their adolescent's messaging sounds credible!

As a senior leader responsible for home–school liaison in Tower Hamlets in the 1990s, I worked with many Bengali parents who faced a language barrier and were self-conscious that their English was not yet fluent. Many of the mums seldom left their estate and were apprehensive of venturing out onto the surrounding streets, let alone into school. Born in rural Sylhet, they had not experienced schooling themselves and had a very limited understanding of the Western education system. However, it is important to note that even parents who are completely fluent in the English language and with UK educational institutions can find the jargon used in school letters and news bulletins incomprehensible and off-putting.

Reflection

How many of these challenges do you recognise from your own school's parent body?

For each communication barrier identified here, jot down one strategy that would be effective in overcoming it. (An example might be offering to find an interpreter for a parent whose English is limited.)

What actions do you take to ensure that parents are encouraged to communicate with your school?

There are, without doubt, some quick wins that schools can employ to improve home–school communication. Janet Goodall, a leading academic in the area of parental engagement, has conducted much action research with school leaders in the south-west of England. Her *Report on the Pilot of a Toolkit for Parental Engagement* (2017b) is a fascinating read about a year-long project involving colleagues from 34 schools, teeming with practical and interesting strategies to develop impactful parental engagement. These include:

- Text message reminders to parents (these are more likely to be picked up during the day than emails).
- Invitations for key events written by pupils rather than members of staff (this is more compelling and emotive than a communication from a teacher).
- Encouraging parents to visit for low-threat, 'feel good' occasions like class assemblies (which are an opportunity to see the class together, have the

advantage of being less formal than an end-of-term ceremony and make it easy to be inconspicuous in the audience).

- Weekly parent thank yous (to show appreciation and acknowledge the importance of the partnership and building a relationship).

I have to admit to having a light-bulb moment when I read the advice about getting staff to stand alone (rather than in pairs or groups) when welcoming children and parents at the gate (Goodall 2017b: 46). In over 20 years as a school leader, I had never stopped to consider that a parent might find approaching one teacher less off-putting than having to talk to two, but it makes sense and is such a simple thing for staff to recognise.

Sometimes, reaching the audience you want requires lateral thinking. At John. F. Kennedy Catholic School in Hemel Hempstead, leaders were finding it hard to communicate with a core group of parents of disadvantaged learners. They decided that if they could not get them into school, the school would have to go out to them, and they devised a PP roadshow.

Case study: John F. Kennedy School

The aim was to affect positive engagement and partnership working. According to the EEF, effective parental engagement can lead to learning gains of three months or more over the course of a year.[1] Yet it can be difficult to involve all parents in ways that support children's learning, especially if parents' own experiences of school weren't positive. Whilst the disadvantage gap is fairly small at JFK in comparison with the national one, it is still a gap that leaders are keen to reduce and eventually eradicate completely.

Staff at JFK recognised the issues stemming from a lack of engagement from many families of children eligible for PP funding. For example, attendance at parent consultation evenings and year group information evenings was generally lower from disadvantaged families, resulting in them missing the aspirational messages that staff share with parents at such events. They also missed individual feedback relevant to their children's progress, and information regarding intervention programmes.

1   See https://educationendowmentfoundation.org.uk/evidence-summaries/early-years-toolkit.

Low attendance rates are partly a result of the school's vast 'catchment' area (covering large parts of Hertfordshire and Bedfordshire). Some disadvantaged students live up to 16 miles from the school, which makes it difficult for some families to travel in for meetings. Equally, the absence of some families at parent events was judged to be due to the formality of the school environment causing discomfort. Whatever the reasons, the fact remains that these parents do not get the same messages as more advantaged families, which appears to contribute to disadvantaged students' underperformance.

In an attempt to engage more disadvantaged families, it was decided to take a fairly innovative approach and to run a PP roadshow. The roadshow involved four information evenings for parents and carers, held in four separate venues across Bedfordshire and Hertfordshire, in places known to be in close proximity to most of the school's disadvantaged families. All meetings were held in church halls, light refreshments were provided to help create a welcoming atmosphere, and the tone was deliberately informal. The deputy head teacher for PP presented at the evenings and was available at the end of each meeting to talk to individual students and parents.

Several families stayed behind to discuss individual circumstances, to gain advice, and to explore how they could be supported further. Many of these conversations had immediate positive effects on the child. One example of such a conversation was with a parent whose child had purchased their own revision booklet from their personal savings, as the family could not afford it. Following the conversation, it was agreed that the school would fund all such revision resources and reimburse the child.

Within the week that followed the roadshow meetings, the PP lead held four one-to-one student meetings and two parent meetings. These meetings were with students and parents who had previously been difficult to engage, and all concluded with clear targets and strategies in place, to support the students to make further progress. Two further meetings were held in the month following the roadshow at the request of the families. Again, these meetings were with previously hard-to-reach families and had positive outcomes in terms of action plans and also building home–school relationships.

Steve Jump

Building staff commitment and expertise

To build and sustain high-quality, long-term home–school relationships requires a significant investment of time and resources. It involves training all staff to appreciate that relationships with parents and carers are precious and must be nurtured. It involves leaders setting very clear expectations with all staff regarding language and tone used in conversations with parents, timely responses to parent queries and availability for out-of-hours meetings. It involves modelling the style and tone of emails and letters, role playing and practising phone conversations and meetings to build staff confidence and assure positive outcomes. It requires a degree of quality assurance to celebrate great practice and to pick up inconsistencies – a quiet word here and there, retraining and coaching where necessary. Very importantly, it requires leaders to prioritise the formation of strong parent relationships and to protect time in the working week for all staff, teaching and operational, to work on deepening these relationships. In 2018, an EEF guide entitled *Working with Parents to Support Children's Learning* cited evidence that few staff get any training in parental engagement: only 28% of school leaders said they currently provided training and 76% of schools in England did not have any plan for monitoring parental engagement. According to the EEF research, fewer than 10% of teachers have undertaken training on parental engagement (van Poortvliet et al. 2018: 11).

Creating a culture in which staff are committed to building strong relationships with all parents (even the hardest to reach and toughest to work with) is not easy. It requires staff to be open to accepting that they could be influenced by what Agarwal (2020) calls 'in-group' bias. In-group bias is a term for the way in which humans tend to empathise with and seek to help people who are similar to themselves – for example, due to race, social class, accent, background or lifestyle. In *Sway*, Agarwal (2020: 56) asserts that we 'favour our in-group automatically' but when people are provided 'with more information about out-group members [this] can reduce their bias towards them' (2020: 76). This is an important observation, especially for those seeking to build relationships with parents of a different ethnicity to their own, those living in poverty or those from otherwise contrasting and under-represented backgrounds.

Research conducted by Keith Herman and a team of researchers from the University of Missouri supports the notion of unconscious bias affecting parental relationships. Herman says:

It's clear from years of research that teacher perceptions, even perceptions of which they are not aware, can greatly impact student success. If a teacher has a good relationship with a student's parents or perceives that those parents are positively engaged in their child's education, that teacher may be more likely to give extra attention or go the extra mile for the student. (Quoted in Hurst 2017)

Of course, Herman suggests, the converse is also the case: a negative perception of the parents is likely to lead to the teacher investing less in their interactions with them and their child.

When I was setting up INA I visited dozens of schools to glean great practice. I was struck (as I still am when I visit schools) by the wide variations in 'customer service' provided to parents and visitors. I have seen school receptions with:

- Freshly percolated coffee available for visitors.
- Copies of the day's broadsheet newspapers.
- Fresh flowers.
- Welcome messages and copies of key policies and documents available in the main community languages.
- Pictures of the staff on display, and information about their role.
- Albums of press clippings and good news stories and copies of school newsletters for visitors to thumb through whilst waiting.
- Digital screens with rolling images of students' achievements and information about upcoming school events.

I have also witnessed:

- Signs declaring that the staff will not tolerate abusive behaviour from visitors (usually in bold and capitals).
- Posters stating that staff will not see parents without an appointment.
- Lists of all the queries that the reception staff will not deal with.
- Signs asking visitors not to put their feet on the seats.
- Reception areas without any seats for visitors.

At INA I stressed to the reception staff that their role was arguably the most important in the school, being the front face and first point of contact. Reception staff underwent thorough training and induction in how to greet visitors, appropriate language, body language, tone and phone manner, and how to deal with a wide range of scenarios. Their line manager and I would observe their practice closely, give feedback and compliment great practice. From time to time I would need to telephone the school when off-site, which was a great opportunity to witness the receptionists' phone manner for myself. I would usually follow their salutation with a quip like, 'Exemplary practice, as always!' Their line manager communicated clear expectations about how the reception area should be maintained – how it should be clean, tidy and uncluttered at all times – and how important it was to provide waiting parents with a drink and to offer to take their coats or buggies. But the most important aspect of the training was getting new recruits to understand why treating parents in this way was so important and how, by doing so, they were making a vital contribution to our collective goal of supporting every learner to achieve great things. So I felt pride when I saw our receptionists look up and address parents coming through the door by their name, ask after their father who had recently been unwell, wish them 'Eid Mubarak', say how much we were looking forward to the child's younger sibling starting school in September, or tell them how well their child had sung in assembly that week. These snippets of conversation were invaluable for forging strong relationships.

Reflection

Do all your staff model quality communications with all types of parents?

How do your staff induction, training, development and learning practices foster this?

What more might you do?

In the summer before INA opened, Sir Anthony Seldon, then headmaster at Wellington College, kindly agreed for me to use his school as a base for some staff induction training. I had sought out this venue specifically because I wanted us to be inspired by how the best independent schools, charging very significant fees to parents, provide customer service. I had a vision of our school providing a comparable quality and standard of care. Each member of my staff experienced an exemplary welcome from the Wellington team. They were addressed by name, asked about their journey, guided to a parking space, offered refreshments and asked whether they had any other needs. It was a powerful experience.

We talked about the need for us all to treat our pupils' families with this level of care, even when they might not be behaving in the most reasonable manner or showing the same degree of courtesy in return. We reminded ourselves that every parent wants the very best for their child, no matter how much their behaviour at times might not demonstrate that motivation!

Very occasionally I encountered a parent who was so aggressive and abusive to staff that I had no option but to serve them with the notification that they were not to come near the school premises. I had a duty to protect my colleagues who were working tirelessly for the students, but it was action that I took with a heavy heart, knowing the damage that it could cause to our relationship with the parent's child. One case was particularly difficult. It concerned the father of a boy who had a serious degenerative condition and was severely disabled. The child's mother had died a few years earlier in tragic circumstances, leaving the father to bring up his two young sons – one at INA and one at a feeder primary. The father had a history of abusive and aggressive behaviour towards staff, which we were warned about by the primary school. Although our relationship with the father started well, it deteriorated when the pupil was in Year 9, and a number of teaching assistants, teachers and the SENCO were on the receiving end of some very unpleasant behaviour.

We tried to deal with the situation empathetically, especially for the sake of the student, but things came to a head one day when the father caused a major disturbance and threatened a number of staff members, including me, in the reception area as parents were arriving for an awards ceremony. The police had to be called and, partly on their advice, a ban was imposed. We worked hard to ensure that all of the student's needs were met and that he was fully included in all aspects of the curriculum, working around his significant disabilities. We took him on trips to the theatre and to a university, supported him to set up a tournament-winning boccia team and included him (in his wheelchair) in a sponsored walk of the London bridges. The intention had been to review the father's ban after a period of time but, in a terrible of twist of fate, I was visited by two police officers a few months after the incident to be told that he had died unexpectedly in his flat. I had to break the news to the older son and take him to his younger brother. I took some small comfort in the knowledge that, whilst the student had witnessed his father displaying some very challenging behaviour at the school, he had never seen staff behaving unprofessionally in response or heard them criticising his father. He had been, and would continue to be, loved and supported by the school community.

At Wellington, the founding INA staff had discussed the importance of establishing and maintaining regular contact with parents and finding every opportunity to feed back positive snippets of news. We had agreed on the need to respond to all calls and emails within 24 hours, even if just with an acknowledgement or holding message. We had role played various scenarios and agreed on common approaches and behaviours that we would all adopt in seeking our collective goal. We even devised a written communication etiquette plan, so emails and letters home would be consistent in tone and style. If parents do not get a quick and efficient response to their enquiries, and time and attention from staff who allow them to talk and demonstrate that they have listened to their worries, the school's protestations about the importance of working with parents will lack integrity. If communication does not flow naturally and habitually between home and school – with efforts made to share good news and celebrate successes, as well as to communicate concerns and resolve issues – the home–school relationship will be strained and less effective.

Reflection

How would you rate the quality of 'customer service' given to parents and carers at your school? How would your parents and carers rate it?

How do you seek feedback from parents and carers? What does it tell you?

So far we have focused on strategies to ensure that parents and carers feel welcome in school and encouraged to communicate with staff. These include:

- Home visits.
- Regular, positive, jargon-free communications (via phone, email or text).
- A parent-friendly phone answering/directing service.
- A quick response to queries from parents.
- A welcoming reception area.
- A translation/interpretation service.
- Invitations to celebratory, low-threat events.
- Ensuring staff are available and approachable at the start and end of the day.
- Roadshow events in the local community.

Of equal importance, of course, is the manner in which the school communicates with parents and carers. In the early days of INA I insisted on reading every letter that was sent home. I was checking for tone, style, jargon and growth mindset language. Because I was encouraging staff to communicate frequently with parents, especially to share good news, this was quite time-consuming. Yet it was invaluable for quality assurance and I quickly gauged whose communications did not need to have an eye cast over them and where to delegate the role to line managers. Like many schools, we produced weekly newsletters – one each for primary, secondary and sixth form. This was a means of keeping families informed about all aspects of our education provision: successes, initiatives and upcoming opportunities. Each newsletter also gave top tips and suggestions for ways in which parents could support their child's learning at home. Again, as many schools do, we supplemented this with a parents' area on the school website, which gave practical advice, key policies, useful links and contact details.

Consulting and seeking feedback

Schools that strive to maintain strong parental engagement work hard to maximise the impact of their feedback to parents on their child's progress and attainment. They consult on the best way to run parents' evenings or progress meetings – for example:

- What is the optimal time of day for such events?
- How long should appointments be?
- What information should be shared and by whom?
- How can the school make reports and data accessible and meaningful?

They set themselves a target of 100% attendance and strive to ensure that they achieve that goal, even if it means deploying additional staff resources: making reminder calls, arranging transport, setting up virtual meetings and mopping up the no-shows the next morning. They carefully consider the format and content of their written reports, seeking feedback on various alternatives from a sample group of parents or surveying entire cohorts. They welcome feedback on their systems and the parent experience and are always striving to improve. The EEF guide to working with parents stresses that:

Communication should be two-way: consulting with parents about how they can be involved is likely to be valuable and increase the effectiveness of home–school relationships. Currently around half of parents say that they have not been consulted. (van Poortvliet et al. 2018: 7)

Schools cultivating an ethos of high performance for all are open to, rather than affronted by, constructive feedback from parents and carers and seek to reflect on how their practice could be improved. They are not defensive; they admit when they make mistakes and are open to apologising when this is the case. If they issue a parent survey, they ask questions about what could be better, they report back openly on the results, they communicate to the parent body what they are going to do differently as a result, and they keep to their word. This demonstrates an institution-wide investment in working in true partnership with parents and generates the respect and trust necessary for them to open up and discuss any challenges they might be experiencing and support they would find helpful.

Consulting with parents and involving them in decision making might involve forming a joint working party, with representation from the parent and staff bodies, to work on a 'hot' issue. At INA one such example was school lunches. We had a policy of requiring all staff and students to eat together in the primary and secondary dining halls. We employed an excellent catering team who prepared a variety of hot dishes (halal, non-halal and vegetarian) daily, from which diners selected and helped themselves. Salads and lighter options like soup and jacket potatoes were available and all dietary needs were catered for. Feedback from a particular parent questionnaire indicated a significant level of dissatisfaction with the lunch arrangements and a sizeable group of parents wanted their children to be allowed to bring in packed lunches. This presented a significant issue for us: it conflicted with our vision around the family dining experience, and we knew that if we allowed food from home, we could not quality assure the content of lunch boxes or limit food to the dining halls. The solution was to invite the parents to select representatives to join a working group, along with some students and the catering manager and finance and resources director, to review and redesign the menus, sample the new recipes and evaluate the improvements. The opinion of the parents quickly changed when they realised that there was a genuine commitment to making family dining work for everyone. They appreciated seeing their ideas and suggestions reflected in the new menus and described the food as 'delicious' when they came in to eat with students.

Reflection

On what issues do you consult with parents and carers? When do you involve them in decision making?

Helping parents to support their child's learning and extending links beyond the school day

Impactful parental engagement is about much more than simply getting parents to come into school for key events, to help out on school trips or to support school policies. It is about working in partnership to influence the home learning environment and so to raise attainment. Smart school leaders realise that what makes the most profound difference is parental engagement with the learning process. This is all about ensuring that parents' attitudes, behaviours, language and routines in the home are conducive to out-of-school learning.

John Hattie (2020), writing during lockdown in April 2020, says:

I have rarely met a parent who does not want to help the child, but some do not have the skills.

He goes on to suggest that learning at home is related less to the structure of the family but more to the parents' skills at assuming the role of teacher. He argues that 'learning should include opportunities for students to give feedback about their learning and to receive feedback about where to go next' and points out that this is a key skill of teachers, but often less so of parents.

It must be assumed that all parents are equally committed, caring and concerned about their child's prospects but there may be variability in how well equipped they are with the tools to best support their child's development. Wendy Berlinger and Deborah Eyre's book *Great Minds and How to Grow Them* (2017) is brimming with practical strategies that parents can adopt to create a great environment for home learning. They cover talk and conversation, reading, feeding curiosity, building empathy, role modelling behaviours, encouraging collaboration and setting expectations. But many parents and carers are not likely to pick up a book like this; they need a helping hand and some guidance from trained teachers.

Schools that have really got to know their families are in a great position to support parents to be involved effectively in their child's learning and, in effect, to train them to be co-teachers, through workshops, online tutorials or webinars, or small group or one-to-one consultancies. In the early years, it is important that parents and carers are supported to understand the benefits of play as well as formal learning activities in underpinning the fundamental elements of key concepts, knowledge and skills.

If efforts have not been made from the outset to work on an equal footing with parents and carers as co-educators, an *approach* offering support can be interpreted as a *reproach,* judging parenting skills or capacity. If the effort is not invested to understand each family individually, it is easy for groups of parents to be treated stereotypically: assumptions can be made that all families eligible for PP funding will lack learning resources or that parents who have not been to school in the UK will struggle to assist with home learning, for example. Too often, well-intentioned approaches can feel judgemental and condescending.

A Sutton Trust briefing by Carl Cullinane and Rebecca Montacute (2020: 1) stated that less than half of parents without higher education qualifications feel confident in supporting their children's learning, whilst more than three quarters of parents with a postgraduate degree and 60% of those with an undergraduate degree felt comfortable doing so. In a humorous lockdown blog about 'parental load theory', Professor Becky Allen (2020) admitted that even highly educated parents find assisting young children with home learning a challenge:

Parental Load Theory starts with the insight that nearly all parents have limited time capacity. In designing resources and instructions, the goal should be to reduce the parental load that is extraneous to the task and carefully craft the load that is intrinsic to the task to ensure that parents are not overwhelmed. This theory is equally relevant to time-poor parents and to time-rich parents who do not feel confident in supporting their children's learning. I posit that the intrinsic parental load of a task are the adult–child interactions required for learning to take place. These include conversational roles, questioning, prompting, support for enquiry, and so on, all of which support students in developing understanding and fluency in concepts and ideas. However, far more significant are the extraneous parental loads that are essential to task completion: the parental role in enforcing engagement, through encouraging the student to start the activity and then persist at it [...] the parental administrative role in interpreting instructions, correcting resource errors, printing worksheets, re-typing in complex log-in details, finding essential resources, and so on.

The lockdown experience has shown us that most parents find at least some aspect of supporting their children's learning challenging and even stressful. For those with children with particular characteristics it can be harder, as Hattie (2020) muses:

We need to be doubly concerned about those students who most need teacher expertise […] students with special needs who require specialized instruction, those who already do not like learning at school, and those who come to school primarily to be with their friends (for them learning alone is a killer).

Over the last decade, I have been inspired by a wide range of initiatives designed to empower parents to support their child's learning and to extend parental links beyond the school day. Every school will do this in a different way, customised to their circumstances and their parents' needs. I shall close this chapter with a reflection on a school visit I made a couple of years ago, and then an extract from a case study about empowering parents through family learning.

Case study: Woolenwick Infant School and Nursery

In 2019 I made a memorable visit to Woolenwick Infant School and Nursery in Stevenage. I was struck by the commitment of the staff to supporting parents as co-educators and their refusal to accept any barrier to that partnership. Woolenwick serves a deprived part of Stevenage, with predominantly white working-class families. The school is a haven for creative, imaginative and enquiry-based learning and its young pupils display an impressive level of self-regulation, maturity and understanding of the learning process.

At the start of the day, parents bring their children into the playground to be welcomed by the staff. They are invited to come up to a table, staffed by an adult from the school, to read the philosophical question of the day with their child. They are encouraged to discuss it together, to decide on their response and then to place a pebble in the 'yes' or 'no' basket provided. The results of the day's survey are publicised at the end of the day at home time, generating further debate. On the day that I visited, the question was 'Do pirates exist in real life?' Head teacher Usha Dhorajiwala explained to me that the initiative is to encourage parents to engage in creative, imaginative and philosophical dialogue with their children, and to support and role model this for them where necessary:

We want the conversations that mums and dads have with their child before school to extend beyond 'Get your coat on, hurry up!' and to give them a topic for conversation on their way home from school too.

Another abiding image I have from my visit to Woolenwick is of a wonderful reading area in a classroom which had a giant Paddington Bear toy as the focal point. As in most schools, staff at Woolenwick emphasise to families the importance of reading each day to and with their children. But, as at many schools, a number of parents and carers lack either the skills or the confidence to do this, so they require support and modelling. Usha explained to me that the staff encourage under-confident parents to come in to take part in the reading sessions, first listening to a teacher or teaching assistant read to the class and then practising reading with their child. The staff entice reluctant parents into the school through piquing everyone's interest in the book in question. When one of the Paddington Bear tales was the focus book, the staff organised an evening screening of the film *Paddington*, on a big screen, outside under the stars and with popcorn. All pupils and parents were invited to take part in the magical occasion. The reading sessions followed on seamlessly from the film night. As in lots of high-performing schools, staff at Woolenwick plan every aspect of the curriculum with care and purpose. The Paddington story was chosen for a variety of reasons, not least because Paddington is a lovable hero from Peru – an immigrant. At the time, leaders were aware of the presence of anti-refugee and anti-immigration feeling in the local community and wanted to challenge stereotypes and support and celebrate children in the school who were immigrants themselves. I came away from the visit with the strong sense that the school was up to something exciting and aspirational, and that leaders were committed to empowering all parents and carers to play a crucial role in supporting their children to be powerful learners by the age of seven.

Mulberry School for Girls serves a vibrant and culturally rich community in central London: 96% of the pupils are Bangladeshi, 56% are eligible for FSM and 98% are practising Muslims. In 2010 I worked with the head teacher and one of her senior colleagues on the G4G programme. They wrote a case study about implementing a strategy for community and family learning.

Case study: Mulberry School for Girls

The aims were to raise attainment by involving parents more directly in their daughters' learning and to overcome barriers to learning caused by high rates of child poverty and social exclusion through effective support of families and the community.

A future leader was appointed, with the remit of developing family and community engagement. In the first year, work began in a small and unobtrusive way. A series of trips were offered to mothers, as for many Muslim women mixed-gender social settings in the local area presented a barrier to participation, but the girls' school was accessible. The school consulted with mothers and the first trips were to the British Museum, Kew Gardens and Brighton. From the mothers who attended the trips, a parent voice group was developed and consultation took place about possible provision for family learning through classes held during the day and after school. One of the parents became a liaison officer and began to build a network of mothers who wanted to attend.

In the second year, a range of classes were offered: fitness, ICT skills, first aid, yoga, badminton, cake decorating, how to set up a small business, advice on parenting, health advice (topics included diabetes, substance misuse, mental health and domestic violence) and English for speakers of other languages (ESOL). A course was introduced to enable parents to start volunteering as a route into employment. A community day was also established and became an annual event, with thousands attending each year.

As teachers began to see the impact of parents' involvement in the school, it was decided that each faculty and year group should set a community target as part of their strategic plan. This meant each team planning for parents' involvement in their daughters' learning. Curriculum workshops were introduced, involving parents and their daughters learning together about the subjects being studied, what they involve and why they are important. A residential science revision weekend was established, at which mothers stayed away alongside their daughters to engage in science learning activities. Parents of girls joining the school in Year 7 took part in transition workshops. Seeing the impact of these initiatives, governors supported the vision for creating a new family leaning centre in partnership with a local primary school. The centre comprised classrooms, a crèche, a health suite, a meeting hall, a small community theatre space and a garden.

Vanessa Ogden and Ruth Smith

Over the four years of the community development strategy, attendance rates and attainment outcomes improved markedly. By empowering parents to understand the school's curriculum and skilling them to better support their children as learners in a Western education system, the school's outcomes became outstanding. Head teacher Vanessa Ogden, writing 10 years on, reflects:

Over the past decade, our community offer has led to employment and enrichment in better times – and the support of very practical needs in hard times. Our evaluations show that building on existing strong relationships through continuous engagement with families by phone during lockdown made a significant positive difference to them. Daily, we provided information, signposting to services and FSM provision, as well as assistance with remote learning. In March 2020, we began running a food bank to deal with hunger and a care essentials service to deal with period poverty, serving 520 families. Schools standing shoulder to shoulder with their communities in hard times reap many benefits for their pupils: strengthened relationships, support for education, and confidence in the quality of provision.

Closing thought

Schools that are serious about striving to achieve excellent performance outcomes for all learners appreciate that they cannot do it alone. They need to harness the support of parents. They recognise that learners spend far more time out of school than in it and that key adults at home are hugely influential in shaping learners and their outcomes. School leaders are relentless in ensuring that their staff are welcoming towards parents, meticulous in maintaining effective and impactful communication and determined to work in partnership with every family. They know that the time invested in building and maintaining parental relationships will be repaid tenfold.

Chapter 5

Creating an environment of high-quality teaching and learning

I never teach my pupils; I only attempt to provide the conditions in which they can learn.

Attributed to Albert Einstein

The goal is to provide rich environments in which to grow better brains.

Andy Clark (2003 :86)

High-quality classroom teaching, perhaps above and beyond every other factor, raises pupils' attainment and accelerates the progress they make. The good news is that the impact of a highly effective teacher is disproportionately great on disadvantaged and vulnerable learners. A Sutton Trust report of 2011, entitled *Improving the Impact of Teachers on Pupil Achievement in the UK – Interim Findings*, found that the difference between the impact of a very effective teacher and a poorly performing teacher is significant:

- *For example during one year with a very effective maths teacher, pupils gain 40% more in their learning than they would with a poorly performing maths teacher.*

- *The effects of high-quality teaching are especially significant for pupils from disadvantaged backgrounds: over a school year, these pupils gain 1.5 years' worth of learning with very effective teachers, compared with 0.5 years with poorly performing teachers. In other words, for poor pupils the difference between a good teacher and a bad teacher is a whole year's learning.* (2011: 2)

This chapter is in two parts. The first explores the features of high-quality teaching. The second considers the importance of high-quality CPD and reflects on how to develop the culture and systems for continuous staff learning and improvement.

High-quality teaching and learning

In an ASCL webinar on 24 June 2020, Marc Rowland asserted that 'what happens in the classroom matters the most.' He warned those striving to close attainment gaps and support disadvantaged learners to 'avoid a supermarket sweep approach' and 'focus energies on learning'.

So what is it that highly effective teachers do to ensure that all learners become high performers?

Creating the right conditions

Firstly, they create the optimal conditions for outstanding learning to take place. The learning environment (both physical and emotional) is crucial, as Clark's and Einstein's quotes at the start of this chapter remind us. Students need to feel emotionally secure and safe: confident to take risks, ask questions, try new activities, take themselves out of their comfort zone, attempt new challenges and make mistakes. This requires staff to be encouraging, sensitive, warm, empathetic and respectful. It requires them to use growth mindset language, model learning and boost self-esteem. It is often taken as a given that those entering the teaching profession will possess all of these qualities. Yet, sadly, many of us will be able to recount a time when a teacher spoke or acted in a way that did not make us feel safe, honoured or understood; some of us have seen colleagues behave in ways that are not conducive to a positive learning environment. Many schools have a staff code of conduct; the best pick up on any behaviours that deviate from it, addressing issues swiftly, proportionately and professionally.

Learners also need to be stimulated and inspired: to have their imaginations and aspirations fired by visual displays, physical resources, examples of excellent practice and attainment. This requires staff to have high expectations, exude optimism, regularly showcase high-level outcomes and give time and thought to the use of a rich range of lesson materials. In Chapter 2, I discussed the power and importance of language. The most effective teachers use the language of possibilities: 'I wonder what would happen if …?' 'How might you change this in your next draft?' 'What does that make you wonder?' 'How do you want to make that even better?' 'Where are you going to take this next?'

Great teachers create a stimulating and inclusive environment and climate for learning. They design rich and exciting physical spaces (indoors and outdoors) and inclusive displays which visually represent all groups that are part of the school's community and showcase the learning journey from wonky first drafts to well-crafted pieces of beauty. They recognise that sometimes students need to be persuaded to want to learn. The experience has to be made irresistible, and the invitation to learn must convey respect, trust and optimism.

Reflection

How conducive to learning is the environment at your school both physically and emotionally?

How do you know? Have you sought learner feedback?

What improvements could you initiate?

The importance of planning

Secondly, highly effective teachers are highly effective planners. They carefully craft lessons, and sequences of lessons, having asked themselves four questions:

1. Where are my students now?
2. What do I want my students to learn and where do I want them to get to?
3. How will my students acquire the knowledge/skills?
4. How will I know when my students have mastered the knowledge/skills?

Answering question 1 involves reflecting on what assessment data tells us about learners' current knowledge/understanding/skills. This then informs the direction of subsequent teaching to best cater for students' needs. Understanding prior knowledge is crucial as we use this to make sense of and learn new information. When we learn new information, we build on and connect it to our previous knowledge or understanding.

Question 2 is about teachers deciding what skills and knowledge they want their students to acquire next. This entails deciding learning objectives and outcomes and giving thought to the optimal sequencing of learning.

Question 3 is about deciding on the most appropriate teaching and learning activities to get the students to the end point determined by the answer to question 2. It involves considering teaching strategies, classroom organisation, resources and the optimal learning environment.

Answering question 4 is the assessment phase of the learning cycle. It involves determining the best method(s) of measuring progress made and knowledge/skills acquired.

In their planning, the most effective teachers consider the specific and/or additional needs of each learner in the group. Importantly, the best teachers see their students as individuals, each with their own challenges, strengths and interests. They work to identify what might help each one to make the next steps in their learning, whether they are performing below, at or above expectations. They seek out and devise bespoke strategies to address individual needs, rather than simply trying to shoehorn learners into existing support strategies. They review their learners' progress every few weeks, looking for any signs of underperformance and adapting their interventions and support accordingly.

Close tracking and timely intervention

Just as the diligent health worker or midwife will check on a mother and baby regularly throughout the pregnancy via scans, blood pressure checks and other screening tools, the best teachers closely track their students' progress through formal and informal assessment methods. They ensure timely interventions. These might include: pre-teaching, reteaching, peer support, one-to-one intervention, revision classes, parental involvement, reading recommendations, revision guides, online programmes, enrichment classes, mentoring and going on a trip or a visit.

The government's billion-pound COVID-19 catch-up grant generated much debate about the impact of various types of intervention on students' learning. The EEF's *Covid-19 Support Guide for Schools* advises that:

There is extensive evidence supporting the impact of high-quality one to one and small group tuition as a catch-up strategy. To be most effective, creating a three-way relationship between tutor, teacher and pupils is essential, ensuring that tuition is guided by the school, linked to the curriculum and focused on the areas where pupils would most benefit from additional practice or feedback. As a rule of thumb, the smaller the group the better. However, both small group and one to one tuition can be effective catch-up approaches. Tuition delivered by qualified teachers is likely to have the highest impact. However, tuition delivered by tutors, teaching assistants, or trained volunteers can also be effective. Where tuition is delivered by teaching assis-tants or volunteers, providing training linked to specific content and approaches is beneficial. (Education Endowment Foundation 2020a: 5)

The following extract is from a case study written in 2018 by leaders at a primary school which introduced daily interventions, led by the class teacher, as a tool to ensure that all learners were truly mastering the maths and English curriculum in Year 1.

Case study: ARK Conway School

Our aim was to ensure that we enabled depth of understanding and accurate application of knowledge for all learners, using the following approaches to our intervention time:

* Pre-teaching children key concepts or language.
* Challenging children on a deeper level regularly.
* Providing additional support to children who demonstrate misconceptions in lessons earlier on in the day, ensuring these are addressed immediately and effectively.

It was evident when children entered Year 1 that some had more gaps in their learning than others. Whole-class teaching was unlikely to cover all of these areas, particularly as, in response to EEF research into setting or streaming, we do not put the children into achievement-based sets. However, we were also mindful that we would not want to slow down the pace of learning of the whole class in order to ensure that all children had mastered a concept.

The decision was therefore made to provide daily intervention sessions to ensure that misconceptions could be addressed immediately, and increased support could be given – based on individual needs – to ensure mastery for all children. The daily interventions were created to provide opportunities for supporting depth of understanding in both mathematics and literacy.

When considering who would be best placed to lead on these interventions, it was quickly decided that it would need to be the class teachers. These were the members of staff who had received the relevant training, planned the whole-class lessons and, along with co-teachers, had used assessment for learning to identify any gaps occurring on a daily basis.

Identifying the right time for the sessions was paramount. There were three clear constraints. Firstly, we knew that we wanted the bulk of English and maths teaching to have taken place prior to the interventions. Secondly, we wanted to facilitate some time for the class team to share assessments and identify which children required the targeted daily support. Finally, with the success of the initiative balancing on the ability of a co-teacher – usually a graduate teaching assistant, who was often new to the school and had little to no whole-class teaching experience – to lead a purposeful lesson with the remainder of the class, there was a requirement to find a lesson that could easily be successfully delivered by a novice. With all this in mind, immediately after lunch was identified as a feasible option, as English and maths lessons were by then completed. There was time at the start of lunch for quick assessment feedback between the class team. Handwriting lessons, which were taught using a prescriptive and heavily resourced scheme, followed immediately after the lunch break.

With the optimal time identified, training followed for both teachers and co-teachers. Teachers were skilled up to identify the purpose of the daily interventions. It was important to confirm that intervention time was to support a small group of pupils to push on to achieve or exceed mastery. There was clear guidance provided which ensured that teachers recognised that if assessments identified large groups, or even the whole class, as struggling with a concept, intervention was unlikely to fix the root cause of ineffective whole-class teaching. Initial training for co-teachers took the form of sharing the handwriting scheme and providing all the necessary resources. This was then followed up with two or three co-taught sessions with a leader.

Focused, immediate and daily interventions have ensured excellent academic outcomes for our pupils, which have been sustained over time. Daily intervention time has positively impacted on pupils' outcomes, with 100% of children finishing Key Stage 1 in 2016 working at or above ARE in reading, writing and maths. Notably, 73% of these pupils were working at greater depth in these three areas.

In addition to academic outcomes for pupils, there have also been pastoral benefits. Working one-to-one with their teacher or within a small group has provided an ideal environment for pupils to gain the confidence and reassurance required to overcome potential barriers in their learning, whether striving to achieve mastery or go beyond. Teachers have also reported that intervention time has enabled them to fulfil our school vision of 'knowing every child', which supports them to tailor learning for the individual, not only during the daily interventions but also within the whole-class environment.

Furthermore, enabling co-teachers to deliver high-quality lessons successfully to the remainder of the class during intervention time has ensured that all of the graduates who have worked within this role have been accepted onto teacher training programmes, and chosen to complete their training at our school.

Rebecca Ross-Wood and Lois Osborne

In a *TES* article, Rob Webster (2020) argues that the most effective interventions:

- Are well planned, with clear objectives.
- Target the learners for whom they will be most beneficial.
- Adhere to explicit delivery protocols.
- Involve brief but regular sessions.
- Are carefully timetabled for consistent delivery and minimal time out of class.
- Are taught by well-trained practitioners.
- Support and relate to what is being taught in the classroom.

> ## Reflection
>
> Consider the seven criteria suggested by Webster. Which of these criteria were used by ARK Conway School in designing their successful intervention system?
>
> If your school utilises out-of-class interventions, how well do they meet these criteria?
>
> Might you make any changes or improvements to maximise their impact?

The power of effective delivery

Next, great teachers are great communicators. They break down information into digestible chunks when they deliver lessons. They explain complex theories and difficult concepts clearly and simply. They design sequences of learning logically and incrementally. They understand the science of cognitive load and use the well-researched strategies of dual coding, chunking and storytelling to ensure that learners, especially those with a less well-developed schema, can process new learning and commit it to long-term memory. The need for teachers to be skilled orators, delivering effective expositions in an accessible way, is perhaps even more critical for remote and digital lesson delivery. Students accessing lessons via an online platform – for example, during a national lockdown or when self-isolating – need clear instructions and for new learning to be confidently presented, especially if the lesson is not experienced live and there is no facility for asking the teacher a clarifying question.

Great teachers support learners by creating time and structures to enable them to process, practise and consolidate new knowledge, concepts and skills. They use the techniques of retrieval and interleaving. Through low-stakes and ipsative testing and regular formative assessment, they determine how well new learning has been understood and committed to long-term memory. They are quick to spot misconceptions and gaps in understanding and to address them before moving on.

It was fascinating to see various schools' approaches to supporting learners on their return to classrooms in September 2020. Some instigated early testing across the curriculum to determine gaps in learning. Others implemented a 'recovery curriculum' in the initial weeks, focusing on mental health, wellbeing and rebuilding relationships. Others adopted a middle way. I visited one secondary school in October 2020 where leaders explained to me that it was important to them that students' return was a positive experience, one that enabled them to regain confidence, and that the curriculum was engaging and joyful. They were keen to avoid a fixation on 'lost learning' and didn't want to worry students with the language of 'gaps'. Instead, they told staff to 'crack on' with their schemes of learning (revised in light of five months of remote learning) and to modify their teaching in response to what they discovered needed reteaching, consolidating or revising. Staff had been advised to use low-stakes testing, little and often, to gauge where to pitch learning. Leaders had arranged staff training focused on:

- Metacognition and memory retention.
- Differentiation in remote learning (which is quite tricky to do in live lessons).
- Impactful teacher exposition and modelling (as live teaching is a big part of their localised lockdown contingency plan).
- Revisiting the basics of structured learning.

Reflection

Did your school adopt an agreed whole-school approach to the curriculum when you returned in September 2020?

What approach did your school take to assessing lost learning and filling gaps? With what effect?

Determination to close gaps

Teachers who are most effective at raising the attainment and accelerating the progress of disadvantaged learners feel a sense of urgency and a moral imperative. They work through barriers to success. Leaders who are passionate about high performance for all allocate their most effective and committed teachers to the groups with vulnerable learners in them.

In order to ensure that every pregnancy results in a safe and successful delivery, medical staff need to be aware of those expectant mothers with an increased risk of complications – for example, older mothers and those with pre-existing conditions which put them at risk. In schools, we know that certain pupil groups are over-represented in the forgotten third: students eligible for PP funding, children in care, those with SEND, children of time-poor parents, those lacking strong learning role models and cultural capital, and those who have gaps in their knowledge and understanding arising from a disjointed educational experience.

Early indications suggest that the combination of economic hardship and reduced face-to-face teaching during the coronavirus pandemic will have had a significant impact on the poorest children and young people in our society. The needs of these children require the planning of our best teachers. But, just as not every older mum will have a complicated pregnancy, not every student in a vulnerable group will be at risk of low attainment. The smartest teachers will identify the gaps wherever they present themselves, and address them regardless of who requires additional support.

In the knowledge that the disadvantaged are disproportionally represented amongst the 'fatalities' of our education system, a colleague of mine at Herts for Learning, Alison Wood, devised the following aide-memoire to assist classroom teachers in addressing the needs of those eligible for PP funding.

Supporting the learning experiences of students eligible for PP funding – a prompt list

Before meeting your student eligible for PP:

1. Have you been briefed on the generic/specific barriers to learning for this PP student from your school's PP lead?

Planning learning for your PP student:

2. Lessons are planned to take into account the PP student's needs – targets shared, careful questioning, engaging activities via media, pictures, music, etc. according to need. What engages a PP student will engage the whole class.
3. The student is seated according to their needs.
4. The teacher provides differentiated resources depending on the student's barriers to learning.
5. Any specific equipment/extra books are provided by the school.

Before the start of the lesson:

6.   The teacher groups the student with specific peers to provide 'stretch' or 'support', or plans to ask the student to assist others to improve their self-esteem.

7.   The teacher gives the student 'advance warning' (perhaps as they arrive to class) that they will be called upon to answer a question when feedback is taken – to ensure that the student is confident in their reply.

Teacher strategies during whole-class learning:

8.   The teacher alters their position whilst teaching (next to, behind, close to the student).

9.   The teacher writes feedback in the student's book to support them/keep them focused.

10. The teacher applies strategic questioning or reduction of questioning in a whole-class context.

Teacher strategies whilst students are working independently:

11. The teacher writes additional supportive targets in the student's book.

12. The teacher speaks with the student to support, encourage, challenge, etc. whilst the class is working quietly. 'I'm expecting you to aim for …'

13. The teacher writes a praise comment.

14. The teacher scribes, if necessary, to help support and focus the student.

15. The teacher initials the student's book to show that the quality has been checked.

16. Whilst the teacher is monitoring the whole class during independent learning, the teacher writes timings in the margin during writing tasks to show how much the student has achieved in, say, five or 10 minutes. This builds up stamina and lets the student know the teacher will keep returning and annotating as a measure of how much they have been able to achieve during the time allocated.

At the end of the lesson:

17. The teacher looks at the student's book and comments on the work done.

18. The teacher asks the student one thing that they have learnt during the lesson.

19. The teacher gives specific verbal praise to the student as they are leaving the lesson.

20. The teacher may write targets in the student's book regarding a specific homework or intervention which needs to be completed – perhaps using an additional personalised book which the student has been bought by the school.

21. The teacher may escort the student to intervention sessions where necessary.

Ways to feed back:

22. The teacher marks the books of students eligible for PP first – and perhaps in more detail.

23. The teacher gives video feedback (e.g. voiceover feedback of a video showing student's work).

24. The teacher and student engage in a conversation via a Google Doc to support learning.

25. The teacher feeds back to the student's form tutor or mentor to enable them to have a conversation with the student about their learning.

The most committed and skilled teachers make a monumental difference to the life chances of disadvantaged learners. The following case study is just one example of a passionate teacher having a remarkable impact on the educational outcomes of a vulnerable learner whom I know well.

Case study: Annie's story

Annie was a smart student, who particularly loved maths and science at primary school. When she was in Key Stage 2 her parents went through a difficult divorce and in the following years she experienced significant disruption to her education, moving school four times and missing big chunks of learning. In Year 10 she developed an eating disorder and became dangerously thin. She was hospitalised for several months and missed almost a whole year of school. In July of Year 10 she came out of hospital and enrolled at yet another school. Her new English teacher took the time to meet with her before the summer holidays to get to know her, to assess where her gaps were and to determine what support she would need in order to access the GCSE course. She had missed studying the two set texts and the poetry anthology. Her teacher set her an individualised study programme, including online learning and informative YouTube clips, for the six-week break to help her to catch up as much as possible. He insisted on meeting with both her mother and father to understand the home situation better and to get them on board in supporting Annie with her schedule. In Year 11, he met with her weekly to coach her. He taught her how to identify her own next steps and analyse her weaknesses. He made her believe that, although she was only scoring grades 2 and 3 for the work she was completing, she had the potential to perform at a much higher level. Gradually, over the weeks, her grades rose. In the summer exams she gained a grade 9 for her English literature GCSE.

High-quality training for teachers

Ensuring that all staff (teaching and operational) receive regular, targeted and impactful training to improve their practice is key to creating an environment of high-quality teaching and learning. The best GP practices and obstetric wards are staffed by medics and maternity staff who are well-trained, lifelong learners whose practice is informed by the latest research into what works and what has impact. The same applies to schools. When teachers' planning and practice is influenced by what enables students to learn most effectively, and the most effective ways of teaching complex material in a comprehensible way, students experience deep learning. When staff understand cognitive load and can recognise and plug gaps in prior knowledge, ground can be covered quickly. Impactful learning results from skilled, bespoke, targeted teaching. This requires a whole-school focus on staff training and learning. It requires leadership which promotes a culture of everyone being a learner, in which adults are visibly developing their skills and knowledge alongside pupils, teachers openly share their personal development targets and their reading and talk comfortably about their learning challenges with their pupils.

In the ARK Schools Trust, of which INA is a member school, 10 days per year were set aside for staff training and development, compared to, typically, five in local authority schools. At INA we created more, through the introduction of independent learning days for students (of which more in Chapter 6). These occasions provided vital space for staff to talk and listen to each other without distraction, for us to take stock of how we were progressing and to work together on our strategic priorities. INSET days (we would often take several consecutively) at the start of the year were used to induct new staff into – and realign existing staff around – our vision, values, culture, language, policies and procedures, so that when our learners returned they experienced a consistent approach from a united staff body. At times we welcomed external speakers to train and inspire staff – we were honoured to host Tim Brighouse, Matthew Syed and Estelle Morris, for example – but mostly we devised our own staff development sessions, led and delivered by a wide range of staff and students.

Days earmarked for staff training are crucial occasions for learning, yet too often they fall flat and are missed opportunities. In a recent session facilitated by David Weston of the Teacher Development Trust, my colleagues in the education services team at Herts for Learning identified a long list of possible reasons for this. It included:

- Ill-chosen focus, not matched to the audience or the priorities of the school.
- Generic CPD that is 'one size fits all' and fails to address any individual's training needs.
- Imposed from the top, failing to connect with the staff body.
- Overly ambitious: trying to pack too much into one day/session.
- Poor delivery, lack of interaction or time for reflection and application.
- Ill-defined objectives, success criteria and next steps.

Weston advises school leaders to start with the end in mind when planning staff training sessions. He suggests that they ask themselves the following questions: 'What is the change we are seeking?' and 'If this training is effective, what is the change that we will see in our learners?'

The challenge with one-off INSET days, however well-crafted and well-delivered they are, is in ensuring that the learning from them is translated and embedded into changed practice that has an impact on the quality of education and on the students' learning. Training only has an impact where leaders have meticulous plans in place to ensure that skills learnt during an INSET day will be revisited and discussed in staff meetings and one-to-one consultations. They ensure that time and space are created for staff to trial, practise, develop and consolidate these new skills and techniques in their classrooms or workspaces.

In addressing this challenge, it is important to remember that training is not just something that happens five times a year on INSET days. There are opportunities for professional development and learning in all school activities – hence the 'C' (continuing) in CPD. In a high-performing school, training is woven into all staff interactions: line management dialogues, team meetings, coaching conversations, feedback from lesson observations and shadowing colleagues as they have conversations with parents and learners. At School 21 in Newham, East London, founding head teacher Peter Hyman built a powerful opportunity for staff development into the school week when he introduced the staff huddle after each assembly. This entailed a few minutes of feedback given to the deliverer by colleagues in attendance about what had been powerful and effective and how they could improve the structure or their delivery next time.

Reflection

How does staff training get planned at your school?

Do you agree your training priorities as a senior team at the start of the year, in alignment with the school improvement plan?

Do you decide when and where you will introduce new learning and then earmark meeting and line management time to discuss and reflect on it so that it is understood and owned by the staff?

Do you ensure that time is provided for staff to trial and practise new techniques in a safe environment?

Do you check that procedures are in place to observe, coach, encourage and feed back?

Do you have clearly agreed goals and success criteria so that you can judge the impact of your CPD objectively? How do you measure your success against them?

What three steps do you think would be most significant for your school to take to enhance the impact of staff CPD?

Collaborative learning

Creating a climate conducive to collaborative learning for all staff is every bit as important as it is for students. At INA we had a number of staffrooms scattered about the school. We called, and labelled, them 'staff learning rooms' and encouraged colleagues from across years, phases and subject teams to use them to get together to discuss teaching and learning. As many schools do, when constructing the timetable we protected time for all members of each subject team (at secondary) and year team (at primary) to co-plan. These weekly sessions were used for designing schemes of learning, creating supporting resources, reviewing and reflecting on lessons taught and revising programmes of study for future delivery. They were occasions for planning targeted pre- and post-teaching for individual learners and for coordination between teachers and other classroom-based adults. Conversations in staff learning rooms would often turn to the professional reading and research that colleagues were engaged in and how they were applying it to their classroom practice. As my colleagues and I said in *The Nine Pillars of Great Schools*:

The more that staff work together in appropriate teams, the more a shared understanding emerges about the complexity of learning and teaching, with the aim of impacting significantly on pupil achievement. (Woods et al. 2018: 80)

Just as we expect our medics to keep abreast of the latest research and medical papers in their chosen field and implement newly tried, tested and improved techniques, we should require our teachers to be well versed in the latest pedagogical debates and to be regularly refreshing their repertoire of teaching techniques. Many high-performing schools form action research groups to trial and evaluate teaching approaches. Others facilitate staff book groups to generate and foster pedagogical discourse. At Walthamstow School for Girls (WSFG), where I was head teacher between 2004 and 2011, members of the staff book club met in the library at lunch times. This was a conscious decision to demonstrate to students that staff were engaged in learning and seeking to improve their knowledge, skills and practice collectively. Over time, we noticed that a number of girls would regularly pull up a chair near to the book club circle, listening in with interest to the discussion. Occasionally, one would decide to read the book being discussed or recommend a future text to the group.

A common feature of high-performing schools is staff who are open to and energised about continuous learning. Adults might talk in assembly about a new technique they are striving to master, or put a notice on their classroom or office door listing the professional reading they are engaged in or the skills they are working on. When school leaders role model this, alongside the rest of the staff, it has maximum impact.

Reflection

In what ways do staff at your school demonstrate to the students that they too are learners?

Could you use or adapt any of the suggestions given in this chapter, or can you come up with better ideas of your own?

Building in regular opportunities for staff to learn with and from peers is key to creating a culture of habitual and routine staff development. At high-performing schools, lesson observation is seen as an entitlement for all teaching staff. Observing other teachers and being observed ourselves is a powerful tool for improving teaching and learning, and is a rich source of CPD. At many high-performing schools, staff make a formal commitment to observe each other's practice, to reflect on it and to offer quality feedback. On a regular basis, every member of staff will be observed teaching by their line manager but may also be observed by peers. In addition, members of staff will choose colleagues whom they would like to observe. Leaders will provide a range of forums for sharing what staff have learnt from their observations.

Developmental coaching and line management

The role of coaching and line management is also key in developing staff. I have long considered that the term 'line management' is an unhelpful one as, when performed well, it is more about leadership, mentoring and coaching than it is about managing. It should not be a hierarchical process but a genuine partnership aimed at maximising the effectiveness of colleagues and their provision for students. I haven't come across many schools with a policy or set of agreed expectations relating to line management, which I find surprising considering the amount of time typically spent in line management meetings. This perhaps accounts for the wide variation in practice and quality often seen.

At INA the senior staff invested a significant amount of time discussing with middle leaders what great line management looks like and why it was so important that the experience of every colleague in the school was of an equally high quality. We started from the premise that all staff were entitled to a great line manager. Line management training was therefore an important part of the academy's CPD provision and all line managers were required to engage in 360-degree evaluation. We agreed that line management meetings should be:

- Regular (at least once per fortnight).
- At agreed times (ideally at the same time/in a regular timetable slot).
- In a suitable location where there will not be interruptions.
- Planned to allow sufficient time for discussion of important issues.
- Purposeful and focused.
- Constructive.
- Professional.

We created a policy that defined the features of great line management, in order that each of us, supported by our own manager, could focus on improving the elements at which we were not so strong. What follows is an extract from that policy.

Great line managers have vision and purpose. They are clear about their role and they encourage those whom they line manage to see the bigger picture and to recognise their contribution towards achieving the academy's aims. They lead by example, act professionally, are enthusiastic about and committed to the role and thus inspire those with whom they work.

Great line managers are fair, consistent and follow agreed systems and procedures. They are also flexible and open to new ideas. They are well organised and come to meetings well prepared and focused on the role. They are excellent communicators and agree clear expectations with those they line manage.

Great line managers are decisive and positive. They facilitate effectively, supporting those they work with to take action and helping them to be in control. They help their colleagues to organise their time and workload, remind them of deadlines and check to see that things have been done.

A key part of being a great line manager is being an effective coach. Great line managers are excellent listeners: they may give guidance or offer advice but more often they will encourage their colleagues to talk about issues, asking pertinent questions and guiding them to think through alternative options in order to come to their own solutions (rather than telling them what to do). They empower their colleagues to feel confident, to take responsibility and make decisions. They respect the professionalism and expertise of the colleague they are line managing.

Also central to great line management is emotional intelligence. Great line managers know when to support and when to challenge. They understand their colleagues' workload, pressures and issues. They show understanding and empathy. They encourage and praise. They celebrate successes. They ask tough questions and act as a critical friend when appropriate but are never confrontational. They do not shy away from difficult conversations but give constructive criticism and honest feedback. They are open to genuinely frank discussions. They are reliable, approachable and available, always making time for those they line manage. They give practical help when required and, if they don't know the answer, they know where it can be found. They help to shoulder the burden in tough times and help colleagues to prioritise and delegate.

Great line managers are trustworthy, have integrity, keep confidential issues confidential, are honest about what is and isn't possible and always behave ethically.

Reflection

Do you agree with this list of qualities of great line managers? What might you adapt or add?

Line management is partly a tool for accountability. However, line management meetings are also an opportunity for rich professional dialogue. Although certain routine matters will invariably need to be discussed and should lead to decisions and agreed actions, line management meetings should be a forum for creative discussion, imaginative planning, generating ideas and sharing great practice.

It is important that colleagues' experience of line management is consistent and of a uniformly high quality. For this reason, I would recommend that:

- Common agenda items are agreed in advance.
- Time is given to review and evaluate how line management is going.
- Training is provided on effective line management.

> ## Reflection
>
> How consistent is the experience of line management at your school?
>
> Is there a clearly defined and common understanding of what great line management looks like?
>
> How might you adapt the INA policy to suit your school?
>
> What action would be most impactful in your setting to train line managers to be even more effective?

When I look back at my time as a head teacher, I regret not prioritising even more time to train line managers to lead impactful coaching conversations with each of their direct reports. Truly developmental organisations ensure that all leaders are skilled in this area. They develop a coaching culture, a climate in which powerful and honest conversations take place in a safe space, where staff feel that their development is prioritised by their leaders and the organisation as a whole. Whilst they will normally have an annual appraisal cycle, smart schools engage in performance development, rather than performance management (note the importance of language, as discussed in Chapter 2) continually throughout the year. The protection of time for this crucial activity is key. If space is created in the hectic rhythm of a school's life to develop staff, the appreciation is enormous and the impact on staff wellbeing tangible. Happy staff who feel invested in are likely to stay at their school for longer and develop their skills further. As Dr Nasser Siabi, founder of Microlink, says:

Imagine what could happen if we gave (teachers) the time and freedom, the opportunity to teach each child like their own. To ask them what they want to do and what they are good at and enable them to discover it. (Quoted in Blandford 2019: 109–110)

In their powerful book *An Everyone Culture*, Kegan and Lahey (2016: 88) write:

It is one thing to be relentless about continuously developing the processes by which work gets done; it is quite another to be relentless about continuously developing the people who do the work.

They assert that deliberately developmental organisations create a culture of trust and safety in which staff can concentrate on practising, learning and growing rather than:

trying to look good, display expertise, minimise and hide any mistakes or weak-nesses, and demonstrate what they already know and can do well. (Kegan and Lahey 2016: 124)

The former is the behaviour of those who embrace a growth mindset; the latter the features of individuals working in a fixed mindset culture.

Reflection

How deliberately developmental of staff would you say your school is?

What actions might you take to make it a more deliberately developmental organisation?

Closing thought

In *What Makes a Good School Now?* Tim Brighouse and David Woods (2008: 96) suggest that:

The litmus test for successful CPD is that any member of staff becomes a better pro-fessional just by being on the staff alone, sustained by a culture that promotes the best quality teaching and learning.

What would a school that achieves this be like? This chapter has explored the answer to this question. Before you proceed to Chapter 6, you might want to sum up the features of such a school in a few words.

Chapter 6

Metacognition and self-regulation

I cannot teach anybody anything. I can only make them think.

Attributed to Socrates

The more the student becomes the teacher and the more the teacher becomes the learner, then the more successful are the outcomes.

John Hattie (2012: 17)

Imagine if the medical, psychological and social care given to expectant parents consisted of simply preparing for the birth, rather than advice on how to maintain general health throughout the pregnancy, how to prepare for the challenges of parenting and how to raise an infant. The schools that succeed in getting almost all their students through their exams with good grades and impressive progress scores tend not to be the ones which simply teach to the test: they teach beyond and abreast of it. They see it as their role to provide a broad, expansive, creative and imaginative education, not to stick to exam syllabuses. They teach students how to learn effectively and independently, and they imbibe their students in a love of learning. The students who attend these schools leave with the learning skills that will stand them in good stead as inquisitive, self-regulating learners for life, just as those who experience great prenatal and postnatal guidance are more likely to become great parents.

What do we mean by metacognition and self-regulation?

There are a number of definitions of metacognition. Put simply, it is the ability to think about one's own thinking, and to learn to be an effective learner. In the introduction to the EEF guidance report on metacognition and self-regulated learning, the then CEO, Sir Kevan Collins, said:

On a very basic level, it's about pupils' ability to monitor, direct, and review their learning. Effective metacognitive strategies get learners to think about their own learning more explicitly, usually by teaching them to set goals, and monitor and evaluate their own academic progress. (Quoted in Quigley et al. 2018: 4)

Students who have well-developed metacognitive skills have a good knowledge of themselves as learners – their learning strengths and weaknesses. They are good at understanding the requirements of learning tasks and the strategies and tools they will need to use to tackle them. They are good at reflecting on and reviewing their progress, planning and directing themselves to move on to new and more complex challenges. Metacognition and self-regulation go hand in hand, in that learners who have developed strong metacognitive skills are able to chunk up and organise their learning effectively. They motivate and organise themselves to tackle the current learning tasks, persevering even when they experience frustration and initial failure. They strategically map out their longer-term plan as lifelong learners. As Bill Lucas and Guy Claxton put it in *New Kinds of Smart* (2010: 139), 'students who are self-regulated increasingly become their own teachers'.

Why are the skills of metacognition and self-regulation so important?

Building students' understanding of learning has a beneficial effect on academic outcomes. In 2011 the Sutton Trust and the EEF published a Teaching and Learning Toolkit, with a view to helping schools decide which strategies are most effective at improving educational outcomes for students from disadvantaged backgrounds.

Available online and regularly updated ever since, the toolkit ranks the effectiveness of different strategies. Topping this league table of educational effectiveness are metacognition and self-regulation, which are described as having 'High impact for very low cost, based on extensive evidence.' As the toolkit explains:

Metacognition and self-regulation approaches aim to help learners think about their own learning more explicitly [...] The evidence indicates that teaching these strategies can be particularly effective for low achieving and older pupils.[1]

In a series of four texts written by Guy Claxton and various colleagues and collaborators – *The Learning Power Approach* (2018), *Powering Up Children* (2019), *Powering Up Students* (2019) and *Powering Up Your School* (2020) – practical advice is offered to primary and secondary school teachers and leaders about how to teach learners to teach themselves, and compelling evidence of the impact that the Learning Power Approach (LPA) can have on learners' skills development and academic outcomes is presented. The authors – and the leaders in the schools they showcase – share a common belief that a major purpose of education is to grow students' well-honed learning skills: to develop students' habits, behaviours and dispositions to enable them to become effective and fully functioning self-regulated learners. They are all committed to supporting students to achieve the highest possible exam outcomes, but they do not see that as the be-all and end-all. Furthermore, they recognise that the LPA accelerates student progress and enhances academic success, but without allowing the dangerous side effect of teacher dependency to develop. In summary, learning-powered schools focus on education beyond examinations, and on developing learning behaviours as well as getting results.

Between 2010 and 2013, James Mannion and Neil Mercer from the University of Cambridge conducted a comparative study in association with a comprehensive secondary school in the south of England which implemented a whole-school approach to 'learning to learn' (L2L). Drawing on a range of evidence-based practices, a team of teachers worked collaboratively to design and deliver a taught L2L curriculum to all students in Key Stage 3. In total, the first cohort (118 students) received more than 400 taught lessons in Years 7–9. The impact of L2L on student attainment was evaluated over those three years, using the pre-L2L cohort (148 students) as a matched control group. By the end of Year 9, a significantly higher proportion of the L2L students were either hitting or exceeding their target grades, compared with the control group. There was also a significant closing of the attainment gap between students eligible for the PP and their peers (2% vs 25% in the control group) (Mannion and Mercer 2016: 264).

Many students, of course, pick up metacognitive knowledge and skills from interaction with their families and peers. Yet others, often those from chaotic background, whose family members have not developed strong metacognitive skills themselves, need support to become effective, self-regulated learners. This would explain why the Mannion and Mercer study and the Sutton Trust evidence show a particularly strong impact when teachers support disadvantaged and low-attaining learners to develop these skills.

Strategies to support learners to develop metacognition and self-regulation

The EEF guidance report on metacognition and self-regulated learning makes seven recommendations to primary and secondary schools:

- *Teachers should acquire the professional understanding and skills to develop their pupils' metacognitive knowledge*
- *Explicitly teach pupils metacognitive strategies, including how to plan, monitor and evaluate their learning*
- *Model your own thinking to help pupils develop their metacognitive and cognitive skills*
- *Set an appropriate level of challenge to develop pupils' self-regulation and metacognition*
- *Promote and develop metacognitive talk in the classroom*
- *Explicitly teach pupils how to organise, and effectively manage, their learning independently*
- *Schools should support teachers to develop knowledge of these approaches and expect them to be applied appropriately* (Quigley et al. 2018: 3)

These strategies also apply to nursery and Reception years, although there is specific advice for early years practitioners in the self-regulation strategies strand of the EEF Early Years Toolkit.[2]

So what is it that LPA schools do to develop these skills? I shall explore three key areas of action in the remainder of this chapter:

1. Developing staff behaviour and pedagogy.

2. Leaders demonstrating commitment.

3. Implementing structures and systems to support student learning.

We will then consider the added importance of metacognition and self-regulation in a remote-learning context.

Developing staff behaviour and pedagogy

Firstly, LPA schools have a clear, codified and commonly agreed view of the teacher behaviours they value and are striving to see demonstrated in every classroom. At INA we articulated this in our teaching and learning policy:

Great teachers are first and foremost learners, and model their learning visibly. They talk about their learning, their learning challenges and the joy of learning – they seek to make every aspect of the learning process as visible as possible. They deliberately share new or contested findings and ideas in their subject with their students. They cheerfully acknowledge when they don't know the answer to a question they are asked. They invite students to throw tricky questions at them so that they can see their teacher thinking on their feet when faced with uncertainty. They are happy to share with their students the task of finding things out. They pause and think aloud when things do not go according to plan.

They plan meticulously but recognise that mistakes will be made. They role model openness, curiosity and non-defensiveness. They review and evaluate and constantly strive to get better as teachers and learners.

Great teachers are facilitators of learning. They know that excellent teaching is more about helping students to find information and figure things out, rather than telling them things. They ask themselves, 'What is the least I can do to get productive

---

2   See https://educationendowmentfoundation.org.uk/evidence-summaries/early-years-toolkit/.

learning happening here?' They give students a central responsibility for their and their peers' learning. They fully involve students in planning, delivering and evaluating lessons. They give students increasingly demanding opportunities to take charge of their own learning.

Great teachers design exciting and varied lessons that intrigue their students (students stretch their learning muscles best when their energy and attention are captured by what they are doing). Students learn best when their teachers adopt a variety of learning approaches in a series of lessons. Learning activities should include: investigation, experimentation, observation, discussion, practical exploration, role play, problem solving, decision making, and pair and group activities.

They talk the language of metacognition habitually with their classes, so that their students can see how the learning activities have been crafted, why they are learning in the way they are, and what skills they are practising. They employ 'split-screen' lesson planning; they are explicit about the learning dispositions being developed in each lesson as well as the subject content and skills being taught. They encourage the students to get involved in co-planning schemes of learning. They coach their students to design and teach starter and plenary activities to their peers or younger learners, progressing to whole lessons and sequences of lessons. Assemblies, and sometimes discrete lessons, focus on the habits of great learners – for example, perseverance, empathy, imagination, collaboration and resourcefulness. Praise, assessment and reporting systems recognise the development of learning behaviours as well as academic attainment.

The behaviours described in this extract are, of course, an ideal. I do not claim for one minute that all of these features were in evidence every day in every classroom at INA. Some colleagues adopted such approaches more naturally and comfortably than others. The key was, of course, to have open and honest conversations with colleagues (as described in Chapter 5) about our goals and how near we were to achieving them, and then to provide bespoke support and training to enable teachers to get continually stronger and more effective in exemplifying the desired pedagogical approach.

Reflection

Thinking about the staff in your school, how many of the pedagogical features described in the teaching and learning policy extract are in evidence in their practice, and how consistently are they applied?

Use the following audit tool (based on the policy extract) to consider and make notes about the pedagogical approach of the teachers at your school (including you). What are your school's strengths? What might be your next priority areas for development?

Audit of teacher behaviour to develop skills of metacognition			
Teacher behaviour	Areas where this is a strength/ visible	Areas where this is a weakness	Next steps to implement
Teachers talk about their learning, their learning challenges and the joy of learning.			
Teachers deliberately share new or contested findings and ideas in their subject with their students.			
Teachers cheerfully acknowledge when they don't know the answer to a question they are asked.			
Teachers invite students to throw tricky questions at them so that they can see their teachers thinking on their feet when faced with uncertainty.			

Audit of teacher behaviour to develop skills of metacognition			
Teacher behaviour	Areas where this is a strength/ visible	Areas where this is a weakness	Next steps to implement
Teachers are happy to share with their students the task of finding things out.			
Teachers pause and think aloud when things do not go according to plan.			
Teachers role model openness, curiosity and non-defensiveness.			
Teachers give students a central responsibility for their and their peers' learning.			
Teachers fully involve students in planning, delivering and evaluating lessons.			
Teachers talk the language of metacognition habitually with their classes, so that their students can see how the learning activities have been crafted, why they are learning in the way they are, and what skills they are practising.			
Teachers employ 'split-screen' lesson planning; they are explicit about the learning dispositions being developed			

Audit of teacher behaviour to develop skills of metacognition			
Teacher behaviour	Areas where this is a strength/ visible	Areas where this is a weakness	Next steps to implement
in each lesson as well as the subject content and skills being taught.			
Teachers encourage the students to get involved in co-planning schemes of learning with them.			
Teachers coach their students to design and teach starter and plenary activities to their peers or younger learners, progressing to whole lessons and sequences of lessons.			
Assemblies, and sometimes discrete lessons, focus on the habits of great learners – for example, perseverance, empathy, imagination, collaboration and resourcefulness.			
Praise, assessment and reporting systems recognise the development of learning behaviours as well as academic attainment.			

In an article for *SecEd* on 30 June 2020, Guy Claxton had the following message for teachers:

You need clear and unambiguous expectations. You need to make your classroom a safe place to grapple with difficult ideas and procedures (so no one groans when you give a wrong answer in good faith). You need to clearly mark when you want your students to be in learning mode, and when in performance mode (and not let them get stuck in performance mode where learning is slowed). You need challenging activities in which students can learn to moderate the level of difficulty for themselves, so they can stay in the amber or the Goldilocks zone. You need to find time for plenty of what Neil Mercer at Cambridge calls exploratory talk or inter-thinking. You need a language of learning, so everyone can talk about what the processes, strategies and attributes of effective learning are. And you need ways of assessing that focus not on snapshots of attainment but the trajectory of improvement.

Reflection

Which of the practical strategies suggested by Claxton to develop students' metacognitive skills do you think would be most impactful? Why?

Which are already utilised by teachers in your school?

How might you embed these practices further at your school?

Leaders demonstrating commitment

In his article, Claxton goes on to stress the 'importance of senior leaders – especially the principal – signalling loud, clear, genuine, frequent and visible support for this pedagogical shift'.

His advice is to:

- Allow time for discussion and airing of reservations, but then get a mandate from staff that leaders can work from.

- Identify, support and, if necessary, promote those colleagues who will be champions and coaches: who are enthusiastic and experienced with this way of teaching, and willing to support others.

- Strengthen a staff (all staff, not just teachers) culture of enquiry: a willingness to experiment, question their own practice, be open to new possibilities, and support others.

- Protect staff, as far as possible, from other innovations and demands, and insist that this will be the only initiative for the foreseeable future.

- Once the mandate is obtained, insist that all staff have to be involved in 'trying something', and hold middle leaders to account.

- Institute a school-wide peer-to-peer professional development system that allows for quick dissemination of 'good ideas'.

- Build leadership capacity in key colleagues so that the new culture will survive the departure of the individuals who instigated the changes.

- Get understanding and buy-in from parents and especially governors – ensuring that the latter really 'get it'.

Reflection

How committed are leaders at your school to developing the metacognitive skills of learners and teaching them to self-regulate?

Reflecting on Claxton's checklist, is there anything you would add in order to (further) support the development of metacognition and self-regulation at your school?

Implementing structures and systems to support student learning

Most schools that are serious about adopting a learning-powered approach to education have a system or structure in place to teach pupils explicit metacognitive strategies. This might be an L2L programme delivered by tutors or a series of timetabled LPA themed days. It is important that it is bespoke to the school, its context and its learners. At WSFG the programme we introduced in 2004 was called Building Learning Power and involved tutors and subject teachers introducing learners to an agreed set of learning muscles – which they would practise exercising – on a fort-nightly cycle. At INA we devised a framework around the acronym 'BRIDGES', which stood for bravery, resourcefulness, integrity, discovery, grit, emotional intelligence and self-discipline.

Case study: INA BRIDGES framework

The acronym BRIDGES derived from the quote often attributed to Isaac Newton: 'We build too many walls and not enough bridges.' The skills and character traits developed in the framework support learners in navigating from one stage of life to the next, bridging gaps in knowledge and experience.

The BRIDGES wheel is a visual representation of the 52 characteristics that INA learners (adults and students) develop over their school life:

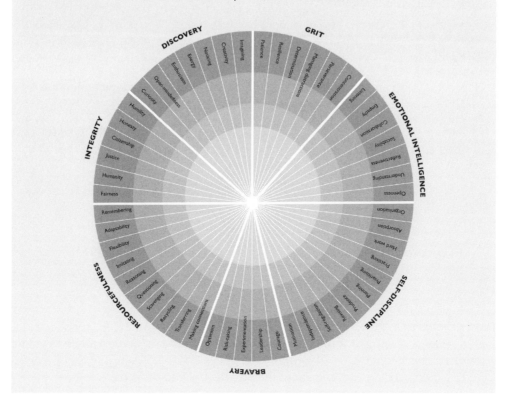

All schemes of learning and all lesson plans – in all subjects – include BRIDGES objectives to complement the curricular goals. Students are introduced to the characteristics by their tutors through weekly BRIDGES lessons, which aim to develop students' understanding of each focus area and its application to their own learning and lives. Each fortnight the school focuses on a different spoke of the BRIDGES wheel, with one spoke from each sector being targeted roughly each half term. This is further reinforced through every subject lesson having a BRIDGES objective, communicated to the students alongside the subject-specific learning objective – for example, understanding why the Normans won the Battle of Hastings using collaboration and curiosity.

In planning for BRIDGES in the primary school, the staff faced the challenge of adapting the secondary model for much younger students. It was decided that BRIDGES was every bit as applicable to younger learners, but that a simplified model was required. The wheel was adapted to just show the seven key learning sectors that were used on the secondary wheel and was modelled on Newton's disc. This focus on the seven key groupings allowed the primary staff to focus on one key learning skill each week, rotating around the whole wheel each half term. This allows for a greater depth of understanding for primary-age children as they revisit each learning skill area six times per year, giving them plenty of opportunity to demonstrate and exercise the habit.

Staff support is vital and all members of staff are involved in our BRIDGES pro-gramme. All staff, both teaching and operational, agree a personal BRIDGES performance development (PD) target with their performance manager as part of the PD cycle; thus they explicitly and actively identify a particular disposition that they wish to develop further during the year. BRIDGES is part of the induction programme for all staff – existing and new – at the start of the year, as well as part of staff induction for mid-year joiners. There is regular CPD on BRIDGES.

At termly awards assemblies, students within each tutor group at secondary, and within each year group at primary, are recognised for the development of one of the seven BRIDGES dispositions and given a badge in recognition. In secondary, tutors seek input from the wider staff body when deciding which student to select for each award. Parental support is important. The BRIDGES disposition of the week (at primary) or fortnight (at secondary) is publicised in the respective news-letters (see Appendix A).

Reflection

Do you have an L2L programme in your school? Is any curriculum time allocated to specifically teach metacognitive skills? If so, how similar or different is your school's approach and practice to that described in the INA case study?

How impactful is your school's programme? How do you know? Might you amend your practice in any way?

If you don't currently have a framework for teaching metacognitive skills, might you consider developing one? What might your first steps be?

The importance of metacognition in remote learning

If there was a need to convince anyone of the arguments for educators playing a central role in equipping students with the skills necessary to learn effectively and independently, the coronavirus pandemic surely provided ample evidence. Distance learning has been practised for hundreds of years in certain remote communities around the globe. However, there are currently very few research studies into what makes for effective remote learning. Most of the research conducted relates to higher education and to older learners. Bettinger and Loeb's study showed that university students from disadvantaged backgrounds 'consistently perform worse in an online setting than they do in face-to-face classrooms' (2017: 2). They added that taking online courses increases these students' likelihood of dropping out and stalls their progress.

Without doubt, the learners who have coped best during the months of home learning are those who already possessed the skills of time management and self-organisation, planning and crafting learning episodes, researching new information, exploring and elaborating, practising and consolidating, drafting and redrafting, revising, designing refresh and retest exercises, and building on and linking prior learning. Well before the pandemic, some schools had scheduled home learning days at regular intervals over the course of the academic year and their staff had prepared and coached their learners incrementally to be equipped to study effectively and independently at home. Imagine how comforted staff in LPA schools must have felt as successive lockdowns and school closures were announced, able to survey their student body, secure in the knowledge that they had taught their learners how to direct their own teaching and learning effectively.

Now more than ever, it has become clear that resilience, flexibility and self-regulation are essential factors in learning. When they teach students face-to-face, most teachers tend to do a lot of the metacognitive work for them. They plan and sequence learning episodes, they monitor how learners are progressing and intervene if necessary, and they evaluate the success of their lessons. When students are learning remotely, unless they are required to attend live lessons at set times (and a diet of back-to-back, synchronous teacher-directed learning episodes is not recommended!), they need the skills to plan their days effectively, deciding for themselves how long to spend on each task and how to prioritise activities. They have to monitor how well they are understanding and executing various tasks and devise strategies to help themselves when they get stuck.

> ### Reflection
>
> How well prepared were learners at your school for the style of remote learning that they experienced during lockdown?
>
> How well did they cope? How do you know?
>
> Were there any noticeable differences between key groups (according to age, gender, socio-economic background, attainment level, etc.)?
>
> To what extent did your staff reflect on lessons learnt from the remote learning experience during the first national lockdown and use this to inform the remote learning strategy going into 2021?

What makes for great remote learning?

In April 2020, the EEF conducted a rapid evidence assessment that examined the existing research (from 60 systematic reviews and meta-analyses) on approaches that schools could use, or were already using, to support learning whilst closed to the majority of their cohorts (Education Endowment Foundation 2020c). The findings suggested that teaching quality is more important than how lessons are delivered or what software or platforms are used. Clear explanations, scaffolding of new learning and quality feedback are more significant than how or when they are provided. This suggests that neither synchronous nor asynchronous lessons are more impactful; both live and recorded lessons can be effective as long as they are pedagogically strong. During the third national lockdown, Twitter was alive with blogs, reports and think pieces about effective remote learning. The core messages were consistent – variety, clarity, simplicity and high-quality pedagogy are key.

The EEF Guide to Supporting School Planning concludes that:

---

explicit modelling of independent learning strategies and guided practice is necessary. For example, prompting pupils to reflect on their work or to consider the strategies they will use if they get stuck have been highlighted as valuable. During the new academic year, integrating these strategies clearly into homework and other study approaches is likely to prove effective. (Education Endowment Foundation 2020b: 12)

In May 2020, the government produced guidance on adapting teaching practice for remote education, including case studies of good practice.[3] It recommended:

- Using teaching approaches that work well in face-to-face teaching, such as revisiting prior learning, breaking down new learning into manageable chunks, teacher modelling, scaffolding, practice and learning checks.
- Using technology and platforms that are familiar to both staff and pupils.
- Using formats that can be viewed by learners on mobile devices.
- Allowing for flexibility and different approaches within and between schools.

Learner feedback from teachers and peers

My discussions in recent months with a wide range of teachers working in a variety of schools, settings and phases have convinced me that the impact of online and remote teaching and learning is determined to a great extent by the strength of the teacher–learner relationships and the regularity and quality of communication and feedback between the two. The Sutton Trust and EEF Teaching and Learning Toolkit identified feedback as one of the most impactful teaching strategies.[4] Communication and feedback become even more crucial in learning environments that physically distance teachers and students.

Going back to our obstetrics analogy, what a patient tells their midwife or doctor is often more illuminating than what tests or physical examinations show; similarly, the discussions that teachers and students have about tasks and activities is often more significant than the finished product itself. Furthermore, in the same way as the best medics listen to their patients, put them at ease and closely observe what they tell them, the best teachers seek feedback not just on students' mastery of the learning but also on their experience of the journey, the strategies they utilised and their metacognitive strengths. Impactful remote learning occurs when teachers and

---

3 See https://www.gov.uk/guidance/adapting-teaching-practice-for-remote-education.
4 See https://educationendowmentfoundation.org.uk/evidence-summaries/teaching-learning-toolkit/feedback/.

students actively and collaboratively assess and reflect on the learning process, using whatever online tools are available to them.

Providing timely and personalised feedback to learners in a remote setting is a new challenge for many teachers. Having said that, in the winter of 2020–2021, faced with having to quarantine books before and after marking to avoid the spread of infection, schools had to adopt digital solutions even with their in-school learners. These included photographing and uploading work, using virtual chatrooms and forums, and adopting software packages designed for submitting, marking and feeding back on work completed by learners. Smart school leaders piloted and evaluated a range of approaches, providing training for staff and support for less confident colleagues, refining their practice in light of their experience and feedback from teachers and students, as well as collaborating with and learning from other schools.

However, importantly, they were striving to keep the dialogue and feedback as regular and personalised as ever, despite the challenges. They recognised that not all learners are equally motivated. Having access to a tablet, phone or other electronic device is not enough to ensure effective remote online learning; indeed, it can distract from learning through providing access to the likes of YouTube, Snapchat and Instagram! These educators appreciated that children are motivated by feedback and incentivised by knowing that their teachers are keeping a watchful eye on their progress, taking an interest in their learning experience and engaging in personalised dialogue about their studies. This type of learning-powered approach and live interaction strongly motivates students.

Reflection

Do staff in your school have a common understanding of what constitutes effective remote learning?

Do you have an agreed strategy for the implementation of effective remote learning, and how have you supported staff with any training needs?

How do you ensure regular and personalised feedback to learners and an ongoing dialogue between teachers and students?

Which aspects of your remote learning provision work best and how do you know?

What are your next priorities and what steps do you plan to take?

Given how time-consuming one-to-one feedback is, especially conducted remotely, the smart teacher will also look to utilise peer-to-peer feedback opportunities. Discussion boards and forums, small group or partner work, online debates, group projects and presentations, peer marking and review, and getting learners to share their approaches to a task or examples of high-quality end products all serve to engage and motivate learners.

Whenever I have visited independent schools in the UK and abroad, I have noted that one of the less obvious advantages that their students enjoy is the structured evening 'prep' time, studying in peer groups with a member of staff on hand to support and stimulate learning. This is something that state schools could aim to emulate through facilitation of out-of-school and remote learning.

Reflection

Have you set up any peer-to-peer support networks?

How regularly do your staff utilise peer-to-peer feedback activities?

Facilitators of out-of-school learning

If you are a school leader and convinced of the importance of out-of-school learning, you might consider taking two key steps. Firstly, you could build 'facilitator of out-of-school learning' into the job descriptions of all of your staff, discussing with them just why it is so important and encouraging them to reflect on the part they could play in supporting effective home learning. Secondly, you might take a long, hard look at everything you require your staff to do in the working week, in order to free up time for them to invest in gaining a greater understanding of all their learners and their home learning environments. You could encourage your staff to consider their students' learning habits and behaviours, with a view to pairing up those who lack strong learning role models at home (older siblings or parents) with learning buddies from their peer group. Some readers might worry that these actions would detract from the core function of teaching great lessons. However, my view is that this time would be well invested, resulting in stronger educational outcomes and learners who are more able to self-regulate and learn independently away from school.

Reflection

Do the staff in your school see themselves as facilitators of out-of-school learning?

What do they do to support or intervene when students are not yet able to operate as effective self-regulating learners?

Closing thought

I suspect that an enduring lesson from the coronavirus crisis will be an awareness of the danger of over-relying on schools – in the sense of the physical buildings in which learning happens. My hope is that more leaders will adopt a learning-powered approach to fashioning their curriculum – prioritising behaviours, language, structures and activities that will support their children to develop the characteristics and dispositions of successful learners. If they do, not only will their students be prepared for the scholarly behaviours required of them should they pursue university study, and equipped as lifelong learners whatever they decide to do, but they will not be knocked off course by the consequences of any future pandemics on their school's ability to provide on-site education.

Chapter 7
The importance of oracy

Mankind's greatest achievements have come about by talking, and its greatest failures by not talking.

Stephen Hawking (Quoted in McGowan 2018)

The limits of my language mean the limits of my world.

Ludwig Wittgenstein (2001 [1922]: 68)

Oracy is the ability to express oneself fluently in spoken language. Those with well-developed oracy skills are able to articulate their ideas clearly and persuasively, deepen their understanding through discourse and engage with and relate to others through talk.

In his powerful chapter on oracy in *The Forgotten Third*, Peter Hyman (2020: 115–116) writes:

They say that, on average, a child speaks for no more than four seconds per lesson. For many it's less. For too many, finding their voice is a quest with many obstacles in the way. Like the heroes of Greek mythology, for the forgotten third, those who find life more of a struggle, it takes the slaying of too many dragons, the endless hacking back of too much psychological undergrowth, before it is possible to find a sense of true identity. The reasons are myriad. Some young people are trapped by the past or get stuck in their heads for fear of venturing forth; cowed by hierarchies and power dynamics. Others are hooked on playing the victim, or the clown, both used as coping mechanisms for difficult lives. We see in our schools every day these barriers to talk.

This chapter explores oracy – why it is so important and how those who work in schools can support learners to develop the skills that it encompasses.

Why is oracy so important?

A great postnatal healthcare professional will ensure that new parents have been taught and understand the mechanics and practicalities of looking after a baby: how to feed, bathe, and change the infant, what warning signs to look out for, and which medical checks are needed at each stage of their development. However, the crucial piece of their work is teaching the new parents how to bond and connect with their baby. Their advice might include holding the baby close, with the parent's skin next to theirs as soon as possible after the birth, chatting and smiling, pulling faces at the baby, singing to and dancing with the infant and stroking their cheek. Helping parents to form a relationship with their baby is crucial; parents who develop postnatal depression often cite difficulties in connecting and communicating with their baby as part of the problem.

Bodily contact and face-to-face conversation are fundamental human needs. We have seen this poignantly during the coronavirus pandemic, with those living alone during lockdown finding phone calls and Zoom catch-ups no substitute for in-person communication. Relatives and friends expressed how hard they found it going for months on end without a hug from their loved ones.

With verbal communication being such an essential human need, articulacy is a crucial skill for human development. When we are able to express ourselves using well-chosen language, we gain satisfaction from making ourselves understood and from understanding the impact that our words have. This raises our self-esteem, increases our confidence and enhances our wellbeing. If we can articulate ourselves coherently and persuasively – even in high-pressure situations, such as when meeting someone significant for the first time, attending a job interview or contributing to a public meeting – we are more likely to convince people to take notice of us and respect our views. Oracy is a skill which is highly valued by employers and highly likely to open doors and lead to exciting and enriching opportunities.

Unfortunately, of course, the opposite is equally true. Reluctant, faltering and clumsy communicators experience frustration and embarrassment. Those who are not at ease and skilled at speaking and listening to and with others find it harder to build and maintain quality relationships. People who lack a wide vocabulary with which to express themselves – or the grammatical grounding with which to construct well-crafted sentences – get overlooked, prejudged and written off. Inarticulacy is one of the most significant barriers to social mobility, and it is a barrier experienced disproportionately by the disadvantaged. If those who face the greatest difficulties and hardships in society can be supported by educators to find their voice, to talk with purpose and confidence, to feel safe and free to speak out, they will be empowered to navigate life's challenges more successfully. They are more likely to achieve, feel fulfilled and be happy.

If that were not argument enough for the importance of oracy, it is a powerful tool for learning and for the development of metacognition. When learners develop the skills to be effective speakers and listeners, and to talk about talk, they are better able to understand themselves, each other and the learning process. Talk helps students to understand, process and embed new concepts and knowledge.

In an article in the Chartered College of Teaching's *Impact* journal, Will Millard and Amy Gaunt (2020) argue that 'Developing classroom talk has a wide range of benefits on students' outcomes during school, and beyond'. They point to cognitive gains, personal and social gains and better civic engagements, 'where students are encouraged to participate verbally and given space and time to reflect upon and discuss complex ideas'.

What evidence is there that disadvantaged learners have less-developed oracy skills?

Academics are agreed that language development affects cognitive development. But is there a link between language acquisition and socio-economic background? Hart and Risley's (2003) now famous study into vocabulary – 'The early catastrophe: the 30 million word gap by age 3' – would suggest so. They analysed the early vocabulary growth of children in 42 families. Over two and a half years, they observed each family for an hour each month to see how they interacted with their 1- to 2-year-olds. They discovered a significant difference in the amount of experience that the children had with language and interaction and a strong link between this and the children's language development aged 3.

They found that the average child on welfare heard around 616 words per hour, compared to the typical child from a working-class background who heard 1,251 words per hour, and the typical child from a professional background who heard 2,153 words. In their research sample, over four years, the average child from a professional background accumulated experience of 45 million words, compared to the average child of working-class parents (26 million words) and the average child of parents on welfare (13 million) – hence the 30-million-word gap.

In summary, the research showed that children from wealthier homes received more encouragement to talk and used a greater range of vocabulary than those from poorer homes. The findings from this US study correlate with research conducted in the UK by the Sutton Trust (2012), which identified a gap of 19 months in performance on vocabulary tests between 4- and 5-year-olds in the lowest income quintile compared to those in the highest income quintile.

Hart and Risley (2003: 6–7) reported:

Before children can take charge of their own experience and begin to spend time with peers in social groups outside the home, almost everything they learn comes from their families […] 86 percent to 98 percent of the words recorded in each child's vocabulary consisted of words also recorded in their parents' vocabularies.

There are several reasons why parents of disadvantaged children often have less developed oracy skills. They are more likely to have experienced a poor quality of education themselves and less likely to have spent as many years in the education system as their wealthier counterparts. They are less likely to work in a career or profession in which the level of oracy of their work colleagues is high. They are more likely to speak English as an additional language, and so their children will often not be exposed to the same rich breadth of vocabulary as their peers whose parents speak it as their first language.

Unless teachers are aware of the likelihood of at least some of their disadvantaged learners requiring support to develop their oracy skills and widen their vocabulary, these gaps are likely to become ever wider. Hart and Risley were struck at how well their measures of accomplishments at age 3 predicted measures of language skills at age 9 to 10. The Bercow Report (Bercow and Department for Children, Schools and Families 2008) stated that a large proportion of students start school with worryingly limited basic communication skills – missing those that are vital for effective schooling – and highlighted a direct link between young children's language and communication skills and their later academic attainment. The Rose Report (Rose 2006) had previously drawn attention to the importance of developing children's speaking and listening skills, so essential in the acquisition of literacy.

To conclude, therefore, it is especially important that learners from poorer backgrounds and homes in which there is limited dialogic and developmental talk have access to a language-rich curriculum with plenty of opportunity for structured classroom discussion and talk that builds confidence and understanding. School closures as a result of the pandemic have made this even more pressing: lockdown will have increased the language gap between children from families who are able to support their children's oracy skills and those who are less equipped to do so. Remote teaching does not readily lend itself to peer discussion, and the types of COVID-secure measures that were in place to limit transmission in schools in the autumn of 2020 saw the furniture in many classrooms rearranged – with desks and chairs facing the front and learners seated in rows, making peer-to-peer discussion more difficult. Emma Hardy – shadow minister for further education and universities and chair of the All-Party Parliamentary Group on Oracy – expressed concern in *Schools Week* that this could lead to a reduction in pupil talk: 'It will certainly make it harder for teachers to ensure high-quality classroom talk can prevail' (Hardy 2020). In the same *Schools Week* article, Hardy also said that 'Recent Parent Ping polling found that 64 per cent of parents agree that school closures reduced opportunities for children to develop their oracy skills.'

On 24 August 2020, Children's Minister Vicky Ford announced a multi-million-pound package of support to boost early language skills by funding one-to-one tuition for key learners, using the Nuffield Early Language Intervention (NELI) programme. Ford said: 'We cannot afford for our youngest children to lose out, which is why this package of support is focused on improving early language skills for the Reception children who need it most' (quoted in Department for Education 2020b).

So what can we do to widen vocabularies and teach the skills of oracy? There are three key aspects to developing oracy in schools:

1. **Creating a climate in which learners feel safe to talk.** And, crucially, are encouraged to do so, building up their confidence until they volunteer their views without prompting or coaxing and enjoy talking in a range of situations. For this, it is key that teachers have developed strong relationships with their students (as discussed in Chapter 3), that all students show their peers respect and encouragement, and that staff know and understand their learners well.

2. **Teaching learners how to articulate themselves fluently.** Here role modelling and staff consistency are crucial. As they become more competent in their oracy skills, students need to appreciate the nuances of language, how to modify their speech in different situations, and the importance of the use of Standard English in certain contexts (of which more a bit later in this chapter).

3. **Teaching learners how to learn through talk.** This can be in short bursts, such as in the 'turn and talk to your partner' technique used from Reception onwards, to 'think, pair, share' activities deployed more typically in upper primary and secondary. It can also involve learners engaging in effective peer discussion and debate for an entire lesson, with minimal teacher supervision. We will look at approaches to dialogic learning in the latter stages of this chapter.

Supporting learners to develop oracy skills

Many schools have developed excellent practice in fostering the oracy skills of learners and training adults to become impactful teachers of oracy. A shining example is School 21, which set up a charity – Voice 21 – in 2015 to train teachers in oracy practice. Voice 21 now works with hundreds of schools nationwide, using a framework developed by teachers at the school in conjunction with Neil Mercer from the University of Cambridge. The framework has four oracy strands:[1]

- Cognitive (content, structure, reasoning – application of thought to what you are saying).
- Linguistic (vocabulary, language and rhetorical techniques – knowing what words and phrases to use).
- Physical (use of the voice and body to convey meaning).
- Social and emotional (engagement, confidence, listening and responding, audience engagement).

Teachers who are skilled at teaching learners how to talk start by showcasing high-quality talk themselves. They form their sentences with care. They use grammatically correct constructions. They choose technical and subject-specific language (explaining it where necessary) and deploy a wide vocabulary. They create a safe and inclusive culture in which every voice is heard (no talking over peers or sniggering at other people's contributions allowed) and all learners are encouraged, supported and expected to talk. They know which of their learners have weaker oracy skills and build up opportunities to talk incrementally for those pupils, starting on home ground by asking them about a topic with which they are familiar or a subject that is a particular interest or passion of theirs. They give reluctant speakers advance notice of when an oral contribution will be requested or required, and acknowledge and praise improvements. They maximise opportunities for talk, so that learners can practise their oracy skills. They plan and structure their talk opportunities carefully; there is no idle chatter. Rather, they explicitly communicate their instructions and their expectations about the type and nature of talk required for the task. They give careful thought to which (and how many) pupils work together, how roles are allocated and what outcomes are expected. These teachers reflect deeply on the effectiveness of their oracy activities. They assess the progress of their learners objectively and forensically, with a clear sense of how oracy skills become increasingly sophisticated, holding themselves to account for the impact of their oracy coaching.

1   See https://voice21.org/oracy/.

The EEF report, *Improving Literacy in Secondary Schools* (Quigley and Coleman 2020), puts forward seven key recommendations related to reading, writing, talk and vocabulary development. The section on effective ways to promote high-quality talk is just as applicable to primary schools as it is to secondary. It advocates:

- *Teachers modelling what effective talk sounds like in their subjects.*
- *Deliberately sequencing talk activities alongside reading and writing tasks to give students opportunities to practise using new vocabulary, develop ideas before writing, or discuss ways to overcome common challenges.*
- *Using sentence starters and prompts to help students to structure and extend their responses.*
- *Selecting questions that are open-ended, well-suited to discussion and allow opportunity for authentic student response rather than direct replication of teaching.*
- *Setting goals and roles, particularly for small group discussions.*
- *Using wait time to develop students' responses, by leaving a pause after they have first given an answer, which gives them a chance to reframe, extend, or justify their reasoning.*
- *Giving precise feedback relating to different elements of accountability.* (Quigley and Coleman 2020: 29)

Reflection

Which of the seven EEF-recommended strategies would you categorise as learning *to* talk and which are learning *through* talk?

Which of these strategies is most embedded in your school? Which might you develop further?

What training or support would teachers require to utilise these techniques more routinely and effectively?

Just as the great teacher has clear oracy goals and high expectations for each pupil, schools that are determined that all learners will develop a high standard of oracy skills set and articulate ambitious expectations from everyone in the school, including teachers and all operational staff. They might well have an oracy policy, and they are likely to devote considerable time to training their staff to be effective practitioners. At INA we had a Standard English policy which we discussed and agreed with staff and revisited at regular intervals. The rationale was as follows:

We believe that by teaching students what Standard English is and how to use it, we empower them to feel confident and at ease in formal situations, to project a positive image of themselves and create strong first impressions which may impact on their educational, career and life chances. We know that the ability to use Standard English appropriately improves students' self-esteem.

All staff were expected to value and celebrate regional dialects but also to guide and coach learners in the use of Standard English in certain contexts. We embraced the use of colloquial and more familiar language in the playground, lunch hall and more social and informal settings, but advised staff as to how and when to challenge these styles of speech. We also asked staff to listen out for 'sentence fillers' in student speech, differentiating between the occasional use of expressions such as 'sort of', which can slip into speech when someone is formulating their thoughts and thinking through how they will verbalise them, and ingrained habits of using words such as 'like' and 'basically' repeatedly in a sentence, as part of an affected style of speech. In the case of the latter, we felt it important that students understood that their means of expression was getting in the way of effective communication, could be viewed negatively by, for example, a prospective employer and so could disadvantage them.

Staff discussed and agreed a range of strategies that could be effectively deployed for supporting students in developing Standard English and using it appropriately. With many of the examples that follow it is, of course, vital that they are used sensitively and only in classrooms in which a strong relationship of mutual trust and respect has already been created between all learners and the teacher and the first stage of developing oracy (getting students willing, confident and keen to talk) has been mastered. So, recommended oracy strategies could include:

- The beep game. Students agree on the colloquial expressions that are banned. Then one student talks for a defined amount of time on a topic and the class beep if they use any banned words or phrases.

- Encouraging students to use alternative 'fillers', such as 'I think' rather than 'kind of' and 'like'.

- Saying 'I really like your idea, but could you say that again, rephrasing it, using Standard English?'
- Encouraging think time.
- Coaching persistent offenders by recording them and playing their speech back to them in a one-to-one session so that they can hear how they sound and self-correct.
- Having a class Standard English monitor.
- Acknowledging and praising students when they use Standard English.
- Giving students the opportunity to try again or to nominate a friend to help them rephrase what they said.
- Building in plenty of opportunities for debates and discussions.
- Building in the use of Standard English as part of the assessment criteria for certain tasks and discussing the rationale behind this.
- Giving parents top tips for them to use to support their child in improving their use of Standard English.
- Holding a session for families of the students who find using Standard English hard, to talk through the reasons why this is a priority and how parents and carers can assist.

Reflection

Do you have an issue in your school with learners not using Standard English in situations in which it is expected/required?

Is there a correlation between use of non-Standard English and disadvantage?

What strategies do you currently deploy to address this?

Might you utilise any of the ideas from the INA list?

If you were planning a staff training session about the importance of Standard English and how to coach students in using it, what activities might you include?

Dialogic teaching

The next stage after teaching learners *how* to talk is teaching them *through* talk. Robin Alexander, Cambridge academic and primary education expert, describes this as dialogic teaching – using talk to engage learners' interest, stimulate their thinking, advance their understanding, expand their ideas, and build their discursive skills.

Between 2014 and 2017, Alexander's Cambridge Primary Review Trust and the University of York, supported by the EEF, conducted a research study into the impact of dialogic teaching on the engagement levels and educational standards of primary children who are socially disadvantaged. Following the trial, which involved 5,000 students in three English cities, the EEF reported that pupils whose teachers had received the dialogic teaching intervention made, on average, two months' additional progress in tests in English, mathematics and science compared with their control group peers. These attainment gains were after an intervention lasting only 20 weeks.

Alexander (2018: 6) suggests that to be effective, dialogic teaching must be:

- *Collective (the classroom is a site of joint learning and enquiry)*

- *Reciprocal (participants listen to each other, share ideas and consider alternative viewpoints)*

- *Supportive (participants feel able to express ideas freely, without risk of embarrassment over 'wrong' answers, and they help each other to reach common understandings)*

- *Cumulative (participants build on their own and each other's contributions and chain them into coherent lines of thinking and understanding)*

- *Purposeful (classroom talk, though open and dialogic, is structured with specific learning goals in view).*

Harkness teaching and learning

There are many examples of dialogic learning structures used by schools with children of different ages, such as talk partners, Socratic circles, Philosophy for Children (P4C), fruit and talk, and circle time. Harkness is one technique that is used by schools that are serious about fostering learners' oracy skills. Philanthropist Edward S. Harkness established the Harkness method of teaching in the 1930s at Phillips Exeter Academy in Boston, USA, developing a style of teaching that encouraged student-led discussion and questioning. Learners sit around an oval or circular table and engage in a seminar-style dialogue. When I was setting up INA, I had the chance to visit Phillips Exeter Academy with my chair of governors, who was an alumnus of the school. I was struck by the quality of dialogic learning that I observed across the curriculum.

Traditional teaching   Harkness teaching

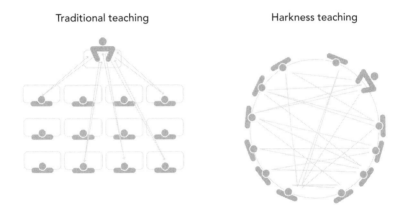

Source: Lucas and Claxton (2010: 128)

The principles underpinning the pedagogy of Harkness teaching are simple: the teacher acts as facilitator; students act as collaborative learners with ownership of the issues being discussed. Harkness places students at the centre of the learning process and encourages them to learn from one another. Under the guidance of the teacher, the instruction focuses on the ideas brought to the table by the students themselves – what happens in the class depends on the reading and preparation undertaken by the students in advance. Harkness is very much akin to the seminar-style discussion that is common in many higher education institutions and, as such, is excellent preparation for university.

Case study: Harkness at INA

We believe that focused dialogue is a key component of learning that develops students' oracy skills. In planning their lessons, teachers are expected to create opportunities for more varied and dialogic interaction patterns to occur, including Harkness discussions and collaborative learning. The Harkness method creates a learning culture of enquiry and collaborative discussion, which goes way beyond the lesson. It requires self-motivation, a love of learning and a willingness to share your own ideas as well as be open to others'. At INA all teachers are teachers of the Harkness method, and Harkness discussions are built into every scheme of learning.

Training teachers in the Harkness method has been the key to its success. Prior to opening, in the summer of 2012, the principal led a Harkness session in which staff participated in a Harkness discussion and explored some of the principles behind it, particularly the role of the teacher as a facilitator. We discussed how to encourage contributions from all participants whilst ensuring that no learners dominated, how to teach learners to take turns and not talk over others, how to coach them to build on each other's responses and link their contributions to comments made previously in the discussion, how to track the dialogue and assess and feed back on participants' skills development. Heads of department then went away over the summer to plan their first schemes of learning, building in a range of Harkness opportunities (at least one every half term). Further staff training took place during the first academic year, and each subsequent year we have included Harkness training in the induction process and delivered further training for existing staff.

In Years 7 and 8, students have one Harkness skills lesson per week, in which they are coached and assessed in the techniques of being a good Harkness learner, as well as taking part in discussions, following the principles, in each of their subject areas. Older year groups learn through Harkness in an increasing proportion of lessons across the curriculum.

Since its introduction in September 2012, we have adapted the way in which Harkness is delivered. The ideal number for a discussion is around 14 students. Originally, Harkness lessons at INA were taught in our Harkness room, around our custom-built oval table, or in our conference room, which also has an oval table with seating for about 14 people. A class would be divided into two groups for their Harkness lessons: a co-teacher or learning assistant would facilitate discussion with one group and the class teacher with the other. We still use this arrangement. However, with the school growing and the desire to embed Harkness more fully into everyday learning, we started to experiment with other practical arrangements so that multiple discussions can take place in various rooms around the school at the same time, and without always relying on having a second adult to take one group.

The 'inner and outer circle' approach is one way of facilitating Harkness with a larger group. Half of the class move their tables and chairs to form an oval for their discussion; the other half sit around the outside of the oval, observing. The students who are not participating in the discussion might be assigned a particular student to observe and feed back to on the quality of their contributions, or they might listen to the discussion and make notes on it to further their understanding of the subject. Another way of facilitating Harkness with a larger group is to have two separate discussions running simultaneously within the classroom, with the teacher seated between the two ovals or circulating around the two groups.

Each year students are interviewed to become Harkness champions. Their role is to promote Harkness learning, by supporting teachers with its delivery and with the planning of lessons within schemes of learning. Each Harkness champion is linked to a subject area. Heads of department can call on them to discuss how to build Harkness opportunities into schemes of learning or to take half a class to facilitate a session.

Leanne Abbott-Jones and Jo Spencer

Reflection

What opportunities do learners in your school have to learn through talk?

How might you introduce more frequent oracy activities?

Do you assess learners' oracy skills in any way?

Looking at the INA class list proforma (on pages 144–145) for tracking the development of Harkness skills, which of these oracy skills might you look to track and assess in your school? How could you do this? Would you add any other oracy skills to this list?

INA Harkness skills class tracker

In Harkness lessons, the teacher closely observes the discussion taking place. They might use a diagram of the Harkness table, with the position of each learner labelled, and draw lines between the participants to record how the discussion flows, which students are most involved and which are quieter. They might use a shorthand or symbol system to annotate the types of contributions made – for example, putting a 'B' by the name of a student who builds on a previous point or an 'I' by the name of a child who interrupts or talks over others. At INA we used a class tracker (see pages 144–145) to keep a log of the particular skills being developed and demonstrated by each student. The names of the learners were listed in the left-hand column and the teacher would annotate the cells relating to the various elements of the four key areas – communication skills; critical thinking and application of knowledge; democratising the classroom; and preparation and follow-up undertaken outside the classroom – to record how students' behaviours and habits were developing. Each learner's profile was shared and discussed with them at regular intervals.

In his chapter in *The Forgotten Third*, Peter Hyman poses 10 questions for school leaders who are striving to develop an oracy culture:

---

1. *In what ways has every child in the school been able to find and express their voice?*

2. *How is each child able to wrestle with the 'great conversation' of every subject?*

3. *Does every teacher include oracy in their lesson plans?*

4. *How are barriers to talk being removed in the school?*

5. *How are teachers being trained in oracy techniques?*

6. *Is talk given the same status and treated with the same sense of purpose as reading and writing? If not, why not?*

7. *Is there an active attempt to give every child a range of contexts and settings in which to explore oracy?*

8. *Are there regular speech-making events with proper preparation time?*

9. *Is oracy homework set?*

10. *How are students being taught to listen?* (Hyman 2020: 122)

> Reflection
>
> How might you use one or more of Hyman's key questions to raise the profile of oracy development at your school?
>
> Could you use them as a prompt for discussion with middle leaders, senior leaders or governors?
>
> Might you address some of these foci in your school improvement plan?

Closing thought

To conclude, I would stress that we ignore oracy development at our peril. In *Scaffolding Language, Scaffolding Learning* (2015: 23) Pauline Gibbons suggests that classroom talk determines whether or not children learn and reminds us that 'a classroom without a well-planned spoken language program denies all students a major resource to learning.' Yet it is those learners who are less well versed in the spoken and written codes of our society who are most disadvantaged:

it would be wrong to assume that children who are not fluent in these codes will automatically acquire them through the process of being in school without specific kinds of support. (Gibbons 2015: 231)

Class: 7P	Communication skills						Critical thinking and application of knowledge		
	Students participate without prompts from the teacher	Students listen closely to comments of others, considering their points carefully before speaking	Students refer to the comments of others, using their names	Students make eye contact when speaking	Students further the discussion with their input, avoiding repetition	Students stay engaged throughout the discussion, demonstrating active listening skills	Students refer to the reading/prep during the discussion	Students use evidence to support their assertions	Students are able to summarise information
Duane S	■	■	■	■	■	■	■	■	□
Rabia K	■	■	□	■	□	■	□	□	□
Matthew S	□	■	□	□	▨	□	□	□	□
Naomi K	■	□	■	■	■	□	□	□	■

Students are able to make connections between others' points and their own	Students incorporate ideas gained from independent reading and thinking into the discussion	Students are willing to ask questions and/or challenge others constructively to deepen understanding	Students avoid dominating the discussion	Students create opportunities for others in the discussion, through making connections to what each is saying	Students actively influence the learning of the group	Students make their voices central to the learning environment	Students work with fellow students to find the answers rather than relying on the teacher	Students address comments to the class (not the teacher)	Students prepare for the discussion by completing independent learning set by the class teacher	Students prepare fully for lessons by reading, annotating, thinking about and generating ideas for discussion	The course readings and discussions inspire students to find out more through further reading, thinking and discussion
				Democratising the classroom					Preparation and follow-up undertaken outside the classroom		
▓	▓	▓	▓						▓	▓	
	▓		▓								
			▓								
▓		▓		▓	▓	▓					

Harkness Assessment

Chapter 8
Developing cultural capital

Kids can only dream things that are known to them.

Michelle Obama (Quoted in Brown 2018)

Fair doesn't mean giving every child the same thing, it means giving every child what they need.

Attributed to Rick Lavoie

In Chapter 5, I made the case that the most effective way to accelerate the progress and maximise the attainment of disadvantaged pupils is by ensuring that high-quality teaching and learning are happening in every classroom across the school. Despite this, I have to admit to feeling disappointment recently when a local authority education manager of a large county told me that, in supporting schools to close attainment gaps, his team of advisers had taken the decision to focus solely on improving the quality of teaching in lessons and had stopped supporting schools with strategies to enrich the experiences of disadvantaged learners outside the classroom.

The All-Party Parliamentary Group on Social Mobility's report, *The Class Ceiling: Increasing Access to the Leading Professions* (2017), concluded that whilst the most important controllable factor in reducing gaps is the quality of teaching, what happens after the school bell has rung is also crucial. I agree. In this chapter I shall argue that we need to find ways to level the playing field regarding out-of-school opportunities and participation in order to ensure high performance and achievement for all. But, more than that, I shall argue that we must pay attention to the entire curricular experience of our learners. We need to focus on what skills they are learning and the knowledge they are acquiring from the moment they arrive in the morning until they leave at the end of the day – in assemblies, clubs, tutorials and other non-timetabled activities. There is simply insufficient formal lesson time in the average school week to ensure that disadvantaged learners acquire the cultural capital to thrive and achieve in ways commensurate with their more advantaged peers.

What is cultural capital and why is it so important?

The term 'cultural capital' perhaps requires definition. When I use the term, I am referring to the skills, norms, behaviours and wider cultural knowledge that give us social, economic and other advantages: the assets that allow us to move smoothly and confidently between different groups or levels in society. The accumulation of cultural capital is a key element of social mobility. If only fostered in middle-class homes and acquired by learners at schools serving the more affluent, this knowledge acts as a gatekeeper for the powerful and perpetuates the existence of a stratified society with an emphasis on class and elites.

Like many school leaders, I was delighted to see that Ofsted's 2019 *School Inspection Handbook* stressed the importance of developing cultural capital:

As part of making the judgement about the quality of education, inspectors will consider the extent to which schools are equipping pupils with the knowledge and cultural capital they need to succeed in life. Our understanding of 'knowledge and cultural capital' is derived from the following wording in the national curriculum:

'It is the essential knowledge that pupils need to be educated citizens, introducing them to the best that has been thought and said and helping to engender an appreciation of human creativity and achievement.' (Ofsted 2019b: 43)

Developing cultural capital is key to widening the horizons and raising the aspirations of children whose life experience is very narrow. It has the effect of boosting their self-esteem and convincing them of both their worth and their right to have ambitious dreams. It goes some way to furnishing them with a bit of the confidence demonstrated so effortlessly by their public-school educated peers.

At both WSFG and INA, my leadership teams and I were determined that the curriculum experience should be as wide and rich as possible at all key stages. We wanted our students to be exposed to a multitude of disciplines – academic and practical, artistic, linguistic, scientific and technical. We championed non-examined and non-tested subjects and activities and ensured that their place in the school day was protected. Participation in weekly enrichment activities was compulsory for all pupils in the early years and at Key Stages 1, 2, 3 and 5 at INA. We didn't consider shortening Key Stage 3 or mandating that students study an EBacc combination of subjects at Key Stage 4. We were convinced of the character and mental health benefits of this approach and the correlation between broad learning experiences and examination success.

We had a clear vision and rationale because we had spent time discussing (and, at times, arguing about!) what we meant by a cultural education and what cultural activities we believed it was essential for all our students to experience. We had the debate with our staff about who gets to determine what type of experiences are non-negotiables and whether a cultural education should comprise skills that the students are interested in – for example, gaming or beat boxing – or be made up of activities that we, with our adult perspective, might believe that they should experience – such as capoeira or cricket. There is a danger that cultural education programmes can acquire a middle-class, paternalistic whiff: 'It's important that everyone can read Latin and appreciate opera.' However, if the range of cultural activities is limited to students' requests, it won't expand horizons or build self-esteem in the same way. Inevitably, we sought to strike a happy medium.

I have to admit to being one of the voices arguing for the inclusion of some activities that could be seen as somewhat elitist – for example, art appreciation. This stemmed from my experience of imposter syndrome as an undergraduate at the University of Cambridge in the 1980s. I came from a middle-class background and attended a state comprehensive and sixth form college in Basingstoke, a new town. My parents were both teachers and, as a child, I was encouraged to read widely and, from time to time, taken to the theatre, concerts and pantomimes. I studied the piano and cello (private lessons paid for by a local authority grant) and, through playing in a county youth orchestra and attending residential music schools during the holidays, I got to meet a number of privately educated people my age.

My cultural capital was by no means deficient compared to most, yet I recall many occasions at university when I felt that I didn't fit in, despite choosing to apply for a 1960s 'left-leaning' college. One such occasion was during a small group seminar with some fellow history undergraduates. We were studying medieval English monarchs and the discussion turned to propaganda through royal portraiture. Suddenly the language became alien to me, and I felt out of my depth. The tutor asked for my view and made reference to gallery visits and art criticism. When I admitted that I had never actually been to an art gallery, I recall aghast looks passing between my fellow students. The episode left me feeling humiliated, belittled and, more than anything, angry. The irony was that the tutor was a forward-thinking, pro-state-school director of studies who gave me lots of opportunities and whom I respected greatly. He would have been mortified to think that his question had affected me in this way. Nevertheless, I never wanted any of my students to go through a similar experience.

> ## Reflection
>
> Do your staff have a common understanding of the term 'cultural capital'?
>
> Do you have an agreed vision about the cultural experiences you want all of your learners to have?
>
> How do you develop cultural capital at your school?

Planning for the development of cultural capital

Before INA opened in 2012, the leadership team crafted the cultural education policy statement, an extract from which follows: a declaration of what we believed all students should have experienced by the time they graduated from Key Stage 4 at INA, and that we were pledging to support them to achieve. This was then expanded with a Key Stage 5 addition, once we embarked on planning the sixth form, and a primary cultural passport (Appendix B), when we became an all-through school.

Cultural education at INA

By the time students reach the end of Key Stage 4 at INA, they should have:

- *Experienced a high-quality and enriching curriculum offer throughout Key Stage 3, including art, dance, drama, design, history, literature and music.*

- *Had an opportunity to learn a musical instrument.*

- *Taken part in workshops with professional artists, craftspeople, architects, musicians, archivists, curators, dancers, filmmakers, poets, authors and actors.*

- *Developed knowledge about a range of different aspects of culture, including an understanding of the historical development and context of art, drama, design, literature and music.*

- *Been encouraged to be adventurous in their choices about cultural activities, by learning about literature, films, visual arts, crafts, heritage, music and dance beyond the scope of their normal everyday engagement.*

- *Developed an understanding of the different forms of each cultural area (for example: literature, including poetry, plays, short stories and novels; music genres, including classical, pop, hip-hop, rock, jazz, folk, musical theatre and world).*

- *Been on visits to museums, heritage sites, galleries and cinemas at each key stage.*

- *Had an opportunity to go on a residential trip.*

- *Had an opportunity to visit a place with a significantly contrasting culture to Ilford.*

- *Travelled on the London Underground into central London.*

- *Sung in a school choir.*

- *Attended professional concerts and plays.*

- *Taken part in an artistic performance to an audience.*

- *Watched and learnt about films from outside the Hollywood mainstream.*

- *Regularly read books for pleasure, rather than only as part of their learning.*

- *Read a broad range of books both by living authors and by authors who may no longer be alive, but whose works are regarded as literary classics. Some of these books might be about subjects that are directly relevant to the readers' lives today, but young people should also be reading books that expand their horizons and show them the possibilities in the world beyond their own direct experiences.*

- *Used a library to access a wide range of books, as well as for other research materials.*

- *Been given the opportunity to study cultural education subjects (art, dance, drama, history, literature and music) to gain qualifications at level 2.*

- *Regularly made use of digital technology to see, read and listen to great culture, no matter where it is situated in the world.*

- *Had their artistic and creative work celebrated in the academy and in the wider community through publication, exhibitions, performance and screenings.*

- *Been supported to take particular strengths and interests forward.*

- *Had the chance to lead or shape an activity at INA – for example, by helping with a club or being a student librarian.*

- *Been able to join a lunchtime or after-school club in areas such as creative writing, dance, drama, art, music, film or digital media.*

- *Given time to a charitable cause.*

By the time students reach the end of Key Stage 5 they should additionally have:

- *Been encouraged to continue to sample a wide range of adventurous cultural experiences during their own leisure time.*

- *Been encouraged to continue to take part in the broad range of cultural events that take place both within their school environment and in the wider area in which they live.*

- *Developed the ability to build on the knowledge which they have acquired about culture to discuss and critique the new cultural works that they encounter.*

- *Had their own personal achievements in cultural activities celebrated in school or in their wider local community.*

- *Been given the opportunity to study cultural education subjects to gain qualifications at level 3.*

- *Had the opportunity to spend time interacting with cultural professionals (such as artists, writers, archivists, musicians, curators, technicians, filmmakers, designers and dancers).*

- *Learned about the wider world of employment and apprenticeship opportunities within the creative and cultural industries, aside from being a frontline performer or creative practitioner.*

It was important to us that this policy didn't just exist as a grand aspirational statement but really shaped the practice and experience of everyone in the school. So we created a 'cultural passport' for each of the year groups, displayed in the students' organisers, of key experiences and activities that they should have participated in by the end of the year. Many schools do this; some call it a student pledge or '20 things to do before you are 16', for example. We made it clear that tutors were expected to design tutorial activities around the passport, to make time for tracking and ticking off completed elements in the student organisers and to provide opportunities for students to share their progress with their peers, inspiring them with ideas and examples. Some classes designed their class assemblies around the cultural activities that they had undertaken.

We encouraged subject teachers to build in opportunities for students to cover elements from their cultural passport during their lessons, and then to ceremoniously tick them off. It will not surprise you to learn that one of the topics we used in the Key Stage 3 Harkness scheme of learning, was 'Which of this year's nominees should win the Turner Prize?' The aim was to encourage students to feel confident reflecting on art and articulating their feelings about modern artists' works, as well as to develop their oracy skills.

> Reflection
>
> What experiences would you include in a cultural passport?

Involving everyone

There was simply not enough time in the formal timetabled day to cover all the experiences listed on the passports. Like every school, INA had a programme of enrichment activities. Most took place at the end of the school day, but some were scheduled for before school, at lunchtime, or at weekends. What was less conventional was our expectation that *everyone* participated in enrichment – staff and students. Right from Reception, children attended one enrichment session per week, changing activity each term.

There were no exceptions for staff: everyone, from catering staff to caretakers, teachers to technicians, got involved in something. It might be a club based around an interest of theirs (for example, the head of maths ran Irish dancing sessions) or they might support a student to run their own club (as we saw in Chapter 2, one Year 7 student, Johal, set up an origami club). Some secondary staff ran enrichment activities for the primary pupils (for example, science club) and some of the primary staff led activities for the older learners (for instance, one Year 2 teacher set up a Key Stage 4 public speaking club). Nervous colleagues with no prior experience were paired up with more confident members of staff whose clubs had a lot of takers. Once the school had a dozen year groups, we were offering over 200 free enrichment activities per week.

Leadership from the top was essential. All members of the senior leadership team were expected to run their own activities: the head of primary had a gym club, the business manager an eco club, and the SENCO a martial arts club. Over a seven-year period, I led a variety of enrichment activities: a Reception and Year 1 art club, a Key Stage 3 running club and the London club. I had first come across the concept for the latter at WSFG where, at regular intervals, one of the assistant heads would arrange weekend trips into the capital to visit museums, galleries and places of interest. She targeted her invites at vulnerable students and those who did not get to experience such activities with their families. I reinvented the idea at INA and, with various colleagues, ran trips on one Saturday per half term to a range of destinations, including the National Gallery, the Tate, Chinatown, the O2, the Natural History Museum, the Science Museum, the South Bank and Borough Market. The trips usually had no cost and were aimed at students who had never ventured into the capital, despite living only a few miles away. These visits gave me some of my fondest memories of my time at the school.

Clarity of purpose

I have often been asked how we managed to persuade all staff to give an hour a week of their time to enrichment. Here we had a big advantage in being a new school. We could build whatever we liked into our school practices, as long as we were explicit with staff, and with learners and their parents, about our expectations. Indeed, as I have said, job offers were contingent on agreeing to our staff expectations policy. We were, in effect, calling on colleagues' discretionary effort – time that does not have to be given, but is offered because the individual chooses to do so. We created engagement through telling a compelling story. We explained to applicants that giving an hour of our time, unpaid, to an enrichment activity was a powerful way of demonstrating our commitment to the school community. We had a clear rationale for enrichment, articulated in our enrichment policy.

The provision of a stimulating, rich and varied extracurricular programme of activities which builds on and extends the taught curriculum, broadens students' educational opportunities and expands their horizons is vital in enabling us to achieve our ambitious goals. Involvement in enrichment activities can improve students' attitude to school, increase students' engagement with learning and improve educational outcomes.

Enrichment opportunities contribute to students' personal and social development and support the development of their learning dispositions – for example, developing leadership skills through engagement in an eco group, exploring creativity in a drama club or fostering self-discipline through practising a musical instrument. In addition, the skills, experience and character gained through engagement in enrichment activities are an excellent foundation for a successful life at university and beyond.

At INA, we believe that extracurricular activities enrich the experience of students in numerous ways, including:

- Supporting the existing taught curriculum and providing opportunities for deep learning (e.g. science club).

- Providing an alternative experience to classroom-based lessons and the taught curriculum (e.g. the London club).

- Providing students with opportunities to take ownership of learning (e.g. student-run activities and clubs).

- Encouraging students to explore activities and subjects they might not have contemplated otherwise (e.g. astronomy club).

- Supporting students to continue with an interest and/or to master a skill (e.g. arts and sporting activities).

- Providing opportunities for students to learn from and with other people, including students of different ages, parents/carers and members of the local community (e.g. local history club).

- Providing students with opportunities to experiment and innovate (e.g. drama club).

The enrichment coordinator – an important post holder – allocated students to clubs each term, monitored the smooth running of activities and, most importantly, evaluated their success. Our structure ensured that all our disadvantaged pupils were taking part in enrichment activities, but we wanted to ensure that this experience was actually increasing their cultural capital. This is hard to measure, but pupil feedback, session drop-ins and tracking the number of applicants to each activity gave us qualitative and quantitative evidence.

Reflection

How many clubs per week are offered at your school? Who attends them?

Are there additional activities that you (and the students) would like to see in your enrichment offer?

How could you increase the offer, the uptake and the impact?

Most schools supplement the cultural education provided in formal taught lessons through assemblies, talks from visiting speakers and educational visits and trips. Some are explicit about utilising these opportunities to close gaps in cultural capital. At The Cranbourne Primary School in Hoddesdon staff have always aimed to address social disadvantage through a knowledge-rich curriculum, but a couple of years ago leaders decided that assemblies should be an integral part of this, as children spend many hours in them over the course of the year. They set about redesigning their assembly programme to develop cultural capital in a more systematic fashion.

Case study: The Cranbourne Primary School

The aim was to give our disadvantaged children knowledge of significant people, places and events that they would not otherwise meet in the curriculum. This would contribute to enabling them to become 'interested and interesting' and give them equity with their more affluent peers, whether within the school or from other localities. Leaders wanted to instil a 'high aspirations for all' attitude, in the knowledge that the disadvantaged children had bigger gaps to fill in terms of cultural capital.

The staff brainstormed significant people, places, events and anniversaries, and found they had enough for a two-year assembly programme in the first instance. People, places and events were chosen specifically because they were not taught in the Cranbourne formal curriculum. They were selected to extend the children's knowledge of broader themes such as diversity, exploration and prejudice, as well as because they are important in their own right. The year was planned out so that the children would meet something new each week, for approximately four weeks. This would be followed by a themed review week, in which the assembly would draw on learning from any point in the programme. Themes have included 'prejudice and discrimination', 'exploration' and 'pioneers'. Staff have been able to incorporate some learning into more than one review topic – for example Alan Turing, who pioneered computer design but also faced prejudice because of his homosexuality.

Leaders carefully planned and sequenced the subjects of the assemblies so that knowledge was revisited and interleaved. For example, key characters in various civil rights movements (Martin Luther King Jr, Mahatma Gandhi, Rosa Parks, Nelson Mandela) were introduced to the children at different intervals, some-times of many weeks. This meant that they had to reach into their long-term memories to retrieve what they already knew to make the links, so strengthening their recall skills.

The initiative has enabled school leaders to extend the 'broadening horizons' agenda and expand the children's cultural capital and general knowledge. This was important for all children, but particularly for disadvantaged pupils, because of their limited learning opportunities beyond school. The impact has been out of all proportion to the effort involved in putting the system into place. It has made assemblies a pleasure to lead, because the children are so motivated and engaged. Assemblies feel like a truly valuable part of the school day.

Rachel Semark and Isla Grayson

Favouring the disadvantaged

At INA, just as the enrichment coordinator tracked which enrichment activities disadvantaged students experienced, the PP coordinator tracked the trips and visits they attended and the opportunities that each child eligible for PP funding was given. Many of the trips involved whole cohorts, but inevitably some opportunities that the school was offered were for limited numbers of learners. When difficult decisions had to be made – for example, which children should be picked to participate in a writing workshop with a visiting author, or to show a leading politician around the academy, or to visit the Bloomberg headquarters, or to attend a Harkness summer school at Phillips Exeter Academy in Boston – we strove to consider which learners would be impacted most significantly and positively. Likewise, when we sourced 180 high-quality work experience placements for our Year 10 learners, we offered the optimal contacts – for example, placements at Goldman Sachs, IBM, or the BBC – to students who would not get comparable experiences through their family connections. We sought out children whose self-esteem needed to be boosted, whose horizons needed to be expanded, and whose sense of entitlement needed to be encouraged.

In effect, we were positively discriminating in favour of the disadvantaged. We did so in the knowledge that there is a significant imbalance of opportunities in society at large. As Dr Lee Elliot Major (2015), the then chief executive of the Sutton Trust, said:

Widening wealth gaps have created a privileged class hell-bent on preserving that privilege for their offspring and armed with ever more resources to enrich their children educationally. At the same time 'working class' kids have been stripped of the traditional places where they once developed cultural capital: the youth club, town hall, local library, or children's centre.

We wanted *all* our students to benefit from rich cultural capital. As the saying goes, 'If you raise the bar, you need to give some children a bigger box.'

A few months ago I was talking with the head of English and his line manager at a secondary school I work with in Hertfordshire. We were discussing the fact that, although the school provides financial support for students to attend theatre trips arranged by the English department, a relatively low number of pupils who are eligible for PP funding apply to go on these trips – and sometimes, having signed up to attend, they fail to show up on the evening. I asked what preparation the English teachers invested in prior to the trip. Did they make a point of having a quiet chat with students who might not have ever been to the theatre before to familiarise them with the experience, dispel the mystique and answer any questions they might have – what to wear, what to bring, the format of the evening, etc.? I asked whether they ever follow up with non-attenders to enquire as to what made them stay at home and what might have persuaded them to turn up. My colleagues admitted that they had not done any of this. I fully understand why such analysis gets missed in the busy life of schools (and I suspect that it also got missed in the schools that I led) but we all agreed that such actions might ensure that more disadvantaged learners see attendance at the theatre as something 'for them', in which they want to participate.

Our discussion moved on to how to maximise the impact of participation in activities like theatre trips for those new to such experiences. It was prompted by a conversation I had had earlier in the day with a high-attaining Year 11 student, who was eligible for PP funding, who had recently been on a school trip to a production of one of his GCSE set texts, *An Inspector Calls*. I had asked him what he thought of the production and his views on the characterisation. The student had found it difficult to respond to my enquiries, despite being on track for a top GCSE grade, and it became apparent that he had not dissected or discussed the production with anyone afterwards. My colleagues and I reflected on the need for teachers to build in time after cultural events to explore the experience with those who might not get the opportunity to do so at home in dialogue with parents or siblings. If we are to open up new worlds to all, and to close gaps securely, we need to provide the space to emulate the 'middle-class dinner conversation' that more advantaged learners get routinely.

Reflection

How do you ensure that your disadvantaged pupils are benefiting from all the opportunities to build cultural capital provided in your school?

How have you successfully provided 'bigger boxes' for them?

What more can you do to give disadvantaged students the (non-financial) support that they need in order to build their cultural capital?

Supporting learner-led development of cultural capital

So far in this chapter, I have discussed ways of developing cultural capital in school and through school-organised activities. But it is also important for school leaders to focus energy on supporting learners to build up cultural capital for themselves outside of school, ideally supported and encouraged by their family members. From the very first contact with new pupils and their parents/carers, schools need to be sending a clear message about the importance of reading regularly and widely; pursuing a range of hobbies, pastimes and interests; exploring and participating in activities in the local area; and visiting places of historical, social and cultural interest.

During our home visits – which, as I mentioned, we conducted with every family joining the academy – staff members shared a suggested reading list, details of recommended documentaries to watch, a gift of a book to read and a document giving details of places to go and things to do and see. A similar document called 'Places to go and things to do and see on a school closure day' was on the school website for parents, carers and students to refer to in cases of heavy snowfall or another incident that would mean closing the site. This document had details of local museums, markets, parks, leisure centres: contact details, opening times and advice on how to get there. For younger children, we encouraged families to make visits and engage in activities together; for older students we recommended small groups taking trips together. Like all schools, we had some learners who embraced every opportunity available and packed their weekends and holidays with a wide range of enriching activities; we had others who were couch potatoes, stuck to their phones and other screens. The challenge was to prise the latter away from their devices. Like lots of schools, before each holiday we set enrichment challenges and targets; the headline messages were delivered to all during assemblies, with tutors having pep talks with key tutees who might need more support.

At the end of the summer term of 2015, a wonderful student in the founding cohort, then in Year 9, died in his sleep one weekend. The school community was profoundly shocked. Ahmed was a 'Renaissance boy': a unique child with an insatiable thirst for learning, respected and liked by all. Ahmed played the piano and trombone, wrote music and poetry, studied Arabic, read voraciously and was curious about science and maths. He exemplified our vision of a learner who embraces every opportunity to develop cultural capital, knowledge, skills and character, and explore personal learning passions. In honour of his memory, the school now sets aside a day each year as the 'Ahmed Al-Khafaji Day'. There is no formal school, but staff and students use the time to explore a passion of theirs. Some make music with their friends, others visit a gallery or exhibition, some curl up with a book that they have been meaning to read for ages, others teach themselves some vocabulary in a new language, some learn how to dive, others write short stories, and so on. Younger pupils are supported by their parents. Where required, older students get guidance about their choice of activity from their tutor. Everyone – staff and students – records details of the activity they engaged in on a small card the next day in school and these cards are arranged into visual displays around the site. This school custom is a fitting tribute to Ahmed, but also a powerful exercise in developing self-reliance in the process of building cultural capital.

I like to think that, challenging as the various lockdowns were for all learners, students who had been taught how to develop cultural capital for themselves, and had been helped to discover the joy of doing so, were better equipped to thrive during the months when they were largely restricted to their homes. I suspect that they were well represented amongst the lockdown cake bakers, up-cyclers, gardeners, music makers, virtual gallery explorers, film producers, charity workers and book devourers. A pandemic like COVID-19 makes a compelling case for educators continuing to focus on what happens outside classrooms every bit as much as on the quality of teaching and learning taking place inside them.

Reflection

What practices at your school support learners to develop their cultural capital independently?

Closing thought

In concluding this chapter, let's return to our medical analogy. Great GPs and midwives assess the strength of the social and educational networks that expectant parents in their care have to determine whether they might benefit from further antenatal and postnatal advice and guidance. They ascertain, for example, whether their patients have joined a National Childbirth Trust group, are attending parenting classes and have read key practical guides on child-rearing. These practitioners introduce novices and those who have fewer contacts to a supportive network that will expand and enrich their knowledge, confidence and expertise. Likewise, great schools see it as their role to provide a broad, expansive, creative and imaginative education through an ambitious and stimulating curriculum. They widen horizons and ensure that all students can access a plethora of rich, fulfilling and memorable experiences. The students who attend these schools leave with a wealth of enrichment that stands them in good stead as inquisitive, creative learners and responsible citizens for life – just as those who experience great antenatal and postnatal guidance are more likely to become great parents.

Chapter 9

Poverty-proofing your school

The shame of being a 'free school meals kid' will always remain with me. It was pain-
fully reinforced by the daily ritual of announcing, during registration, that I was 'free
dinners', before collecting a token that I was made to hang on a peg inside the school
office. It's funny what you remember about school and the impact this has.

Rob Carpenter (2018: ix)

Talk to any adult who was entitled to FSM as a child, prior to the introduction of PP funding by the coalition government in 2011, and you are likely to hear a similar story to Rob Carpenter's. But I suspect that if you were to talk to any of the children and young adults who have been eligible for PP funding since then, you might also hear some stories of shame and pain. Not because staff at their schools were as insensitive to students' feelings or as thoughtless about administrative systems as those at Carpenter's, but simply because it is not easy to poverty-proof a school, and even harder to do so without exposing children from disadvantaged backgrounds.

A picture of poverty

We need to remember, of course, that there are far more children in our schools who are living in real poverty than just those eligible for PP funding. The Child Poverty Action Group reports on its website that there were '4.2 million children living in pov-erty in the UK in 2018-19. That's 30 per cent of children.' It reminds us that '72 per cent of children growing up in poverty live in a household where at least one person works.'[1] COVID-19 has simply accelerated an already-worrying trend. According to the government's own statistics:

on 30 September 2020 the number of households in temporary accommodation was
93,490, up 7.0% from 87,390 on 30 September 2019. (Ministry of Housing, Communities
and Local Government 2021: 1)

1   See https://cpag.org.uk/child-poverty/child-poverty-facts-and-figures.

From April to September 2020, the Trussell Trust, the UK's biggest foodbank network, gave out 1.24 million emergency food parcels to people in crisis (compared to 1.9 million in the whole of the previous year).[2] On average, 2,600 parcels were distributed to children every day in the first six months of the pandemic (Trussell Trust 2020).

The impact of the virus on child poverty levels is certain to be significant. In April 2020 alone there was a jump of 856,500 claims for unemployment benefit (the largest increase since records began in 1971 and the highest total since 1996), as reported by *Reuters* (2020). Redundancies reached a record high of 370,000 in the three months to October 2020 (Sharma 2020). Unemployment for September to November 2020, as reported by the Office for National Statistics (2021a) on 26 January, was 5%, despite the protection of the government's furlough scheme. In a powerful interview with BBC political editor Laura Kuenssberg, Dame Louise Casey – who spearheaded the government's taskforce on rough sleeping during the pandemic – suggested that the UK was heading for a time when families would not be able to afford to put shoes on their children's feet. She said: 'We are looking at a period of destitution.' (*BBC News* 2020) As mortgage holidays came to an end on 31 October 2020, the Joseph Rowntree Foundation warned that 1.6 million households (20% of Britain's mortgage holders) would struggle to pay for their homes in the subsequent months (Hetherington 2020).

Exposure of those living in poverty

The ugly wrangling over FSM provision during periods of lockdown and school holidays – an ongoing feature of the pandemic, in which Marcus Rashford rose to heroic status as the champion of disadvantaged families – is evidence, if needed, of the stigma that the poor face in our society. Fears voiced by Tory politician Ben Bradley about increasing dependency on the state give an insight into the views of those MPs who, in October 2020, voted to reject a plan to extend FSM provision into the autumn half-term school holiday, despite an embarrassing government U-turn in the summer. The pictures that hit social media, and subsequently the news, in January 2021 of insultingly meagre and low-grade food parcels delivered to families eligible for FSM by government-approved meal providers led to understandable criticism. Many questioned the motives behind the policy that favoured food handouts over vouchers or cash payments to disadvantaged families. In a blog entitled 'Myths about poverty

2   See https://www.trusselltrust.org/news-and-blog/latest-stats/end-year-stats/.

must be refuted so that parents on benefits will be trusted with £20 and not half a pepper', Sam Freedman asserted that:

The reason the Department hasn't done the simplest, cheapest thing and just give [sic] parents a bit of extra cash is because they don't trust them to spend it properly [...] distrust of those on benefits remains strong; the belief that poverty indicates moral failing runs deep.

As this book went to press, the Westminster government was sticking firm to its decision not to provide FSM over the February 2021 half-term break.

A charity called Children North East, in conjunction with the North East Child Poverty Commission, has been working with young people and schools for a decade, auditing poverty levels and exploring the ways in which children from economically disadvantaged backgrounds can be unintentionally stigmatised by the school staff who are trying to support them. Luke Bramhall, the school research and delivery lead at the charity, explained, in a *TES* interview in October 2019, that his staff make a point of talking to every child in the schools they work in:

We ask 'Do you know who's poor in the school?' says Bramhall. The answer is always, 'Well, yes, and this is how we know.' (Quoted in Edkins 2019)

The charity found many examples of ways in which PP children were exposed by well-intentioned school systems and practices – for example:

- A symbol denoting children's FSM status appearing by their names when the class register was displayed on the whiteboard each day.
- Food technology ingredients for PP children being left at the front of the classroom for collection.
- Class teachers publicly distributing free revision guides in class to PP learners.
- FSM packed lunches being put in easily identifiable 'uniform' brown bags by catering staff for collection when classes were going on trips.

The charity suggests that schools are mostly unaware of the impact of these routine practices and the coping mechanisms that students employ as a result. Children – who are keen social observers – also notice economic signifiers. Students from poorer families are inevitably exposed by the brand of shoes they wear, the type of pencil case and pens they have, the quality of materials they bring in from home for practical lessons or show-and-tell activities, how quickly their now-too-small uniform is replaced, what weekend and holiday activities they mention and the home and area they live in.

In 16 years of headship, I asked my students thousands of different questions but, I am ashamed to admit, never questions around their awareness of economic hardships amongst their peers or the effectiveness of the school's poverty-proofing attempts. Had I done so, I suspect that I might have been supplied with many insights into need, of which I was not aware, and into school practices that I had no idea were causing my vulnerable students pain and shame.

Reflection

Do you know which of your students are living in poverty?

How do/could you sensitively audit the levels of economic hardship experienced by your learners?

How could you get feedback on whether any practices at your school might be unintentionally exposing or stigmatising your poorer learners? Could you ask your students questions that would elicit honest feedback? How could you ask? Which members of your staff could you ask to speak to the students?

The hidden costs of the curriculum

It is easy to assume that, in the state system, our schools give equal educational provision to all learners because the vast majority of curriculum experiences are fully funded for all students. Stories of 'requests' for termly parental contributions to school funds, insisting on parents buying uniform items such as plain white shirts from expensive suppliers, and having exhaustive lists of compulsory equipment (including atlases, religious texts and sets of art pencils) send a clear message about the type of families that some schools welcome and those they are happy to deter from applying. Thankfully, these practices are less common now than 10 years ago, but they still persist.

Yet a 'cost of the school day' project in Scotland, led by the Child Poverty Action Group in conjunction with Glasgow City Council, found that various school costs place pressure on family budgets, leading to unequal access to opportunities and poverty stigma (Spencer 2015). Another significant research project (Farthing 2014) – commissioned by the British Youth Council, the Child Poverty Action Group, Kids Company and the National Union of Teachers in 2013 – was discussed in a fascinating article by Laura Mazzoli Smith and Liz Todd (2019). I want to dwell on two key findings of this research which showed how keenly children from poorer families feel the hidden costs of the curriculum.

Firstly, the joint research found that 14% of low-income students chose not to study art or music due to the associated costs of these subjects (Farthing 2014: 10). All schools work hard to implement strategies to minimise the impact of poverty, but they also face significant budget constraints and have to manage resources carefully, including the PP grant.

Let's look at the example of music. The EPI's 2020 annual report revealed that disadvantaged learners are 38% less likely to study music for GCSE than their more affluent peers and that at the end of Key Stage 4 they are 20 months behind those who are not eligible for PP funding (Hutchinson et al. 2020: 13). Why is this? Well, to achieve a strong pass grade in music at GCSE and A level requires proficiency on a musical instrument, which ordinarily results from years of private tuition with a significant associated cost. In fact, to get to grade 8 proficiency (the standard equated with A level success) was estimated – by Greg Coughlin, the head of music at my last school – to cost between £8,000 and £15,000 in tuition per student. At INA we were in the extremely fortunate position of having a generous benefactor who funded the purchase of an instrument for every pupil, and the school committed the staffing resources to provide small-group tuition for an hour every week, thus simulating conditions akin to those typically enjoyed only by middle-class children from affluent backgrounds. The results were staggering: 40% of the founding cohort (which had a predominantly Muslim, working-class profile), instilled with a love of music from their Key Stage 3 experience, chose to take GCSE music. The results speak for themselves: 100% gained a strong pass grade and 53% achieved an A* or A, placing the department in the top five in the country for value-added. This despite the fact that no more than a handful of the children had ever had a private music lesson. How different would the picture have been without that enhanced funding?

The national statistics regarding Key Stage 4 participation and outcomes for disadvantaged learners are as bleak for PE as they are for music: disadvantaged learners are 46.5% less likely to take PE at GCSE, and end the course 17.7 months behind their non-PP peers (Hutchinson et al. 2020: 12). The PE teachers at INA were also very conscious of the hidden costs associated with high performance in their subject. With a sizeable practical assessment element at GCSE and A level, students who belong to sports clubs outside of school, whose parents pay for regular lessons and/or who have the opportunity to participate in activities with significant costs (horse riding or golf, for example), are unfairly advantaged. The language, behaviours and etiquette associated with sports like cricket and tennis, for example, can be off-putting to those on the outside, sending a message to poorer children that this is not 'for them'. Staff need to be keenly aware of these issues. Our PE teachers worked proactively to break down the mystique and sense of exclusivity surrounding certain sports by including them on the curriculum, providing opportunities for students to practise with the equipment and a coach before and after school, and teaching the rules and vocabulary to all.

Poverty-proofing the curriculum

Like most heads, I was always very keen to keep the day-to-day costs of the school experience to a minimum for parents and carers. I was also determined that those living in economic poverty, for whose benefit initiatives like the following were designed, should not be highlighted. So, we implemented these approaches:

- A school shop sold stationery and maths equipment at cost price to everyone.
- Water was the only drink allowed on site and fountains were situated around the site for topping up bottles with chilled water.
- Free fruit was provided to anyone who wanted a piece between afternoon lessons and end-of-day enrichment activities.
- Free breakfasts were provided to all students before sitting public exams.
- On non-uniform days, although a contribution of £1 per person was suggested, students threw their contribution into a bucket as they passed through the school gates, rather than having their money counted off and checked.
- Packed lunches (for which non-PP students paid a fixed price) were provided for all when classes went on trips.
- All equipment, including sketch books and pencils, was provided for learners in the art rooms.
- Whole class sets of curriculum texts were purchased by the school and loaned to students.
- Considerable care was taken to use a uniform supplier that provided high-quality, affordable uniform and whose staff committed to meeting termly

with students and parents to discuss ways in which the offer could be further improved.

- Items like school shirts and socks could be purchased from the high street.
- For a number of years, parents could purchase uniform directly from the school to keep costs down and, in cases of hardship, free new uniform was provided for certain families.
- Free school lunches were provided for a few individuals who might not qualify for PP but were living in poverty.
- GCSE geography coursework was designed so that it could be completed in the local area at no cost.
- All the texts on departmental recommended reading lists were stocked in the school library for free loan.
- All after-school enrichment clubs were free to all and provided all necessary equipment.
- The computer rooms were open to students from 8am until 6pm every weekday.
- Students were provided with a printing allowance each term.

Yet I am sure that we could have done more to poverty-proof the school. Without doubt we were guilty, at times, of introducing initiatives that were well-intentioned but caused stress for, or even excluded, economically disadvantaged learners. A good illustration of this is Christmas Jumper Day, the annual fundraising campaign organised by Save the Children in the UK where, on a specific Friday in December, people are encouraged to wear a festive sweater and make a minimum donation of £1. We embraced this initiative at INA, and ensured that, by collecting donations from students in buckets at in the school gates, it was not a requirement that every child paid £1. We encouraged festive dress, which could simply involve the inventive use of tinsel. Yet, on reflection, we didn't address the peer pressure surrounding having a Christmas jumper. A *TES* article (George 2019) reported findings from the Open Data Project, which was conducted in the north-west of England and involved around a dozen schools in Lancashire, Liverpool and Manchester sharing and analysing their data. In all of the schools there had been a spike in the number of disadvantaged learners absent from school on 14 December 2018: Christmas Jumper Day. As Duncan Baldwin from ASCL reflected:

What we have identified [...] is that days that are 'fun' and good for causes are not necessarily fun at all if you don't have a Christmas jumper. The net result is that a noticeable proportion of disadvantaged youngsters didn't come to school on that day. (Quoted in George 2019)

As the head of one of the schools included in the audit exercise reflected: 'No matter how well you think you are doing, you'll still be doing some of these things wrong'. Another added, 'or doing the right things in the wrong way' (Mazzoli Smith and Todd 2019: 360).

Reflection

Have you analysed the GCSE and A level subject choices that your disadvantaged students make? Are there subjects that they are less likely to choose? Are there any discernible patterns over time?

What are the hidden costs associated with your curriculum? And with your enrichment activities?

What strategies do you utilise to poverty-proof the curriculum?

Are there ways in which you could further reduce the hidden costs of the curriculum without stigmatising learners?

Do you take part in any initiatives – for example, Christmas Jumper Day – that might exclude economically disadvantaged leaners? How might you overcome this unintended consequence?

School trips

The second key finding of Farthing's (2014: 16) report was that 57% of low-income students had missed at least one school trip due to the cost and felt the impact of missing out. School trips are the main exception to the 'rule' of a free education for all in state schools. There is no doubt that the opportunity to view artists' master-pieces through visits to galleries – or to see a professional performance of a play you are analysing in drama or English, or to touch historical artefacts relating to an era being studied in history – can enhance students' experience of the curriculum, improve their knowledge retention, deepen their understanding and generate a life-long love of learning. But such experiences generally come at a cost that schools are unable to cover for whole cohorts.

When keen teachers come to leaders with innovative and exciting trip proposals, meticulously researched and thoroughly planned, of course we want to support and encourage them. It's important, though, to be aware of the pressures that trips with charges can and do have on families living in poverty. A survey conducted by the NASUWT (2014: 12) found that almost a quarter of secondary aged children were unable to participate in educational trips and activities because the costs were prohibitive.

At INA, leaders were determined that all students should have their horizons broad-ened by access to musical and theatrical performances, art galleries, places of worship, museums and sites of historical interest and notable geographical features. But we were committed to keeping the cost of such experiences down – for all fam-ilies, not just those on the PP register. We worked hard to source free opportunities – to museums without an entrance fee, to universities and open lectures, to local churches, mosques, temples and gurdwaras. We invited professional musicians in to give performances at the school, in return for the use of our premises for rehearsals. We invited touring theatre groups onto the site, which was considerably cheaper than transporting our audience of students to the West End. We sourced bargain base-ment tickets for a range of events, we used staff connections and we called in favours – for example, with transport companies.

There were, of course, compelling reasons for running some off-site trips which had an associated cost. We tried to plan our visit programme for each year group a year ahead, tracking the cumulative cost to parents and ensuring that it did not exceed an agreed amount. We then publicised the planned trips well in advance to give families maximum notice, and provided parents and carers with an opportunity to pay in weekly or monthly instalments. We always used PP funding to subsidise the cost for families eligible for FSM and at times were able to pay the full amount for certain families. I don't think there is anything revolutionary about our practice, but I do believe that managing subsidies for trips with associated cost can be problematic for school leaders and their staff and that it is sometimes done poorly. A random trawl of school websites shows some questionable practices.

Reflection

Read the following school trip letter, imagining that you are a parent or carer struggling financially or a student living in poverty. What messages does it give that could cause anxiety for the reader?

How would you adapt or improve the wording to make it more inclusive?

---

25 March 2019

Dear parents,

We are pleased to announce that the RE department is arranging a trip to St Paul's Cathedral in central London on 24 April 2019.

We will be travelling by coach. The cost of the trip is £15.00 (entrance to the cathedral and travel costs). Please pay online or by cheque by 8 April. If we do not have sufficient parental contributions, the trip will not be able to go ahead. If you will have problems paying this cost, please contact us to discuss.

There is a shop at the cathedral and your child may wish to buy souvenirs. We would suggest that £10 spending money should be sufficient.

Please supply your child with a packed lunch and enough drinks and snacks for the day. Your child can wear casual clothes and we would recommend trainers as we will be doing a lot of walking.

Yours faithfully,

There are 10 issues I have with this letter:

1. The lack of advance notice and expecting parents to pay within two weeks.

2. Why has the school chosen a trip to a place of worship with an admission fee when there are so many free alternatives?

3. Why not take advantage of free student travel on public transport in London?

4.   What is the educational benefit of building in a visit to the souvenir shop? By suggesting a recommended amount of spending money, the letter puts pressure on families to find an additional £10, making the cost of the trip £25.

5.   The juxtaposition of the sentence warning that the trip will not go ahead if insufficient contributions are received with the one about contacting the school to discuss difficulty with payment discourages parents from coming forward – maybe this was the intention?

6.   'If you will have problems paying this cost, please contact us to discuss.' This sentence does not reassure a parent/carer that they will necessarily receive financial support if they come forward.

7.   It is not made clear what the criteria for any financial support might be.

8.   Which member(s) of staff should parents contact about financial support and how do they reach them?

9.   Why invite children to wear their own clothes and trainers? The letter assumes that all students have trainers and adds to the likelihood that children without designer leisurewear will feel nervous about being stigmatised on the trip.

10. Stressing the need for plenty of snacks and drinks has cost implications and presents an opportunity for differences to become apparent between those with generous food budgets and those without.

Here is a suggested rewording of the letter (assuming that the school is determined to go ahead with their chosen destination!):

---

4 January 2019

Dear parents and carers,

As you will remember from the trips plan we sent you in September last year, our RE department trip to St Paul's Cathedral in central London is coming up on 24 April 2019.

We will be travelling by tube. A packed lunch and drink will be provided for all students.

The cost of the trip is £9.00 (entrance to the cathedral and lunch), or £7.00 for those eligible for free school meals. This can be paid online in full or in weekly instalments of £1 over the coming weeks.

If your child is on the PP register or you would like to discuss financial support options available, please do contact [staff member] by emailing [staffmember@

school.co.uk] or phoning on [school number]. We really want every student to come on the trip!

Please also remember that all students should wear full school uniform.

Yours faithfully,

A while ago I was having a conversation with a member of my extended family who is a Key Stage 3 student and eligible for FSM. She lives with her mum and three siblings, and money is tight. It was near to the end of the summer term and I asked her what end of year activities were planned at her school. She said 'There's a day trip for the year group. It's to a museum but it's really expensive so my mum says we will say I am ill on that day and I'll just stay at home.' I changed the subject, but her comment haunted me. I wondered how she really felt about missing out on the trip. And how she would feel on the day, imagining the fun that her friends were having without her. How would she cope when they fed back about the trip afterwards? Would it result in her feeling isolated or socially removed from the group? I wondered whether the school was aware that the trip was prohibitively expensive for my relative, and perhaps others, and whether any provision had been made for families facing economic hardship. I wondered whether her form tutor would think it strange that she was ill on the day of the trip, when her attendance is usually 100%.

How important is the nuance of the wording of a trip letter? Would my amended letter really make any difference to students and parents/carers? I believe so. It is easy for teachers from financially comfortable backgrounds to underestimate the nervousness that children from poor backgrounds feel about presenting their parent with a letter about a prohibitively costly trip (often they don't even take it home). It is also easy to underestimate the fear that some disadvantaged students have of 'standing out' on trips, which can lead them to find excuses not to attend. Teachers often fail to consider the social impact of non-attendance on such days. Any steps that schools can take to level the experience for all participants increase the likelihood that disadvantaged students will participate in and enjoy the occasion. I would recommend that all trip letters are quality assured by a senior leader or the school's PP lead, to ensure that the language is inclusive and that measures have been put in place to ensure that everyone is supported to attend.

Awareness of poverty and the behaviours it leads to

I am a keen advocate of school leaders providing regular training on the impact of poverty on learners, helping all staff to develop an awareness of where it exists in the school community and strategies to mitigate its effects. Many staff have a limited concept of the lives lived by their students. I was reminded of this recently when observing a PE lesson being delivered by a newly qualified teacher in a school serving a deprived council estate in a new town. She was introducing the group, a low-attaining set with many students on the PP register, to trampolining. She wanted to find out how many of them had any experience, but the question she asked – 'How many of you have a trampoline in your garden?' – showed her lack of awareness of these children's homes. Not surprisingly, no hands went up – no one had a garden, let alone a trampoline.

After being involved in a powerful Institute of Education action research project around community cohesion whilst head teacher at WSFG, I determined to build familiarisation with the local area into the induction programme for all staff. The school's catchment area was small: it comprised some gentrified Victorian streets but also some high-rise council estates that had amongst the highest levels of socio-economic deprivation in the country. I encouraged new recruits to take a half-hour walk around the local streets to see for themselves the homes the girls came from, including the stark tower blocks with no green space and signs reading 'No ball games'. At INA we started each school year with a data presentation to all staff. As well as sharing information about our students, we included data on the employment rates, literacy levels, home occupancy statistics, crime figures, higher education participation rates and drug hot spots in the wards our school served. We gave time for staff to reflect in mixed groups on the information presented and consider its implications for us as educators.

We endeavoured to train staff to look out for and be alert to indicators of poverty. This is by no means easy as many children are very good at hiding it! To complicate matters further, parents living in poverty – painfully aware of what their children lack and the potential for them to stand out – might be more partial to splashing out on showy material goods for their children, to compensate. I can think of a number of students who would periodically appear at school with a flashy new watch, bike or pair of trainers. Because we carried out home visits to all families, I had seen first-hand the abject poverty that these particular children were living in and, knowing the shady company that some of their elder siblings kept, could speculate as to how the expensive items may have been acquired. However, to the uninitiated, such students would not necessarily appear to be financially needy.

Mazzoli Smith and Todd (2019) found that poverty can impact on students' attendance, self-esteem, socialising, relationships and extracurricular participation. Typical student behaviours include: concealing poverty to preserve self-esteem, lack of engagement and application, self-isolation (due to fear of humiliation), ostentatious displays of material goods, highlighting the poverty of others and feeling anxiety about sustaining friendships (craving acceptance).

Staff need to be made aware of these behaviours, and those of the child's parents and carers; all too often the emotional and psychosocial dimensions of poverty are not understood or addressed by schools. If staff do not have an appreciation of why, for example, a parent with a child eligible for FSM might buy them designer trainers but claim not to be able to afford a school blazer, frustration and resentment can ensue. A while ago I overheard a head teacher say, 'This mum will take her kid out of school for a week to go to Florida but then we are expected to fund him going on school trips.' She was understandably frustrated, but her comment revealed a lack of empathy for the family's situation and her misunderstanding of the mother's behaviour. This matters as it has the potential to impact on the school's treatment of the child: you will remember the University of Missouri study (Hurst 2017) which I touched on in Chapter 4.

Reflection

Do you ever discuss the phenomenon of unconscious/unintended bias with your staff?

Do you carry out any staff training on poverty in your school community, including its impact and implications for your school?

Resourcing out-of-school learning

So far in this chapter we have considered what school leaders can do through their in-school curriculum to compensate for the economic inequalities that their students experience in their home circumstances. However, COVID-related school closures have served as a reminder that, without school to act as a leveller, the educational inequalities that result from economic hardship are painfully apparent.

The Children's Commissioner's (2020) report, which I referred to in Chapter 4, reminded us of some of the ways in which disadvantaged children are at particular risk of falling behind their wealthier peers without the daily routine of school. Many learners contend with overcrowded living conditions, no desk space, insufficient access to devices, lack of Wi-Fi connectivity, limited stationery and supplies, and no adult able to support them at home. These children will find it harder to complete online work set by their schools and to engage with resources specifically designed for lockdown learning, such as the Oak National Academy. Many websites and services cannot be properly accessed on a mobile, and downloading or uploading content can be extremely slow.

It was interesting to see how schools responded to address these inequalities during the first national lockdown from March 2020. In their identification of 'vulnerable pupils', some schools assessed those without a space conducive to learning in their home environment as meeting the criteria, and invited these children into school, alongside those with EHCPs. Others provided learners without access to a computer with a school laptop or an old PC on loan. Where access to broadband was the issue, dongles and similar devices were delivered to families to provide internet connectivity. Schools without the resources to provide devices ensured that the online learning experience could be replicated through books and printed work packs, delivered to the home.

Schools that already had accurate data relating to whether learners had access to a computer and printer at home were able to act far more swiftly and in a more targeted fashion. The scramble that took place at some schools in April 2020 to respond to the government's request for details of Year 10s without home computers revealed that collecting knowledge about their students' home learning experience was just not something that had, up to that point, been on their radar. In other institutions, it is normal practice to engage in dialogue with families eligible for PP funding about resources that would enable their child to learn more effectively out of school. Hitchin Girls' School in Hertfordshire is a good example. Here school leaders invite eligible parents to submit bids for equipment and resources that their child would not otherwise be able to access, to be paid for from the PP fund.

Case study: Hitchin Girls' School

The aim of this initiative was to develop parental engagement and to provide interventions that have a meaningful impact for students and their families, through addressing issues that they identify as barriers to learning, or by giving access to opportunities that would otherwise be out of reach.

In order to provide some kind of equity in opportunity, we decided to allow parents to bid for a proportion of their child's PP allocation to spend on an opportunity, activity or item that they felt would give their child a better chance of reaching their full potential. Importantly, this approach would give parents a real voice – their suggestions would be directly acted upon – and ensure that they were not experiencing an initiative that was merely being 'done to them'.

The system allows parents of all PP students to bid for £250 of their PP allocation. The PP panel reviews the bids and determines whether or not they meet our criteria of supporting either the student's educational or wider development. A wide range of activities and opportunities have been supported by the bidding initiative – examples include: rail fares for travel to school, music lessons, musical instruments, laptops, computer software and one-to-one tuition.

James Crowther and Frances Manning

A Sutton Trust report of April 2020 found, not surprisingly, that many parents with the means to do so were likely to make use of private tuition and to purchase other learning resources to minimise the impact of school closures on their children's educational progress (Cullinane and Montacute 2020). In the first week of lockdown alone, they report:

14% [of parents] had spent more than £100. 19% of children from middle class homes had £100 or more spent on them, compared to 8% in working class homes. For households earning over £100,000 per year, a third of children had more than £100 spent on their learning. (Cullinane and Montacute 2020: 1)

Assuming that these disparities remained a feature for the duration of the various lockdowns, the impact on the attainment gap will have been significant.

Closing thought

Emerging from the coronavirus pandemic, many schools know their disadvantaged learners and families far better than they did in March 2020: they distributed meals, they formed strong relationships with those vulnerable children who were in school, they made home visits to drop off computers and dongles or to deliver learning to, and collect it from, families who did not have IT provision. My hope is that this enhanced and enriched knowledge will result in leaders reviewing the way in which they organise learning and allocate their PP funding, and lead to schools employing even more strategies to minimise the effects of economic hardship on their disadvantaged learners both in and out of school.

Chapter 10

Preparing learners for successful transitions

The transition between phases of education – notably early years to primary, and primary to secondary – is a risk-point for vulnerable learners.

Education Endowment Foundation (2018: 16)

Transitions from one phase of education to another, and especially from one school to another, are momentous and stressful for all young people. The way in which transitions are handled by schools can have a significant impact on a child's capacity to cope with change in the short and long term and will affect the progress they make from their starting point. When schools work with each other – and with learners and parents – to make transitions as smooth as possible, there is less chance of a dip in performance or an adverse effect on wellbeing.

Smooth transitions are especially significant for children from deprived backgrounds, who may lack the resilience and emotional support required to navigate such changes successfully. Smart schools carefully manage educational transitions – from nursery to Reception, from primary to secondary school and from sixth form to higher education – in the knowledge that, for some learners, these are just a few of what may be a considerable number of changes they have to face. Families eligible for PP funding are less likely to own their own home than more affluent ones. If they live in rented housing, the chances are they will move more frequently. If they are residing in local authority accommodation, or temporary housing, a change of home may well necessitate a change of school. And each time learners change school they are required to adapt to a new curriculum, to join classes in which the students will be at a different point on the learning journey. They will have to establish themselves with a new set of teachers, form new relationships and demonstrate afresh what they know and can do. They may well experience a period of boredom as their new class covers learning which they have already experienced, or anxiety as they struggle to get up to speed with a class which is ahead of them in the curriculum.

In-year transitions

A sobering study from the RSA, *Between the Cracks: Exploring In-Year Admissions in Schools in England*, showed that disadvantaged learners are more likely to move school within phase as 'in-year' admissions. Indeed 46% of in-year admission between 2007 and 2012 were learners eligible for PP funding (Rodda et al. 2013: 4). Moreover, the report showed that:

The attainment of pupils who make in-year moves is markedly lower than their peers, and lower still among pupils who make multiple in-year moves. Only 27 percent of pupils who move schools three times or more during their secondary school career achieved five A* to C grade GCSEs, compared to the national average of 60 percent. (Rodda et al. 2013: 5)

However, this correlation between multiple school moves and under-attainment in examinations is not an inevitability. You may recall Annie's story from Chapter 5 – a student eligible for PP funding who attended four different secondary schools and spent most of Year 10 in hospital. Her wonderful English teacher at the school she enrolled at in the final weeks of Year 10 identified and addressed her learning needs, supporting her to achieve the top GCSE grade a year later.

The best schools have robust and well-conceived systems to ensure that transition is as smooth as possible for learners moving school in-year. This may involve:

- One named member of staff overseeing the process and acting as the champion for in-year entrants.
- Ensuring that each new arrival has a well-chosen and well-coached buddy to befriend and induct them.
- Clear and comprehensive communications to staff about the prior education of the learner and strategies to utilise to support the induction.
- A review after a few weeks to get feedback from the learner and their parents/carers about how they are settling in and to assess that they are in the right groups and classes to ensure that they make optimal progress.

For the majority of learners, however, the key transitions that they will navigate will be between stages and phases of education. In this chapter I shall address each in turn.

Transition into early years

In the first few months of life, infants are at their most vulnerable and impressionable. Their experiences and environment mark them, like the stamp on a freshly minted coin. The early childhood environment has a significant effect on children's social and emotional development. Therefore interventions aimed at improving health, parenting skills and the home learning setting can have benefits for both the short and longer term. In 2003, Feinstein showed that the link between cognitive development and family deprivation begins at a very early age, with gaps in attainment detectable as early as two months. A 2016 EPI report identified a gap of 4.3 months of development between disadvantaged and non-disadvantaged pupils at the age of 5, as measured by EYFS outcomes (Johnes and Hutchinson 2016: 5). Deborah Eyre (2016) explains that children of more highly educated parents, from homes where learning is highly valued, are internalising these parental values and expectations as they form a concept of themselves as learners. Early years expert and head teacher Julian Grenier (2020) states:

Parents at all income levels can provide a positive home learning environment. But it is much more difficult for parents in disadvantaged circumstances. Research suggests that poverty, poor housing and high levels of crime and violence in a neighbourhood are all associated with poorer health and learning for young children (Blair and Raver, 2014). [...] Whilst every parent has the potential to create a positive home learning environment for their child, it's much harder for some parents than others. The research suggests that disadvantaged children, and boys in particular, get less support for their learning at home.

Schools that are serious about avoiding attainment gaps in the early years strive to influence infants' pre-school life experiences. The following case study is a great example of such action.

Case study: Reach Academy

Reach Academy in Feltham, south-west London, is a high-performing all-through school which opened in 2012. It was founded on the belief that schools can and should play a wider role in the community without losing focus on providing high-quality education. Indeed, its leaders believe that the only way to develop the academic potential of all is to broaden the school's offer: if it is to achieve the best possible outcomes, the school has to support its students – and their families – to navigate the complexities and difficulties of life, as much as they support them with the curriculum, because the former can prove a formidable barrier to the latter. Staff strive to build deep, trusting relationships with students and families, which are consistent throughout the school, without the often-jarring transition from primary to secondary education (which, in too many cases, is a transition from a family-oriented and community-focused primary to a more distant and impersonal secondary).

Inspired by Harlem Children's Zone in New York, the academy's founders have developed the Reach Children's Hub to meet the wider needs of as many local families as possible, acting as an anchor institution for a range of connected community support initiatives. Two early observations were particularly powerful motivators: the extent of the gap in skills and knowledge seen on children's entry into nursery, and the extent to which complex difficulties outside of school formed significant barriers to learning for students of all ages. The conclusion was that schools are necessary but not sufficient enablers if young people are to flourish. High-quality education is essential, but it has to be supplemented by broader support for the student as a person, and for their family, especially in the early years. The school and hub work together to provide cradle-to-career support for the children, young people and families in the local community.

In recognition of the vital importance of supporting families from the earliest possible moment in their children's lives, the most developed element of the hub's current provision aims to support infants from birth to the age of 2. Through collaboration with local midwifery and health visiting services, the hub offers free antenatal education for new parents, as well as a support group for young mums in the local area. This builds on a peer support programme which was delivered by the National Childbirth Trust through the hub in 2018 and 2019. Leaders have developed an innovative project with Save the Children and the Feltham Early Learning Community, which includes a range of activities to support families' home learning environments in their children's earliest years.[1]

The hub has begun to play a role supporting local systems and services for children, young people and families. Reach Academy hosts an Early Help Panel, through which local professionals meet to coordinate support for local families

1   See https://www.reachacademyfeltham.com/page/?title=Early+Learning+Community&pid=62.

who fall below social care eligibility thresholds. As part of the Feltham Early Learning Community project, leaders convene an early years network, which provides free training, support and networking for staff working in nurseries and primary schools locally.

Adapted from a case study written by Luke Billingham,
with the permission of Ed Vainker

A 2016 EPI report warned that the entitlement to 30 hours of free early years childcare or education for working parents of children aged 3 and 4 might actually exacerbate the disadvantage gap (Johnes and Hutchinson 2016). This initiative meant a doubling of the provision, from 15 hours, for those who were eligible. Eligibility requires parents to be earning the equivalent of 16 hours per week at the national minimum wage: the unemployed therefore do not qualify. In June 2018 Sir Kevan Collins, then CEO of the EEF, predicted that offering 30 hours of free early education to relatively well-off families would widen the attainment gap between disadvantaged children and their more affluent peers:

When children are 5, [they] have a 4.5 month gap in their learning. Now we are giving extra hours for more learning to people who already have advantage. […] I think one unintended consequence of the policy [is] we are seeing children who are disadvantaged who were getting more than 15 hours having it reduced so that other people can have a place who are getting their 30 hours. (Quoted in Ward 2018)

The impact of early education on a child's development is significantly greater when the provision is of high quality, and particularly so for disadvantaged children. High-quality early education has the potential to narrow the gap. In *Closing Gaps Early*, Stewart and Waldfogel (2017) argued that high-quality early years provision, delivered by qualified professionals, is crucial for boosting the development of the poorest 2- and 3-year-olds. The 30 hours' free entitlement does not necessarily offer the quality that would be required to close the gap significantly. The entitlement to increased hours has put a strain on some providers, who have prioritised accommodating children who qualify for the full 30 hours at the expense of the free entitlement for disadvantaged 2-year-olds. This is concerning given evidence that duration of attendance at pre-school has a significant impact on subsequent outcomes.

The early years education landscape has, of course, been further impacted by the coronavirus pandemic. Montacute (2020: 4) states in her report for the Sutton Trust that there is a considerable risk that the crisis will further open up the early years' attainment gap in both the short and the long term:

In the short term, having providers temporarily closed is likely to have the biggest impact on the poorest children, who benefit most from structured provision and are less likely to have the suitable home learning environment needed. This could also have a long term impact if providers do not receive enough support and are forced to close permanently, and provision is slow to recover once the health crisis passes.

All of this evidence supports the idea that transition into nursery and Reception needs to be managed skilfully, particularly for disadvantaged and vulnerable children.

The early years team at Herts for Learning places a significant emphasis on supporting schools and settings in implementing effective transition practices. Materials available in a transition toolkit for schools provide guidance on best practice that will enable 'ready schools', 'ready families' and 'ready children', influenced by UNICEF's school readiness conceptual framework (Rebello Britto 2012). This takes the premise that 'ready schools' focus on the learning environment, along with practices that foster and support a smooth transition. The transition toolkit adopts a holistic information-sharing approach focused on criteria that indicate a child's level of need in making a smooth transition. The materials are designed to support schools in identifying potential barriers to learning at the point of transition, with a wealth of materials to aid engagement with families.

Case study: the Herts for Learning early years transition toolkit

The Herts for Learning early years team has designed a comprehensive toolkit to support practitioners, parents and children with the transition from home or pre-school to the nursery/Reception setting. The toolkit provides advice, strategies and resources to ensure best practice is established. It includes criteria of potential barriers to transition, indications as to the type of support a child may need when they start school and documents outlining procedures for supporting smooth transitions for children identified as having varying levels of need at the point of entry to school. The resources include:

- An example of a transition policy, which schools can adopt or embed into their own policy to ensure all staff are aware of the importance of best practice when supporting smooth transitions.

- A PowerPoint for schools to adapt to show parents/carers during the induction.

- A document that explains how to host an effective induction meeting, along with a model evaluation form.

- A top tips document to support staff carrying out home visits, and an exemplar home visit policy.

- A proforma for practitioners to use when carrying out home visits to ensure that pertinent information is gathered about the child and their family.

- A document for schools to use to risk-assess home visits.

- A proforma for practitioners to use when carrying out visits to previous settings, to ensure pertinent information is gathered about the child and their family.

The toolkit has a selection of activities to evaluate how children are feeling about the upcoming transition. The guide to consulting children enables practitioners to use children's feedback confidently to inform and adapt provision.

The parental resources include a parent guide to home visits, an early years libraries leaflet and book lists to guide parents towards the benefits of early reading, a leaflet with information about the first day at school, and various transition activities to complete at home – such as practical activities to practise during the summer holiday.

The early years team is currently working with a significant number of early years settings and schools in Hertfordshire on a transition project. The aims are to:

- Build on current good practice and encourage consistency across Hertfordshire.

- Develop a pathway which will help schools receive pertinent information about a child's level of need.

- Support schools and settings to complete and share information about children's potential barriers to learning, using specific criteria around the level of need.

- Identify schools with cohorts that have high levels of need and provide them with advisory and, where relevant, specialist support.
- Provide professional development opportunities and contact with specialist professionals who can offer advice with cohort needs.

The project is designed to further improve the early identification and support for all children, particularly those with potential barriers to learning, who are at risk of not getting off to a good start in their early education.

Reflection

What learning might you take from the two early years case studies to implement in your school and community?

The early years to Key Stage 1 transition is also a key change that needs to be navigated carefully. As Hendry and Nicholson (2020) argued in an article for the *TES*:

If the transition to Year 1 is overly abrupt, and does not consolidate and further develop core EYFS principles, children's social, emotional and academic developments can be negatively impacted [...] children from disadvantaged backgrounds [...] are disproportionately more likely to experience a negative transition from Reception to Year 1.

Each school will approach the gradual move from mostly play-based to more teacher-led learning in its own way, to meet the needs of the cohorts it serves. Some schools incorporate quite a significant amount of formal whole-class or group teaching from the start of Reception; others move towards a Key Stage 1 style of adult-led teaching and learning in the last months of the Reception year; some do not start the shift from child-initiated learning until the start of Year 1. With several months of lost schooling during COVID-related closures, practitioners were required to revisit the transition experience with fresh eyes. Some retained elements of learning through play into Year 1. Hendry and Nicholson (2020) recommend that, where staffing allows, the early years lead co-teaches alongside Year 1 teachers 'to help to embed a play-based pedagogy and to develop a shared understanding of fundamental EYFS principles'.

They advocate a Year 1 classroom environment with sufficient space and resources for play, and additional adult support to facilitate play-based learning.

Transition from primary to secondary

In my experience, schools have vastly different approaches towards managing the transition from primary to secondary (or first to middle or middle to upper) school. Some plan the process in detail, with a timeline of activities that kicks in from the day that school allocations are published. Others are much more laissez-faire, and some almost apologetic for troubling the feeder school for details about the learners. I observed with interest the contrasting responses of heads in Hertfordshire to the realisation that Year 6 learners were not going to be able to visit their new secondary schools during the summer of 2020. What was energising to watch was the creativity shown by leaders in making the transition process as smooth as possible, despite the constraints imposed by the pandemic.

At the start of June 2020, Geoff Barton of the ASCL invited leaders to email him with details of their transition arrangements. This led to the union publishing an uplifting array of imaginative ideas supplied by members. One email response, from Dawn German, assistant head teacher and raising standards leader at Harrow Way Community School in Hampshire, struck me as particularly impressive.

Case study: Harrow Way Community School

We thought long and hard about how we would manage the transition process this year. We have liaised carefully with all the primary schools who will be sending children to us so that no child is left out. We've created a number of resources to share with schools, who in turn will share them with any child who is unable to attend. They include:

- A virtual tour of the school, led by the head of year. As he walks around the school, he shares little tips to allay normal worries that Year 6 children have about the transition (getting lost, workload, being bullied, etc.).

- Short messages recorded by current Year 7 students (past students from each primary school) about their experiences of transition, to comfort and to reduce Year 6 anxieties.

- Meet-your-tutor videos: all the new tutors have recorded a brief introduction so the children can get to know them. In turn, they ask questions and have encouraged the children to write to them with information about themselves.

- A who's who puzzle activity: a presentation with all the key faces that the students will meet in September, with a series of puzzles to 'test' their memories and help them become familiar with our staff.

- A visual timetable. We usually make these for students who have a diagnosis of autism, but we thought this might be helpful for all the children to see how the school day is broken down. We included a map of the school so the children could plot the route from one classroom to another.

- Your curriculum videos: heads of departments have made short videos to inspire the children and give them a glimpse of the learning opportunities they will have in September.

- Virtual Q & A. The head of year will use Google Meet to 'appear' in classrooms and talk to Year 6 pupils about coming to our school. The pupils will also have the opportunity to ask questions.

- Giving the children a book on induction day that they will study in September (we do this every year). This year, we printed labels saying, 'A gift from Harrow Way', stuck them in the books and took them to the primary schools. The head of English recorded himself reading each chapter of the book, so the children can listen to or read along with him if they choose.

Dawn German

Imagine how well supported you would feel if you were transferring to this secondary school and how reassured you would be as a parent of a Year 6 learner heading to Harrow Way.

There was a wealth of other great ideas supplied to ASCL by school leaders across the country, including:

- A Year 6 induction page on the school website, complete with FAQs.
- An induction handbook.
- Secondary staff and students visiting primary schools to see the students who are transferring.
- A series of video messages from different staff, including the tutors, heads of department, librarian, chef, school nurse, etc.

- Inviting Year 6s to create 'This is me' collages with photos, pictures, hobbies, interests, etc. and collating them into a book for each tutor group.
- A virtual transition day.
- Videos of taster lessons.
- Letters to new students from current Year 7 students.
- Mini tasks centred around the school's values and expectations (e.g. uniform and rewards).
- Phone calls home to all parents by the transition coordinators.
- Online book readings by the literacy group.
- An e-prospectus.
- A remote meeting with staff from every feeder school to discuss the students individually.
- A remote meeting with the students, facilitated by their feeder school.
- A card and individual message from the new form tutor and fellow tutees (where there is vertical tutoring).
- A booklet about 'what to do if …'
- A booklet for parents – changes to expect when moving to secondary school.
- Transition activities and challenges to be completed at home.
- Images of uniform – what to wear and what not to wear.
- A dedicated email address for Year 6 parents to ask questions, to be answered by the pastoral team.
- A weekly blog about life at the school, featuring quotes from Year 7 students.
- A short clip for incoming students with EHCP featuring the SENCO giving a virtual tour of the department and staff who specifically support learners with SEND.

Although the circumstances in which schools facilitated transition from primary to secondary school in the summer of 2020 were far from ideal, the requirement for all arrangements to be virtual led to the generation of an impressive array of activities and resources which work well when delivered and utilised remotely. They can be recycled in the future for in-year admissions and in cases where new students are arriving from far afield.

> ## Reflection
>
> How many of the transition activities listed do you have in place at your school? Are there ideas here that you might adopt to good effect?

Many schools have a transition handbook to support learners and their parents in the move from primary to secondary. It might contain key policies and include information on school systems and procedures, as well as summer holiday activities to prepare for the move to secondary.

> ## Reflection
>
> What would you include if you were designing a transition booklet for learners and parents joining your school? Make a list. Think carefully about how you would go about supporting the smooth transition of disadvantaged learners.

The Nuffield Foundation's School Transition and Adjustment Research Study (STARS) was a research study based at UCL and Cardiff University which aimed to find out what helps children to make a successful move to secondary school. The study (Rice et al. 2018) followed a group of around 2,000 pupils from south-east England as they made the transition from primary to secondary. It collected information from pupils, parents and teachers throughout the transition period and asked about pupils' well-being, academic achievement, and views about school and relationships with friends and teachers. The research concluded, unsurprisingly, that great transition arrangements incorporate both pastoral and academic elements. Results suggested that an effective approach to supporting pupils might involve a combination of strategies delivered to all pupils that aim to deal with common concerns, with additional strategies for vulnerable individuals delivered on a case-by-case basis according to their needs.

The following case study describes the development and implementation of a Key Stage 2 to 3 transition strategy at Ashlyns School in Berkhamsted, designed to promote positive achievements for all, but especially to enhance outcomes for disadvantaged students. The strategy incorporated improvements to pastoral transition and parent–school partnerships, as well as increasing the rigour of the school's academic transition. The key intent was to provide disadvantaged students with a positive wrap-around experience, to give them the best possible start to secondary school, and to affect a sustained impact on their engagement and outcomes in secondary education.

Case study: Ashlyns School

The aim was to provide a broader and more inclusive transition experience for all students, but in particular for students eligible for PP and their families.

Strengthening pastoral transition

The leadership team decided that it would benefit the transition process to have a fixed head of year and learning mentor (pastoral support colleague) for Year 7. This would enable these members of staff to accumulate expertise and to operate effectively year on year at this critical transition point. Supporting PP students is a specific focus within their roles: focusing on early identification of need, key strategies for support and communication with key partners.

It was decided to employ a PP support worker to be a key point of contact between the school and PP students and their families. To ensure the smooth running of the pastoral transition process, this colleague calls all PP parents before the uniform sale and Year 6 transition evening. She also calls parents who have not responded to the summer school invitation. Parents who have not returned the admission form by the deadline are offered assistance.

The school runs a transition day for all students, supported by existing students, who act as buddies. All PP students with SEND have the additional support of an extra transition day and after-school tours as well. A week-long transition summer school is also offered, specifically for PP students. Each day of summer school includes English and mathematics, a foundation subject, and new activities to cultivate a growth mindset, such as sailing. The summer school enables students to familiarise themselves with the school building, expectations, staff and other students. It helps to promote confidence and reduce anxiety during the critical first few weeks of September. It also allows staff to get to know the students' likes, social skills and individual needs.

Early in the first term, the school runs a trip to the Peak District. Virtually all the Year 7s take part in this important bonding experience. Every effort is made to ensure that this includes all PP students (for whom the trip is heavily subsidised), including targeted encouragement and reassurance by the Year 7 team, administrative support for parents from the PP support worker and, in one recent case, support with childcare for a student who initially wasn't going to be able to go because they helped care for their younger siblings.

Developing parent–school partnerships

Families of PP students are issued a separate uniform letter, with an invitation to meet the PP support worker at the uniform event. This establishes initial contact and helps develop a positive relationship. Following the parent information evening in July of Year 6, two follow-up events are scheduled in the subsequent days to ensure that absentees have the opportunity to receive the important messages. This sends a clear and supportive message to those families of the school's expectations of parental involvement.

All parents of PP students are called before parent consultation evenings (in advance of the booking system going live) to make appointments. The head of year arranges extra priority appointments with these parents to discuss any emerging areas of difficulty or need, and to offer support, advice and guidance. Non-attendees are followed up. Before the autumn term 'meet the tutor' evening, parents of PP students are invited to an additional event earlier in the evening to hear a presentation about the support they can receive and to meet key members of staff – such as the PP support worker, the SENCO and the literacy intervention teacher. One-to-one ICT support sessions are offered and arranged for parents and, in addition, all reports for PP students are printed out and sent home (other students receive these digitally).

Enhancing academic transition

The student learning ambassadors programme began with a group of Ashlyns students delivering an English lesson to one feeder primary school, and has grown to encompass all of the larger partner primary schools and one infant school. Ashlyns students deliver lessons over a range of subjects, aiding academic transition in two ways. Firstly, it familiarises the teachers who accompany the students on their visit with the pedagogy of a Key Stage 2 classroom and the standards that are expected of the students. Secondly, it helps with transfer of subject knowledge, as Ashlyns staff are familiar with the students and their learning experiences before they arrive at secondary school. The programme has expanded to include student language leaders, who deliver French lessons. Sports leaders from all year groups also deliver lessons, sports days and sports events successfully to a large number of local schools.

To support teachers (and remind students) of expectations regarding written work, each child selects a piece of their 'best' work from primary school. Copies are made and distributed to subject teachers for students to stick in the front of their books, for reference and benchmarking.

Student-voice focus groups (related to transition) always contain at least two PP students – any issues raised here are acted on immediately. For example, if a student raises issues with home learning, they are immediately referred to the home learning club, with a phone call home to discuss the provision with parents.

Termly reports are produced for PP students in Year 7, which include data on strengths and difficulties, wellbeing, attitude to learning, attendance, behaviour, SEND and prior attainment. This overview is discussed with the head of year, which helps to identify barriers to learning and whether there is an impact on progress, and ensures that support strategies are put in place. This includes some positive discrimination for PP students in subjects where setting is used.

Hash Khalil and James Shapland

Reflection

Using the Ashlyns case study, note down the strategies adopted at your school to ensure effective pastoral *and* academic transition. Is your school equally good at both? If not, what more could you do to redress the balance?

Transition from school to higher education

Ben Gadsby's Teach First report – entitled *Impossible? Social Mobility and the Seemingly Impossible Glass Ceiling* – reminds us of the under-representation of dis-advantaged learners in higher education:

24% of pupils eligible for free school meals attend higher education, compared to 42% of non-free school meals pupils, and over a quarter of this participation gap arises from students within the same neighbourhood and with the same GCSE attainment. (Gadsby 2017: 24)

The statistics around how dramatically a university education improves life chances are well known: studying for a degree can give a wide range of economic, social and cultural benefits and is the gateway into most high-status professions. But of more concern than the disadvantage gap in enrolment figures is the data on retention rates. In her book *Social Mobility: Chance or Choice?*, Sonia Blandford (2019: 75) presents the statistic that 26,000 students in England who began a degree in 2015 did not make it beyond the first year. This represented 1.6% of all first-year undergraduates. For disadvantaged undergraduates, the proportion was 8.8%. Gadsby (2017: 26) presents equally depressing data: '1 in 12 freshers from poor families drop out of university each year compared to 1 in 20 of their classmates'.

There will inevitably be a number of factors accounting for this disparity, of which economic pressures will be one. However, it is likely that imposter syndrome – a feeling of not belonging or deserving to be in this environment and a fear of being 'found out' as a fraud – features amongst the causes too. In families where previous generations and older siblings have not studied beyond A level or equivalent, it is more likely that university will seem an alien and unfamiliar environment. Many learners from disadvantaged backgrounds describe feeling a sense that they don't belong or lack the right to study at university. In contrast, affluent freshers who have progressed from public schools that are feeders to, and enjoy well-established links with, certain Oxbridge colleges and Russell Group universities are likely to feel a sense of entitlement and familiarity, born from family tradition and oft-told inter-generational stories.

Another common reason for undergraduates dropping out of degree courses is an inability to cope with the scholarly expectations, resulting from a lack of preparation during their schooling for the styles of learning common at degree level – such as learning from lectures, seminar-style discussions and self-regulated learning. Again, students are less likely to be adequately prepared if they do not mix in circles in which transition to university is commonplace. I discussed in Chapter 6 the rationale behind incorporating Harkness-style discussion into Key Stages 3 and 4 – or even earlier – to coach learners in oracy skills, and in Chapter 7 I reflected on the power of developing learners' metacognitive skills to facilitate independent learning.

It was to ensure that no INA student ever felt that higher education 'wasn't for people like them', that the academy introduced a number of key initiatives to facilitate transition to university and other post-18 education providers:

- Every child visiting a university in Key Stage 3.
- The Saturday stretch programme.
- A super curriculum policy.
- A sixth form speakers' programme.

Let's explore those components in more detail.

University visits

From the outset, there was a determination amongst staff that learners should not see university as the domain of the rich and privileged but as a valid aspiration for each and every one of them. The school served an area of considerable deprivation and a number of wards with low levels of adult education. If we wanted students to feel comfortable about the concept of university – to be able to visualise what a university lecture theatre, hall of residence and student union looked like – it was going to be important to take our students to see them with their own eyes. To reinforce our message of everyone's entitlement to aim for university, if that was their preferred progression route, it was essential that we took entire cohorts.

In the first year, with just 180 Year 7 students, we looked around for a university which was prepared to host us. Most of those we approached turned us down gently, saying that they didn't host visits for students below Key Stage 4. But we wanted to put a fire in the bellies of our learners at an earlier age, before they made their GCSE option choices, which could impact on their progression routes. I struck lucky when I contacted my former director of studies for the first time since leaving Churchill College, Cambridge, 25 years earlier. He agreed to set up a visit for all 180 students and 40 staff, including a talk from undergraduates and the admissions tutor in the lecture theatre, tours of student accommodation and lunch in the refectory.

So, on a sunny June day, the whole school (all students and staff, including premises managers, catering staff and midday supervisors) boarded three double-decker buses and headed for Cambridge. We arrived by 9.30am and walked the Backs in the morning sun, popping into some of the older colleges' first courts and visiting the Senate House where a graduation ceremony was taking place that day. We passed the punters on our way to Churchill College and assembled in the lecture theatre. We had arranged, through contacts of members of our music department, for the Cambridge University Jazz Orchestra to come to Churchill to perform a concert for the INA students (all of whom were studying a big band instrument back at school). The band members then talked about the courses they were studying (interestingly, none of them were music students) and how music fitted into their university lives. The day was a powerful and unifying experience, often referred to in the following years, and it was really satisfying when one of the pupils who had been on the trip was accepted to study physics at Cambridge six years later.

Having arranged one successful university visit, it was easier in subsequent years to persuade other universities – the University of Buckingham, Royal Holloway and Queen Mary, University of London, and Wadham College, Oxford – to host our whole cohort of Key Stage 3 students.

Reflection

Which of your staff still have contact with tutors from their college or university? Does your borough or county have links with particular universities? Who on your staff body might take on the responsibility for setting up university visits?

Saturday stretch

Another way of exposing students to undergraduates is, of course, to invite university students into the school. I wanted our Key Stage 3 learners to have a chance to find out about, and get a taste of, the wide range of courses on offer at university, beyond the national curriculum subjects. I wanted them to be able to talk informally to undergraduates from the local area – with the same backgrounds as theirs – about the daily and weekly routines at university, study expectations, living away from home, social activities and the practicalities of finances and student loans.

From these aims the Saturday stretch programme was born. One Saturday each month we hosted a couple of undergraduates who led a three-hour taster session for Key Stage 3 learners to get an insight into their degree course. Typically, they would start by giving some context about their subject, they would talk about what they had studied at secondary school, why they had chosen the university course and what they loved about the subject. Then they would engage the INA learners in a range of activities related to their course. At the end they would take questions and talk more generally about university life. The undergraduates were contacts of staff members. Our preference was to involve students from Ilford who had studied at local schools – to reinforce the message that university was a natural progression route for students like ours – but in the first year a number of sessions were facilitated by relatives of staff members from further afield. Now that the school has alumni, it is easy to invite former INA students back to lead sessions. We paid travel expenses and a small fee, which made the role attractive to students who were planning to come home for a weekend anyway. Students came from universities all around the country, giving insights into courses from criminology to linguistics, and engineering to dentistry.

The students invited to attend the Saturday stretch sessions were chosen by leaders from related curriculum areas. They looked for learners who showed a passion for the subject and those who did not have family members who had been to university, always remembering those on the PP register or otherwise disadvantaged. The Saturday stretch programme was run by a different junior leader each year; the coordinator role being a great first step into middle leadership.

Reflection

What higher education links does your school have?

Do you have regular visits from undergraduates and, if so, how do you utilise them and with whom do they work?

Do you arrange university visits? If so, who attends and how do you evaluate the impact?

The super curriculum

The INA super curriculum policy defines the super curriculum as 'extracurricular activities that relate to the subjects that are being studied'. Examples of super curricular activities include:

- Reading texts that are not part of the standard curriculum/syllabus but that are related to the subject.
- Listening to TED Talks/podcasts.

- Attending public and university lectures.
- Visiting cultural sites that are related to subject areas.
- Entering national or university-based competitions.
- Setting up an enrichment activity related to the subject area.

The policy outlines the rationale as follows:

Engaging meaningfully with super curricular learning will support our students in becoming outstanding Key Stage 5 learners. It will ensure that they can choose their university course, higher education placement, apprenticeship or profession based on their interests and passions. It will ensure that they develop skills around independence, rigour of thinking and openness to new experiences. Super curricular experiences will also lead to students accessing the highest possible grades and to open access to the most competitive courses. Ensuring that the sixth form is an environment in which our students are cultivated to become independent and passionate learners is fundamental to the realisation of this aim. Supporting our students to become outstanding Key Stage 5 learners will ensure that they develop a lifelong love of learning and an openness and confidence to experience novel situations, and that they live a self-determined adult life which is enriched and fulfilled.

To realise these aims, clear expectations of staff, students and parents/carers were outlined:

Expectations of sixth form teaching staff/subject teams:
- Ensuring that a super curricular reading list is available for students to access for individual topics as well as for their subject more widely.
- Supporting the library by sharing the super curricular reading lists.
- Role modelling to sixth form students by demonstrating a passion for the subject area and having excellent subject knowledge.
- Arranging for a subject-related speaker to attend INA once a term.
- Arranging a trip at least once a year for each year group.

Expectations of sixth form tutors:
- Publicising opportunities with tutees.

- Encouraging students' engagement with opportunities and providing support to tutees with the transition to independent engagement.
- Tracking engagement with super curricular activities.

Expectations of students:

- Engaging with super curricular activities, initially with teacher/tutor support but, in time, independently.

Expectations of parents/carers:

- Encouraging engagement with opportunities.

The speakers' programme

Shortly after opening INA, I was fortunate to visit Eton College for a day. The aspect of the school's provision that impressed me the most was the extracurricular programme, and specifically the incredible array of high-profile and inspirational visitors and speakers – mostly invited by the students themselves – who visited the college each term. I was struck by the wealth of additional knowledge and understanding that the Eton boys would be gleaning from listening to and debating with such individuals. Yet these students, from mostly very advantaged and well-connected backgrounds, didn't need this exposure to anything like the degree that my learners did, coming predominantly from a very parochial and working-class Ilford community. We needed to widen the horizons of our learners and show them the plethora of vocations and professions open to them if they were successful learners. We started to invest time in wooing inspirational speakers from a wide range of careers and professions to the academy, including Jim Al-Khalili, Mishal Husain and Ian Hislop.

As we started our planning for the new sixth form, we committed to having a fortnightly speaker session. This was partly inspired by my own experience of a similar scheme – college hour – at the sixth form college that I had attended in the 1980s in Hampshire. On Thursday afternoons the college would assemble to listen to a visiting speaker. I remember hearing from politicians, a football manager, a business leader, and various musicians and actors. They were memorable occasions and a key element of my education.

The INA sixth form speakers' programme supported the school's mission – 'to equip students with the knowledge, learning power and character necessary for success at university and beyond' – by:

- Inspiring students through hearing about the journey taken by the speaker to their current role.
- Developing a curiosity and openness around professions and cultural experiences that might not sit within their chosen Key Stage 5 subjects.
- Helping students learn more about universities, career-based apprenticeships, different careers, and topical and world issues.

Identifying and then contacting possible speakers can be a time-consuming job. Whilst it is helpful to have one person in charge of an initiative like this, it is made much more manageable if all staff and parents can be encouraged to rack their brains and check their networks, offering suggestions of people to invite and providing contact information. Shared responsibility also builds expertise, and continuity in the event of a sole organiser leaving. At INA, effort was made to ensure that the background of the speakers invited represented the profile of the student body, and that a range of subject disciplines and a wide array of career routes were showcased. The diverse list of speakers to date has included:

- Ranjit Sond: a solicitor and president of the Society of Asian Lawyers.
- Jay Rayner: journalist, broadcaster and musician.
- Ed Husain: author of *The Islamist*.
- Harkiran Kalsi: mural artist.
- Stuart Gordon: Harvard University (who explained the process around applying to US universities and how it differs from the UK higher education process).
- Lord Paddy Ashdown: politician and diplomat (who spoke on Brexit, the UK voting system, property prices, women in politics, environmental challenges and the rise of anti-fascist groups such as Antifa).
- Alex Blower: UK student recruitment and outreach officer from the University of Southampton.
- Katherine Rundell: prize-winning author.
- Charlie Dark: DJ, producer, poet, teacher, night-runner, founder of Run Dem Crew and brand consultant.
- Kuldip Singh: CEO of Mr Singh's Sauce.
- Muhammad Kashif: cardiac physiologist.

- Jennifer Williams: US diplomat for more than 10 years, primarily focused on Middle East policy.

In the early days, the head of sixth form made most of the arrangements, with the plan being that over time students would come up with their own ideas of people they would like to invite and take responsibility for writing letters of invitation, sorting logistics, hosting the guests and chairing the Q & A sessions.

Reflection

If you don't currently have a speakers' programme at your school, how might you go about setting one up?

There are hundreds of sixth forms up and down the country working away at innovative and imaginative strategies for smoothing their students' transition into higher education, often with a particular focus on disadvantaged and vulnerable learners. I end this chapter with a case study from a fascinating sixth form college, Harris Westminster – a selective mixed sixth form in central London which was established with the goal of increasing the rate of entry to top universities amongst students from areas of socio-economic deprivation.

Case study: Harris Westminster

James Handscombe is the principal of Harris Westminster and a visionary leader. Handscombe and his staff are preparing their students to be successful at university interviews and, more importantly, when they take up their places on undergraduate courses. He says:

What do the university admission tutors want? Potential. Students who can benefit from what is on offer. Who want to learn. Who know how to think. Who have the foundations of knowledge from which to build and who are able to communicate their understanding well enough to take part in the academic community. These are skills that all students should have! Universities want people with academic potential – those who can know much more at the end of three years than at the start. Those who have knowledge beyond the core and the syllabus. What can we do to give more state-school and disadvantaged children these skills and a real choice as to whether they want to pursue higher education?

James and his staff explicitly develop a culture of hard work and scholarship. He says:

Students should work hard doing hard work. Hard work and stress are different. Hard work can be the solution to stress. I want students to wish there were more hours in the week. I want them to feel gutted they can't fit more in. So they have to use the hours available, wisely, to maximise them! I tell them, 'Don't just make notes, write an essay. Don't just do questions, solve problems.'

Handscombe wants his learners to pursue scholarship. He tells them that 'Learning is intrinsically pleasurable but not an easy pleasure – like a hike when the drizzle sets in. If you trudge on, there are great panoramas but it is easy to give up.' He reflects that:

You need motivations around you. Do those around you value learning? Do you get praised for learning? Do you have examples around you of how learning can lead to desirable ends? Do your teachers ooze with excitement about the learning process? Is learning offered to you as a good in itself or just a way of passing exams? We need to keep it exciting!

At Harris Westminster the library is stocked with challenging texts. Tutors support students to develop scholarship: knowledge that is extensive and exact, and thinking that is scrupulous and critical. To be called unscholarly is an insult.

The teaching and learning at Harris Westminster is deliberately challenging; staff encourage debate and supplementary questions. Teachers challenge students; students challenge teachers and each other. They uncover the joy of hard thinking, logical arguing and the satisfaction of winning a debate. They look for patterns, make predictions and solve problems. They are turning knowledge from facts into a tool that can be used. 'Education is not just a process of absorbing the knowledge of sages and regurgitating it,' says Handscombe.

To develop deep knowledge in the subject area that they wish to pursue at university, learners join a society for one period per week. They take turns to deliver a lecture and take questions on it. They are coached and required to conduct research off and beyond the A level syllabus. They invite others to pick holes in their presentation, comfortable in the knowledge that this will develop their learning.

Handscombe and his staff tell the students that vacations are for reading, revising and reviewing in equal measure: 'You vacate the site, but you are still a scholar. You read voraciously for pleasure and improvement. You read for the sheer joy of it.'

Reflection

Are there elements of Harris Westminster practice that would be effective in your school for preparing sixth formers for university applications and interviews?

The vision at Harris Westminster is to create a 'community of scholars'. How do you foster a community of scholars in your school?

Closing thought

The best antenatal practitioners recognise the key transitions that new parents will need to navigate in the first few weeks with their baby – coming home from hospital, coping without additional support, the return of a parent to work after maternity/paternity leave, etc. – and support them through these challenging times. Likewise, the best educators take the utmost care in preparing their learners fully for transitions from one phase of education to the next, and from one school to the next. They take pride in their legacy and in knowing that they have sent their learners off fully prepared to thrive in their next educational adventure.

Chapter 11

Getting to the root
of the problem

The important thing is not to stop questioning.

Attributed to Albert Einstein

Vision without execution is hallucination.

Attributed to Thomas Edison

In this chapter we will address the practicalities of writing, implementing and evaluating an action plan to affect high-performance outcomes across a school and to close gaps between disadvantaged learners and their more advantaged peers. We will explore four key steps required for an impactful action plan:

1.   Ensuring clarity about the barriers faced by learners.

2.   Agreeing objectives, targets, success criteria and milestones.

3.   Designing an effective implementation plan.

4.   Reviewing, evaluating, adapting and re-implementing.

Step 1. Ensuring clarity about
the barriers faced by learners

Up to this point, we have explored a range of barriers faced by learners and reasons why there is such a significant number of fatalities in our education system. These have included: limiting assumptions about what some learners can achieve, inconsistencies in the quality of teaching and learning, lack of parental engagement, economic hardship and a deficiency of cultural capital. All of these play their part in explaining why so many learners fail to graduate from school with the skills and knowledge required for standard passes at GCSE or the equivalent. But not every factor will apply to every disadvantaged or low-performing learner, to every cohort of learners or in every school. As Daniel Sobel (2018: 25) says, 'Schools that succeed in narrowing the gap are those that recognise the deeply compound nature of the issue.'

It sounds so obvious, but the first step – diagnosing the specific problems – is one that too many schools fail to execute with sufficient care and precision. Leaders need to be clear about what is actually going on in their schools and communities before they can effectively deal with it. It is important that they are sure of the reasons for fatalities in order to design an effective plan to mitigate these issues. We know that vulnerable learners and those at risk of underperforming are not a homogenous group. Some are eligible for PP funding and some are not. Some learners who are eligible for PP funding are not at risk. The disadvantaged face a range of barriers and challenges. Yet it is easy for staff members to assume a stereotypical view of disadvantaged learners, and not infrequently have I heard such phrases as 'She's a typical PP child.'

A couple of years ago I designed a simple audit tool for leaders to use to assess the barriers faced by their disadvantaged learners. In a seminar attended by two leaders from each of the 28 participating Hertfordshire schools, I asked the pairs to fill in the table that follows to indicate which barriers were faced by disadvantaged learners in their school and how significant each barrier was to that cohort. You will see that the table includes the key barriers discussed in the preceding chapters of this book, but subdivides these categories to identify a number of different challenges within the wider category. This is to encourage those completing the audit to think in specific rather than generic terms about the precise issues at play.

Audit of the barriers to disadvantaged pupils attaining and progressing as well as their peers		
School name:	Number of PP pupils:	Percentage of cohort:
Complete the table below to indicate the significance of each barrier (in bold) in your school now: high, medium, low, and the percentage of the disadvantaged cohort that the factor affects. Tick the features present (in italics) that contribute to that barrier.		

Barrier	Significance
Economic hardship	
Crowded home, not conducive to learning	
Lack of food, clothing, bedding, etc.	
Insufficient funds for resources	
Parental disengagement	
Low engagement with school	
Poor attendance at key events	
Poor attitude to education	
Conflicting values/priorities with the school's	
Negative relationships with staff at school	
Low parental aspirations for the child's educational outcomes	
Gaps in parenting skills	
Lack of boundaries at home	
Lack of educative conversation at home	

Barrier	Significance
Parent(s)/carer(s) not acting as educators	
Parent(s)/carer(s) not spending time with the child	
Parent(s)/carer(s) not fostering learning behaviours	
PP status coupled with other needs	
EAL	
Specific learning difficulty	
SEMH	
Child protection (CP)	
Child looked after (CLA)	
Disrupted education	
Frequently absent	
Frequently late	
Truants	
Away for extended periods	
Lots of appointments during the school day	
Transport difficulties	
Lack of cultural capital	
Not attending clubs/activities out of school	
Not taken to theatre, museums, galleries, etc.	
Lack of books at home	

Barrier	Significance
Not engaged in enrichment activities	
Attitudes of some staff	
PP underachievement isn't a big issue here	
Some PP gap is inevitable	
We can't be expected to act as parents	
The barriers faced by our PP pupils are particularly tough	
Other (please specify)	

The activity led to an interesting debate about two issues. Firstly, who in the school was best placed to complete such an audit, because they had the most reliable data relating to barriers faced by disadvantaged learners. Secondly, which students should be counted as disadvantaged, and therefore included in the cohort described in the audit.

On the first point, some delegates decided to ask middle leaders and senior leaders to complete the audit together; others felt that phase leaders or heads of year were better placed; a further group advocated that tutors or class teachers should be involved.

Reflection

Who in your school would be best placed to complete this audit accurately? Would different groups produce very different returns? Why? What information would you draw on in order to complete the audit?

On the second point, I would suggest that how a school determines the cohort depends somewhat on to what end the audit is being completed. Although not all learners eligible for PP funding will be low attaining or even vulnerable, it is important to track the progress and attainment of each student in the PP cohort closely at all times, to ensure that the additional funding is utilised to enable them to reach their full potential and to intervene if there is any change in their circumstances. However, a school's cohort of disadvantaged or vulnerable learners is highly likely to include a number of students who are not on the PP register, and it is important that their barriers are addressed too in order that they do not become educational fatalities. Of course, the exact composition of the 'disadvantaged' group will be fluid, changing from term to term.

Reflection

How does your school assess which learners are disadvantaged and vulnerable at any moment in time?

What criteria do you use?

How regularly is the cohort list reviewed and updated?

The PP audit tool shown here has now been completed by around 120 schools in Hertfordshire. The power of the tool is less in the completion of the table but rather in the conversations that the exercise generates and sharing different staff members' responses and judgements. The audit tool has also been used by class teachers and heads of department to look at the needs of the disadvantaged students in their classes. It could equally be completed by a team of tutors or all the teachers in a phase.

One interesting area of discussion to emerge from examining responses is around the importance of identifying, and then dealing with, causes rather than the symptoms. The following extract from an action plan is an illustration of a school which appears to be focusing on tackling symptoms rather than identifying causes:

Barrier to learning	Group affected	Action	By whom	Cost
Lateness to school, leading to missed learning	5% of pupils are late by more than 20 minutes two or more times per week	Buy an alarm clock for all pupils in this group	Heads of year to purchase and distribute	50 clocks @ £6 each = £300

Identifying lateness to school as a barrier to high performance is absolutely valid, but the fact that the school is addressing it by purchasing an alarm clock for every tardy student suggests that no one has investigated the reasons for each of the 50 students' lateness. For some it may well be that there is no reliable way of waking them each morning, but what about the girl whose dad gets her up but then heads out for work himself, trusting that his daughter will leave on time for school? Or the boy who is late because he drops his younger sister at the infants' school first and the gates do not open until the time he is due at his school? Different interventions will be required to support these learners to be on time.

Step 2. Agreeing objectives, targets, success criteria and milestones

Having gained a clear picture of what the main barriers to high performance are in the school at that moment, school leaders need to decide on their key areas of focus and agree some SMART (specific, measurable, achievable, realistic, time-related) objectives and success criteria. Most PP expenditure plans have objectives, but they can sometimes be quite woolly and, in my experience, they often do not define what success will look like or how long the school is giving itself to reach its goal.

A target of 'Improving parent attendance at Key Stage 2 parents' meetings from 80%' is likely to be much more effective if written as:

- **Focus area:** Improving parent attendance at termly Key Stage 2 parents' meetings with the class teacher. Attendance currently stands at 80% for all families, but only 65% for PP families.

- **Target:** For attendance to reach at least 95% by the end of the next academic year, with no gap between PP and non-PP families.

- **Milestones:** Minimum 85% attendance overall (and 80% attendance for PP families) in the autumn term, 90% in spring (87% for PP families) and 95% for all by summer.

In this second example, the school has assessed the current position regarding attendance rates, and identified that there is a particular issue with learners on the PP register. It has committed itself to a defined goal of 95%, against which success can be measured. It has recognised that progress is likely to be incremental and that increasing the attendance rate of families eligible for PP funding may be harder. Importantly, though, the aspiration of closing the PP gap is set out for all to see. The school is holding itself to account. The public declaration of goals is, in itself, a powerful step towards reaching them. In *Imperfect Leadership* (2019), Steve Munby talks of the importance of making public commitments in order to reduce the risk of failing to deliver. He tells a lovely story of entering the Great North Run one year to help him to get fitter. He quickly realised that this aim alone was not sufficient motivation to get him up in the early hours on dark, wet mornings to train. So he signed up to run for a charity very dear to him, for which he would raise money through sponsorship. But even that wasn't enough motivation to get him running in the mornings. What ensured that he trained daily and fulfilled his commitment was telling all of his friends and work colleagues that he was doing it: he couldn't lose face by not delivering!

It's one thing committing to public targets and setting clear success criteria, but how do leaders know where to pitch their targets to ensure that they are challenging but achievable? Was 95% attendance a realistic target for our example school to aim for? Was it overly ambitious to aim to reach that goal within a year? Were the milestone markers set appropriately? The answer to these questions has to be that there will always be a degree of uncertainty when setting goals, as it is impossible to see into the future and consider all the circumstances that might unfold. The best way to approach target setting is to be informed by evidence. When pitching their targets, smart leaders combine findings from research, information gained from conversations with colleagues from similar schools and settings, and their own professional expertise. *The EEF Guide to the Pupil Premium* advises that:

Taking an evidence-informed approach to Pupil Premium spending can help schools to:

- *Compare how similar challenges have been tackled in other schools*
- *Understand the strength of evidence behind alternative approaches*
- *Consider the likely cost-effectiveness of a range of approaches* (Education Endowment Foundation 2019: 4)

In deciding whether targets are too ambitious or too comfortable, leaders can compare their school's PP performance with that of similar institutions.[1] When deliberating around targets to close PP gaps, it is worth remembering that in many schools nationally, attainment of learners eligible for PP funding is above the national average for *all* pupils. It can be done, and it is being done by thousands of teachers, departments and schools up and down the country.

---

1   See https://educationendowmentfoundation.org.uk/tools/families-of-schools-database/.

Ultimately, every school's context is different. A wise leadership team will:

- Assess their barriers and ensure that they are confident of the cause.
- Decide how many priorities they have the capacity to tackle at once.
- Agree upon which are the most pressing and will have the greatest impact.
- Research what is possible and has been achieved elsewhere.
- Through assessing their ambition against their resources, set a target and end date for achieving the goal.
- Consider the journey towards the end point and set some milestones.

The EEF, in *Putting Evidence to Work* (Sharples et al. 2018), advise leaders against selecting too many priorities to work on at one time, suggesting that there is a greater likelihood of success if the number of strategies being implemented is kept to a manageable limit. On the question of setting milestones, it is important to remember, of course, that cohorts vary considerably and that progress will not always be linear. In the case of the target to improve parent attendance at Key Stage 2 parents' meetings, it might well be appropriate for the milestones to be stepped up incrementally as the school's strategies gain momentum and impact. But a target around, for example, the number of PP students transferring from sixth form to university might fluctuate from cohort to cohort if the number of disadvantaged learners in successive year groups, or their destination ambitions, vary considerably.

Reflection

Take a look at your school's PP or catch-up premium plan.

How SMART are the targets?

How appropriate are the success criteria?

Are there clear, unambiguous milestones?

Step 3. Designing an effective implementation plan

Once a school has set SMART targets, agreed its success criteria and identified some milestones, the next step is to choose the strategies that will produce the desired outcome. Again, the role of research, published reports and surveys is key here. Wise leaders seek out examples of impactful practice at other schools and talk to their colleagues about what has and hasn't worked for them. The EEF Teaching and Learning Toolkit is useful in this task, providing thousands of meta-studies into the impact of various initiatives to raise attainment and close gaps.

Leaders need to know that the strategies they choose will be targeted at the students who need them the most. Data should be used to identify the groups or individuals who most need an intervention, and then staff and other resources should be deployed appropriately. This is exactly the process that leaders went through in September 2020, as schools opened their doors to all learners after the spring/summer closure and discussed the optimal ways of utilising their COVID catch-up premium. It was important that they had an open mind when diagnosing which learners had the most significant gaps in learning, avoiding assumptions that it would be the low-attainers, those with SEND or those eligible for PP funding who had got left behind.

In the past, there was a requirement for schools to demonstrate that they were spending their PP funding directly on PP-eligible students. This led, in many schools, to PP funding being used on interventionist rather than whole-class strategies. Many academics argued that it would be better spent on improved classroom instruction, suggesting that it is possible to teach in a way that disproportionately benefits those from disadvantaged backgrounds. The restrictions on how leaders can deploy their PP funds has now been lifted. *The EEF Guide to the Pupil Premium*, published in June 2019, is designed to support schools in spending their PP grant to maximise the benefit for their students. The report recommends that schools take a tiered approach to PP spending, making high-quality teaching (including professional development, training and support for early career teachers, and recruitment and retention) their top priority. It argues that targeted support for identified pupils should also be a key component of an effective PP strategy, alongside strategies designed to improve attendance, behaviour and social and emotional support (Education Endowment Foundation 2019).

As stated in Chapter 5, quality teaching helps every child. The EEF guide reminds us that:

Good teaching is the most important lever schools have to improve outcomes for disadvantaged pupils. Using the Pupil Premium to improve teaching quality benefits all students and has a particularly positive effect on children eligible for the Pupil Premium. While the Pupil Premium is provided as a different grant from core funding, this financial split shouldn't create an artificial separation from whole class teaching. (Education Endowment Foundation 2019: 5)

In *Narrowing the Attainment Gap* (2018: 131–132), Daniel Sobel also encourages school leaders to consider using their resources in a layered or tiered way. He used the image of an egg, where the eggshell represents the whole school (on the outside are strategies that ensure great teaching and learning for all), the white represents all underperforming students (beneath the whole-school approaches are interventions and support to enable underperforming students to catch up), and the yolk those eligible for PP funding (at the centre are the targeted use of additional funding to overcome barriers).

Let's go back to the example of the action plan focusing on improving parent attendance at Key Stage 2 parents' meetings. Take a look at the full action plan, with the intervention strategies outlined:

Action	Person responsible	When?	Cost/resource
Publicise parents' meeting and open the booking system. Communicate expectation of attendance to all staff, children and parents via staff meeting, assemblies and newsletter.	Deputy head teacher	Six weeks before	Two hours

Action	Person responsible	When?	Cost/resource
Email/letter reminder to all parents about parents' meeting, including all PP parents.	Office manager	Three school days before event	One hour
Check non-attenders against sign-in lists.	Class teachers	On the day	15 minutes
Make calls to express disappointment to any PP parents who did not attend.	Deputy head teacher	Next day	Approximately three hours
Rerun the above for next parents' meeting but call the PP parents who did not attend ahead of the event.	Deputy head teacher		Approximately three hours

Reflection

How confident do you feel that the implementation of this plan will result in the school improving parent attendance at parents' meetings?

How could the plan be improved? You might like to have a go at drafting a smarter plan yourself before taking a look at my suggestions, which follow.

I would rework this plan like so:

- **Focus area:** Improving parent attendance at termly Key Stage 2 parents' meetings with the class teacher. Attendance currently stands at 80% for all families, but only 65% for PP families.
- **Target:** For attendance to reach at least 95% by the end of the next academic year, with no gap between PP and non-PP families

- **Milestones:** Minimum 85% attendance overall (and 80% attendance for PP families) in the autumn term, 90% in spring (87% for PP families) and 95% for all by summer.

Action	Person responsible	When?	Cost/resource
Design and administer a survey of Key Stage 2 parents to see what the most convenient time would be to hold parents' meetings. Set the time according to the majority preference.	Deputy head teacher	Two months ahead	One day of staff time
Phone/meet with each parent from the class who did not attend one or more parents' meeting last year to find out the reasons why. Feed back reasons to deputy head teacher.	Each teaching assistant/class teacher	Two months ahead	Average six conversations per class = three hours Half a day provided for activity
Take steps to remove barriers identified by consultation above.	Deputy head teacher	Once feedback in. At least six weeks before first parents' meeting	Will be contingent on the results. May include: provision of crèche, provision of interpreter, etc.
Publicise parents' meeting and open the booking system. Publicise response made to consultation (e.g. provision of crèche, interpreter).	Deputy head teacher	Six weeks before	Two hours

Action	Person responsible	When?	Cost/resource
Communicate expectation of 100% attendance to all staff, children and parents via staff meeting, assemblies and newsletter.	Deputy head teacher	Six weeks before	Two hours
Track to ensure that every parent has signed up for parents' meeting by one week before. Alert class teacher to any gaps. Call home to arrange appointment time with those that haven't signed up and check that there are no logistical problems with attendance.	Admin assistant	One week before parents' meeting	Half a day per term (reducing over time)
Speak to any parent who has not made an appointment at home time to stress the importance of the event and to explain that an admin assistant will be calling to fix an appointment time.	Class teacher/ teaching assistant	One week before parents' meeting	Approximately three conversations
Email/letter reminder to all parents about parents' meeting. Make personal call to poor prior attenders.	Office manager Class teacher/ teaching assistant	Three school days before event	Two hours in total

Action	Person responsible	When?	Cost/resource
Print off appointment lists for each class (with parents' phone numbers) for class teacher and admin staff. Ensure 100% sign-up and chase up any gap, alerting class teacher and deputy head.	Office manager	One day before	One hour
Sign in parents against class lists, alerting office manager to anyone who is more than five minutes late. Phone them immediately to check that they are on their way and stress the importance of attending.	Office manager and admin assistant	On the day	Three hours
Check non-attenders against sign-in lists. Make calls to express disappointment and to reschedule within 48 hours.	Deputy head teacher/class teacher	On the day, after the event	Approximately three hours (reducing over time as parents realise the importance of the event and the fact that attendance is an absolute expectation)

I would suggest that there are five key differences:

1. Clearly communicating an ambitious target (aiming for 100% attendance in order to achieve 95+%).

2. Involving a wide range of staff, all playing their part in reaching the goal.

3. Investing time in listening to parents, assessing the barriers to attendance, putting plans in place to address and overcome them, and communicating the action taken.

4. Leaving nothing to chance and taking every possible step to get 100% attendance at the parents' meetings, especially targeting parents who have a track record of non-attendance.

5. Striking whilst the iron is hot and getting in touch immediately with any parent who failed to attend in order to reschedule the session straight away – thus communicating a clear message that attendance is not optional.

Step 4. Reviewing, evaluating, adapting and re-implementing

I am confident that a school adopting a plan along the lines of the last example could significantly increase attendance at parents' meetings. But it might be that not every element of the plan worked as smoothly as hoped or that stubborn pockets of non-engagement remained. It would, of course, be important for leaders to track attendance patterns closely, term by term, and revisit their action plan if progress stalled, asking whether the original strategies were the right ones or needed adapting and revising in light of developments. This self-evaluation stage of action planning is crucial and can easily be forgotten.

Sometimes when I look at a school's PP strategies over a number of successive years, I note that the school is focusing on the same barrier year after year. There is nothing wrong with that per se. If a school has an over-representation of disadvantaged boys in its exclusion figures, the imbalance may well take more than one year to eradicate. But if the school's action plan does not change from year to year, it is not likely to have an impact. It may be, for example, that if the key focus is on improving student behaviour, and the initial action was to amend the school's behaviour policy, it is now time to invest in staff training. Perhaps, once staff have had this training, key students would benefit from a personal mentor or some more positive role models, or perhaps the rewards policy could do with an overhaul. What is clear is that if we keep on doing the same things, we will get the same results.

There is an old adage, attributed to James Baldwin, that says, 'You can't fix what you will not face.' In high-performing schools, staff review progress every few weeks, in order to check that the strategies being implemented are having the intended impact, that staff energies are being well invested and to spot any signs of underperformance so that they can be addressed swiftly. There is a confidence to admitting, without apportioning blame, when things aren't working and to learning from experience and mistakes. There is a culture of all teachers engaging with the data themselves: inputting, analysing and using it to inform their teaching. Just as the diligent health worker or midwife will check foetal development regularly throughout a pregnancy via scans, checking the mother's blood pressure and other screening, the best teachers closely track their students' progress, through formal and informal assessment methods. They ensure timely interventions and use the data collected to determine who will benefit from pre-teaching, reteaching, peer support, one-to-one intervention, revision classes, supported parental involvement, reading recommendations, revision guides, online programmes, attendance at enrichment classes, a mentor, and trips and visits.

Many schools have a PP coordinator or champion for disadvantaged learners, whose role it is to track the interventions put in place for each student on the PP register or disadvantaged list. They monitor the success of the support strategies implemented and report back to the senior leadership team, making evidence-based recommendations about whether these interventions are proving effective, require adjustment or should be replaced.

Most schools are good at describing how they are using their PP grant, but few are as effective in assessing the impact of the deployment. This is perhaps not surprising. It is hard to know the extent to which any changes we observe in attitude, behaviour, progress and performance are a result of the actions that we have taken. Also, unless we have a control group, we cannot assess the counterfactual – what would have happened had we not done what we did.

Yet holding ourselves to account against our original success criteria is important, and seeking external input to the review process can be beneficial, ensuring rigour and objectivity. Many schools use leaders from other schools – or perhaps an adviser, consultant or school improvement organisation – to review their action planning or to conduct a review of provision for learners eligible for PP funding. It is also crucial that the governing body takes an active interest in pupil progress, especially that of disadvantaged learners, and that governors ask for forensic evaluations of the impact of interventions and engage in robust dialogue based on this data. In order to execute their accountability function effectively, governors need to be trained in matters relating to the PP grant and impactful practice to raise the performance of disadvantaged learners. Having a lead PP governor who liaises closely with the staff PP lead can be an effective way of skilling up the governing body.

Ofsted's *Education Inspection Framework* (2019a), and the accompanying *School Inspection Handbook* (2019b), rightly place an emphasis on judging schools according to whether there is a high ambition for all pupils, and ensuring that 'the school does not offer disadvantaged pupils or pupils with SEND a reduced curriculum' (2019b: 41). To be judged outstanding, the school's curriculum must be successfully adapted or constructed to meet the needs of all pupils and to:

---

give all learners, particularly the most disadvantaged and those with special educational needs and/or disabilities (SEND) or high needs, the knowledge and cultural capital they need to succeed in life. (Ofsted 2019a: 9)

This should ensure that 'pupils consistently achieve highly, particularly the most disadvantaged' (Ofsted 2019b: 49). Conversely, one of the criteria for an inadequate judgement is that: 'progress that disadvantaged pupils make is consistently well below that of other pupils nationally and shows little or no improvement' (Ofsted 2019b: 52).

Governors need to be prepared to answer the following questions:

- How are decisions made as to how the PP grant is allocated?
- What impact is this funding having and how do you know?
- How are your disadvantaged learners performing and what are your next priorities?

Reflection

How confident would your governors be in answering these questions?

What action could you take to ensure that they would give detailed, accurate and well-informed responses to such a challenge?

Closing thought

To end this chapter, I've included a diagram from the EEF's very helpful guidance report, *Putting Evidence to Work* (Sharples et al. 2018). This is an excellent aide-memoire for leaders to use when implementing a new initiative. The 'explore' phase relates to steps 1 and 2, the 'prepare' and 'deliver' phases are concerned with the third step, and the 'sustain' phase is relevant to the fourth step. The 12 instructions it contains, if followed carefully, should support schools in designing and implementing an action plan that leads to higher performance and reduced fatalities.

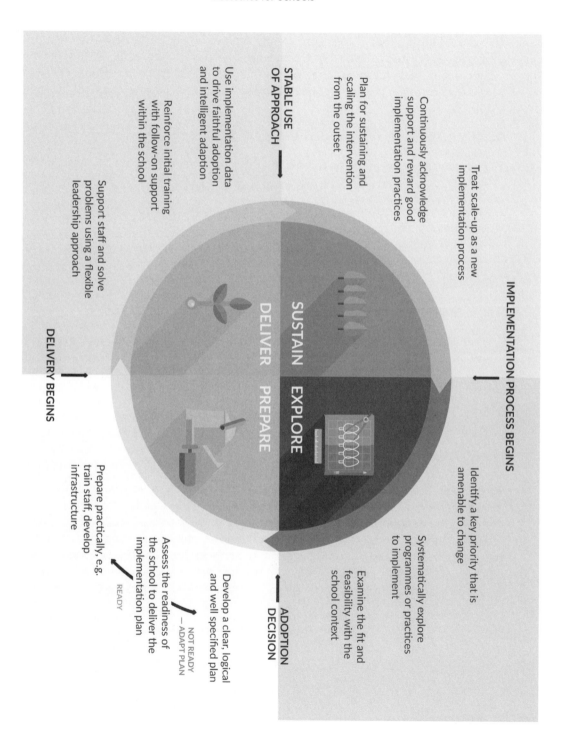

IMPLEMENTATION PROCESS BEGINS

Identify a key priority that is
amenable to change

Systematically explore
programmes or practices
to implement

Examine the fit and
feasibility with the
school context

EXPLORE

ADOPTION
DECISION

Develop a clear, logical
and well specified plan

Assess the readiness of
the school to deliver the
implementation plan

NOT READY
— ADAPT PLAN

READY

Prepare practically, e.g.
train staff, develop
infrastructure

PREPARE

DELIVERY BEGINS

Support staff and solve
problems using a flexible
leadership approach

Reinforce initial training
with follow-on support
within the school

Use implementation data
to drive faithful adoption
and intelligent adaption

DELIVER

STABLE USE
OF APPROACH

SUSTAIN

Plan for sustaining and
scaling the intervention
from the outset

Continuously acknowledge
support and reward good
implementation practices

Treat scale-up as a new
implementation process

Source: Sharples et al. (2018: 8)

226

Conclusions

Excellence is never an accident. It is always the result of high intentions, sincere effort, and intelligent execution.

Aristotle

It always seems impossible until it's done.

Attributed to Nelson Mandela[1]

And so we come to the concluding pages of this book. If you have got this far, I am confident that you are determined to do all that you can to eliminate fatalities in the education system. You will appreciate the magnitude of the task ahead, but you will be up for the wonderful challenge that Roy Blatchford (2019: 63) gives in *The Three Minute Leader*:

Dream more than others think is practical. Expect more than others think is possible.

You are likely to be one of the leaders whom Blatchford (2019: 63) describes as dreaming 'that a project can be realised when all around them share doubts.' History is full of optimistic dreamers achieving. As Blatchford (2019: 63) says, 'School leaders who expect more than others think is possible very often deliver outcomes […] that leave observers speechless.' Just as there are some obstetrics wards with no infant mortalities, there are some classrooms, departments and schools with no gap between the outcomes of the most advantaged and the most disadvantaged, and almost no educational fatalities.

So the task is not an impossible one. If you have a SMART plan (as discussed in Chapter 11) and you pace yourself, taking things one step at a time, you can achieve amazing results. As St Francis of Assisi is thought to have said: 'Start by doing what's necessary; then do what's possible; and suddenly you're doing the impossible.'

---

1   See https://quoteinvestigator.com/2016/01/05/done.

In May 2018, a DfE research report entitled *School Cultures and Practices: Supporting the Attainment of Disadvantaged Pupils* compared practices adopted by high-performing schools that had negligible attainment gaps with the practices observed in lower-attaining schools that had bigger disadvantage gaps (Baars et al. 2018). In the high-performing schools, the researchers found that staff shared a strong sense of common purpose, had consistently high expectations of all learners (including the disadvantaged) and enjoyed good relationships between staff, parents and students. These schools had well-developed parental engagement strategies to support disadvantaged learners at home.

Staff in these schools recognised barriers but didn't view them as insurmountable. They were strikingly consistent in the way in which their ethos, aims, vision and purpose were articulated. The high-performing schools recruited staff who shared the school's values and vision – they looked for a good fit – and let staff who were not aligned go. The focus of their induction training was on high expectations. In contrast, the culture in the lower-performing schools was less positive. Staff tended to use barriers as an excuse for gaps and talked about narrowing, rather than closing, the gap. They had vaguer expectations and aspirations. Staff in the low-performing schools were less likely to believe in the potential of their disadvantaged learners to achieve outcomes in line with or above the national average. In the low-performing schools, staff tended to cite low parental engagement as a barrier. Parental workshops were less frequent and less impactful; they tended to be information sessions rather than interactive workshops.

Reflection

These features of high-performing schools relate to ground covered in Chapters 2–4. How many of them do you recognise in your own school?

The high-performing primary and secondary schools studied by the researchers were smart about putting early support in place for learners who were falling behind in certain subject areas. They recognised that learners would need targeted and specific support in order to achieve their goals. Their staff tailored teaching to the individual learner and set more challenging work for those who progressed quickly. They deployed effective marking. They focused attention on developing pupils' non-cognitive skills, such as confidence and resilience. They developed pupils' speaking skills, their ability to think critically and to ask well-formed questions. They introduced pupils to new topics and experiences. They created a space to develop ideas and explore difficult concepts.

The targets set were challenging yet realistic because they were backed up with interventions, staff CPD and forensic analysis of data. The lower-performing schools were slower to pick up on learners' needs and had generally weaker teaching. In the high-performing secondary schools in the study, the aspirational targets were backed up with a range of strategies and practical support measures, such as bursaries for higher education, careers interviews and one-to-one coaching. The high-performing schools felt a sense of urgency to intervene. They constantly reviewed the composition of each intervention group. They acted swiftly on what the data told them. They stepped in before problems became entrenched. The low-performing schools were less likely to use peer-to-peer support, foster a love of learning or effectively support those with SEND. The high-performing schools made more extensive use of extracurricular opportunities for philosophy, oracy and debating. They deployed reading buddies, introduced one-to-one reading with a teacher, small-group reading sessions and book talk discussions, gave extra maths tuition, had well-resourced libraries, timetabled literacy sessions and encouraged literacy activities as part of free play. They placed an emphasis on high-quality support staff, prioritising support teachers' career development and providing them with individualised CPD. Staff development was seen as a tool for improving disadvantaged pupils' outcomes.

Reflection

You should find quite a close correlation between these features and those discussed in Chapters 5–7. How many of them are strengths of your school?

The high-performing schools in the study tended to subsidise trips and visits for disadvantaged children. They provided more opportunities for horizon-broadening activities. Those located outside of London welcomed visitors into school more than taking their children out on visits. They looked for every opportunity to celebrate achievement and involved parents in this. They were more likely to reassure parents regarding financial contributions, making payment in instalments an option and being open to discussing financial difficulties and solutions. In these schools, children participated in multiple clubs and activities each week to ensure a well-rounded education. Some of the clubs were targeted interventions based on curriculum learning for disadvantaged pupils. Breakfast clubs were open to all but provided a space for disadvantaged children to study at school. Libraries were open into the evening. After-school tuition and homework clubs were key features. The primary schools directed resources to early years. They praised high attendance publicly. They gave financial aid to parents of children eligible for PP. They worked closely with local secondary schools to ensure smooth transitions. These schools involved their local communities in the delivery of extracurricular activities. They often had a member of staff with specific responsibility for outreach whose role was to support parents and families. Leaders were personally involved and active role models. Senior members of staff took specific responsibility for the outcomes of disadvantaged learners.

Reflection

These features relate to the strategies discussed in Chapters 8–11. How well does your school shape up against these characteristics of high-performing schools?

Some of these strategies – for example, appointing outreach staff – require considerable financial resources. But many don't, relying far more on perceptions, attitudes and mindsets. As the Aristotle quote at the start of this conclusion reminds us, high intentions, sincere effort, and intelligent execution are the key drivers. The fact that the disadvantage gap has not reduced significantly in the last 10 years, since the introduction of PP funding, suggests that there is a poor correlation between the provision of additional funding and closing attainment gaps.

There is no blueprint for success. Every cohort is unique and every school context is different. Dylan Wiliam (2018: 2) famously mused that 'Everything works somewhere and nothing works everywhere.' The key is to work out what will work for you and your learners. As you read this book, some of the barriers discussed will have resonated with you more than others. You will doubtless have scored your practice and that of your colleagues highly in many areas, but perhaps there were some strategies suggested that you have not yet tried that might have a positive impact?

At times, identifying the key levers that will effect change and close disadvantage gaps can be extremely taxing. Sonia Blandford uses a lovely analogy in her book *Social Mobility: Chance or Choice?* (2019: 25): she likens this research to groping around in a room in a dark, unexplored mansion, feeling for the furniture and trying to find the light switch. She warns that, when you do finally identify an effective strategy, it might only have an impact for a limited period of time, given that schools are dynamic communities. It is like finding the switch and illuminating the room, only to enter the next room in the house where you are plunged back into darkness. Blandford (2019: 26) reflects:

We must fearlessly journey together through our own dark unexplored mansion. There will certainly be mistakes and missteps along the way, but I believe that creating a more equal society that ensures that every child and young person is provided with chances and choices to succeed is within our grasp, if we so wish.

Just as navigating your way through a darkened house would be easier if you were accompanied by others, I would strongly advocate collaborating with colleagues (in your school and in others) on strategies to eliminate educational fatalities. To share challenges, theories, readings, reflections and ideas with people as passionate as you are to effect change is invigorating, therapeutic and affirming. The delegates from the three cohorts of school leaders (approximately 130 heads and deputies of nursery, primary, secondary and special schools) on the Hertfordshire Great Expectations programme would attest to the impact of peer-to-peer discussions and the power of mutual support. As the horse in Charlie Mackesy's wonderful book *The Boy, the Mole, the Fox and the Horse* (2019) says, 'The truth is, we're all winging it.' In response to the question, 'What is the bravest thing you've ever said?', the wise horse says 'Help'. If we are brave enough to ask our peers for help, we are far more likely to succeed collectively.

What is noticeable in examining the national picture of attainment levels and gaps is that where there is one high-performing school doing well by its disadvantaged learners as well as its more advantaged ones, there are often several. This is no surprise. Ambitious and aspirational teachers and leaders connect and compete with their local colleagues. It's difficult for less-aspirational practitioners to argue that good outcomes for all is an impossible dream if the school down the road, with a similar intake and context, is making it a reality. Our challenge is to ensure that these pockets of high performance spread like a rash, until we reach a tipping point which challenges the current formulas determining grade distribution in public exams and such attainment patterns can become the norm rather than the exception. At this point, societal attitudes around failure rates should shift.

Creating a culture of high performance for all is not easy to do, but neither is safely delivering a baby. School leaders are struggling with reduced budgets, staff recruitment issues, time-poor colleagues, ever-diminishing external agency support and the impact of the coronavirus pandemic. But so are our colleagues in the NHS – arguably more so! The moral imperative to ensure that our students leave compulsory education with the qualifications that will set them up for healthy, happy and successful lives is too great for us not to feel a sense of urgency to reduce the number of fatalities to the occasional exceptions.

Sample BRIDGES newsletters

BRIDGES in the Primary Phase

"We build too many walls and not enough bridges."

Isaac Newton

BRIDGES are habits of mind or learning characteristics that develop a pupil's character and learning power and enable him/her to grow into a well-rounded individual and resilient learner.

There are seven BRIDGES habits that we will be working on, which will rotate on a weekly cycle throughout the year. The BRIDGES habit of the week will always be introduced at the beginning of the week during the Monday assembly and reinforced throughout the week across the curriculum. Each class teacher will award a certificate to a pupil that they feel has demonstrated the BRIDGES focus for the week.

Each week we will update you on the BRIDGES habit that will be introduced in the coming week and offer some top tips on how to reinforce the habit at home too. Please also refer to the Primary BRIDGES wheel below.

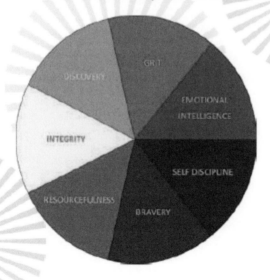

Week commencing 26th February 2018

Self Discipline

Self Discipline comprises seven dispositions:

Organisation	Absorption	Revising
Prudence	Motivation	Practising
Hard Work	Independence	Self-Regulation

At School

- We would all like to see the children develop the habits listed above, as they are all essential lifelong skills that are needed for us to successfully manage our way through school, college, and university and certainly throughout our work careers. It is really important that, whilst the children are young, we help them develop these habits as quickly as possible – especially organisation, independence and hard work.
- At school we ensure the pupils understand that every action has a consequence and that when we work hard it can often reap satisfaction and reward. Our pupils work hard day to day to earn their merits for making good choices and demonstrate their efforts.
- To help the children understand the structure of each day and become better organised, we always start with a visual timetable in Reception. A picture represents each part of the day; this helps the children to understand the daily routines.
- It is important that that we teach the young people to become more organised and check that they have all of their belongings with them each day.

At Home

At home the children need to practise getting dressed and undressed, managing buttons on shirts and coats etc. and generally become more independent. Helping your child to get organised the night before will ensure they have everything they need for their day. It may help to create a visual/pictorial timetable at home to help your child become more organised and to think about when they need their PE kit, home learning, guided reading book etc. This could be displayed in your child's room or in a central place like the kitchen where you can both check what is needed the night before, ready for the following day. This will allow your child to become more involved in preparing for their learning and gaining independence. It is also good to remind your child, as we do in school, to check regularly that they have all of the belongings with them.

Congratulate your child's effort when you see them working hard and for showing an increased motivation with their home learning or reading. Talk to your child about how your own effort to practise and work hard at something led to success and a good feeling of achievement.

23 FEBRUARY 2018   PRIMARY NEWSLETTER   17

Sample primary BRIDGES newsletter spread

Roald Amundsen
(1872-1928)

'The difference between the impossible and the possible lies in a person's determination.'

The first expedition to reach the geographic South Pole was led by the Norwegian explorer Roald Amundsen. With single-minded determination, Amundsen set his plans and priorities on winning the race to the South Pole. Amundsen and four others arrived at the pole on 14 December 1911, five weeks ahead of a British party led by Robert Falcon Scott. Both Amundsen and Scott's team were determined to be the first to the South Pole, battling temperatures of -56 °C. Eventually Amundsen party's mastery of the use of skis and their expertise with sledge dogs ensured more rapid travel and they beat Scott by 34 days. Amundsen and his team returned safely to their base, and later learned that Scott and his four companions had died on their return journey. However, both teams showed exceptional determination to achieve their goal.

8

DETERMINATION

What is Determination?

Having an unshakable belief that you will reach your goal.

Behaviours

Ensuring that you achieve your goal, even though it may require a long time and many different approaches to complete. An absolute belief that you can achieve an understanding or skill. Concentrating on your learning, making it your only goal. Having an understanding about what is really important to you and ensuring you succeed at this learning.

TOP TIPS:

Students

- Set yourself a tough yet achievable challenge that you want to accomplish by the end of the year.
- Volunteer and stick to your volunteering commitment.
- Make a poster that you will display at home to remind you regularly to drive your determination.
- Show determination by completing a challenging reading book or practising a difficult sport or instrumental skill.
- Consider what you are determined to achieve for your future career/life.

Parents

- Discuss the targets your son/daughter has set him/herself. Refer to it regularly and support him/her in finding strategies to remain determined.
- Review your son/daughter's latest report and discuss how he/she can use determination to meet or exceed the targets in all subjects.
- Discuss with your child something you are determined to achieve in the next year/5 years.

Students who have shown great Determination in their learning:

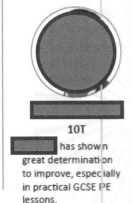

10T

has shown great determination to improve, especially in practical GCSE PE lessons.

9I

Through sheer hard work, ▮ is determined to improve his attainment in history amongst other subjects.

7E

is determined to always do the right thing.

INA BRIDGES

Sample secondary BRIDGES newsletter spread

INA primary cultural passports

At Isaac Newton Academy, we believe that cultural activities are a vital part of life and play a very important role in children's social development. The pupils will participate in a range of cultural activities organised by the academy, to enrich their lives and create great memories. Some cultural activities may also be completed in the children's own time outside the academy, with family and friends.

There are three cultural passports to complete during the children's time at Isaac Newton Primary Academy: one for Reception, Year 1 and Year 2; the next for Years 3 and 4; and finally one for Years 5 and 6.

Within each passport there are a range of cultural activities to complete and they are split into the following categories:

- *Outdoor and nature.*
- **Community.**
- Creative.
- <u>Global</u>.

Role of the pupils

Every pupil takes part in planned cultural activities within school. They use writing, drawings or photographs within the relevant pages of their cultural passport to recount and reflect upon their experience. The pupils present their record of the experience to their class teacher in order to receive a sticker of acknowledgement. The children are given planned lesson time to complete their record of their experience and hand it in to their class teacher. The class teacher then acknowledges with the relevant sticker. If the pupil chooses to complete the cultural activity at home, they need to record their reflections at home. The children then present this to their class teacher, either through a conversation, or the class teacher could ask the child to present to the class or group. The child then receives an acknowledgement note (e.g. Went on a family bear hunt), with the teacher's initials, date and the relevant sticker, on the back page of the cultural passport.

Role of the class teachers

At least half-termly, class teachers plan the agreed cultural experience to take place within school time. They give the children time to reflect upon the experience within the relevant pages where they can write, draw pictures or add photos. Once the experience has been recorded, the class teacher awards each child with the relevant sticker. If a child completes a cultural activity in their own time, the class teacher reviews the child's reflections, which they would have completed at home. If the class teacher wishes, the child could present to a group or whole class. The class teacher is to record the acknowledgement of the activity on the back page of the passport, where they note the experience and add their initials, the date and the relevant experience sticker. The class teacher then updates the cultural passport tracker spreadsheet to note the completion of the experience along with the date.

Role of the year team leader

Year team leaders map out the different cultural activities to be covered over the academic year. There should be at least one covered each half-term. The year team leader will also oversee the cultural passport tracker spreadsheet, to ensure that updates are made by class teachers accordingly. This spreadsheet is kept on the shared area, as class teachers and year team leaders from different year groups will need to access the same spreadsheet as the passports span over multiple year groups.

Role of the parent

Parents are aware of the cultural experiences that are in the cultural passport for their child's phase, which will have been communicated through parent workshops and newsletters. Parents encourage their child to carry out cultural experiences at home linked to the passport. If a cultural experience listed in the passport is carried out in the child's own time – out of school – parents support their child in recording their experience in words, diagrams, drawings, labels and/or photographs, and rehearse how they will present their evidence to their class teacher/class. Parents are informed of the presentation and recording system of activities carried out at home, and of those activities that are carried out in school. Parents are also informed that there are planned opportunities for the children to have their listed cultural experiences during school time, therefore discouraging the idea that every experience needs to be covered and recorded outside of school time.

The tables that follow list the activities that will be covered in each academic year.

Term	Reception	Year 1	Year 2
Autumn 1	**Go on a bear hunt.** Eat an exotic fruit or vegetable.	*Grow and care for a plant from a seed. Create some wild art.*	**Promote healthy eating.**
Autumn 2	**Take part in a traditional celebration.**	*Go for a boat ride.*	Visit a pantomime.
Spring 1	*Make a mud pie.*	Design and make a game or toy.	**Donate to a charity.**
Spring 2	*'Grow' and release a butterfly.*	Meet and put questions to an author.	Learn to play a musical instrument. **Take part in a charity event.**
Summer 1	**Have a picnic.**	*Create a minibeast house.*	**Visit a library.**
Summer 2	*Visit a farm.*	Visit a museum.	*Build a sandcastle. Collect shells on a beach.*
When appropriate over the year		Perform in a class assembly.	

Key: • *Outdoor and nature*   • **Community**   • Creative   • Global

Term	Year 3	Year 4
Autumn 1	*Hunt for fossils and bones.* *Hold a scary beast.*	Create big art.
Autumn 2	**Help to prepare for a traditional family celebration.**	*Go pond dipping.* Communicate in a language other than English.
Spring 1	Play a song on a musical instrument.	Build and float a model boat.
Spring 2	Invent something. Have a pen pal in a different country.	*Fly a kite.* Identify flags of different countries.
Summer 1	**Volunteer.** *Build a den.*	*Climb a tree.* Visit an art gallery.
Summer 2	Read a classic novel. **Join a library.** **Learn to ride a bike.**	**Make a meal for someone.** **Promote healthy living.** *Cook food you have grown yourself.*
When appropriate over the year	*Learn to swim.*	Perform in an event across the academy.

Key: • *Outdoor and nature* • **Community** • Creative • Global

Term	Year 5	Year 6
Autumn 1	Publish your own work.	Go to a ballet or an opera.
Autumn 2	Design and write a computer program.	Bake a cake.
Spring 1	Read a classic novel.	Learn and perform a circus skill.
Spring 2	Feed and care for an animal.	Create 3D art and have it displayed.
Summer 1	Catch a fish in a net. Build a raft. Find your way with a map and a compass. Cook a hot meal for a group of people.	Visit an unusual geographical feature.
Summer 2	Organise a charity event. Promote a safe and healthy lifestyle.	Go rock pooling. Climb a huge hill. Find a geocache.
When appropriate over the year	Represent a sporting team. Perform on stage outside of school.	Travel abroad. Request food in a shop abroad.

Key: • *Outdoor and nature*   • Community   • Creative   • Global

Bibliography

Agarwal, P. (2020). *Sway: Unravelling Unconscious Bias* (London: Bloomsbury).

Alexander, R. J. (2018). 'Developing dialogue: genesis, process, trial', *Research Papers in Education*, 33(5): 361–398. Available at: http://robinalexander.org.uk/wp-content/uploads/2019/12/RPIE-2018-Alexander-dialogic-teaching.pdf.

Allen, B. (2020). 'Parental load theory', *Becky Allen: Musings on Education Policy* [blog] (29 April). Available at: https://rebeccaallen.co.uk/2020/04/29/parental-load-theory.

All-Party Parliamentary Group on Social Mobility (2017). *The Class Ceiling: Increasing Access to the Leading Professions* (January). Available at: https://www.suttontrust.com/wp-content/uploads/2019/12/APPG-on-Social-Mobility_Report_FINAL.pdf.

Andrew, A., Cattan, S., Costa Dias, M., Farquharson, C., Kraftman, L., Krutikova, S., Phimister, A. and Sevilla, A. (2020). 'Educational gaps are growing during lockdown', *Institute of Fiscal Studies* [press release] (18 May). Available at: https://www.ifs.org.uk/publications/14849.

Association of School and College Leaders (2019). *The Forgotten Third: Final Report of the Commission of Inquiry* (Oxford: Oxford University Press). Available at: https://www.ascl.org.uk/ASCL/media/ASCL/Our%20view/Campaigns/The-Forgotten-Third_full-report.pdf.

Association of School and College Leaders (2020). 'ASCL team webinar: September reopening of schools – what will our disadvantaged children need?' (24 June). Available at: https://vimeo.com/432158429.

Baars, S., Shaw, B., Mulcahy E. and Menzies, L. (2018). School Cultures and Practices: Supporting the Attainment of Disadvantaged Pupils – a Qualitative Comparison of London and Non-London Schools. Research Report (May). Available at: https://assets.publishing.service.gov.uk/government/uploads/system/uploads/attachment_data/file/730628/London_Effect_Qual_Research_-_Research_Report_FINAL_v2.pdf.

BBC News (2020). 'Covid: UK "faces period of destitution", warns Louise Casey' (5 October). Available at: https://www.bbc.co.uk/news/uk-politics-54545158.

BBC News (2021). 'Covid: Disabled people account for six in 10 deaths in England last year – ONS' (12 February). Available at: https://www.bbc.co.uk/news/uk-56033813.

Bercow, J. and Department for Children, Schools and Families (2008). *The Bercow Report: A Review of Services for Children and Young People (0–19) with Speech, Language and Communication Needs* (Nottingham: Department for Children, Schools and Families). Available at: https://dera.ioe.ac.uk/8405.

Berlinger, W. and Eyre, D. (2017). *Great Minds and How to Grow Them* (Abingdon and New York: Routledge).

Bettinger, E. and Loeb, S. (2017). Promises and pitfalls of online education, *Evidence Speaks Reports*, 2(15). Center on Children and Families at Brookings.

Blair, C. and Raver, C. C. (2014). 'School readiness and self-regulation: A developmental psychobiological approach', *Annual Review of Psychology*, 66 DOI: 10.1146/annurev-psych-010814-015221.

Blandford, S. (2019). *Social Mobility: Chance or Choice?* (Woodbridge: John Catt Educational).

Blatchford, R. (2019). *The Three Minute Leader* (Woodbridge: John Catt Educational).

Boaler, J. (2009). *The Elephant in the Classroom: Helping Children to Learn to Love Maths* (London: Souvenir Press).

Brighouse, T. and Woods, D. (2008). *What Makes a Good School Now?* (London: Network Continuum).

Brown, M. (2018). 'Michelle Obama tells London school she still has impostor syndrome', *The Guardian* (3 December). Available at: https://www.theguardian.com/us-news/2018/dec/03/michelle-obama-tells-london-school-she-still-has-imposter-syndrome.

Carpenter, B. and Carpenter, M. (2020). 'A recovery curriculum: loss and life for our children and schools post pandemic', *Evidence for Learning* [blog] (1 May). Available at: https://www.evidenceforlearning.net/recoverycurriculum.

Carpenter, R. (2018). *A Manifesto for Excellence in Schools* (London: Bloomsbury).

Carr, J. (2020). 'We fear next summer's exams, say lockdown heads', *Schools Week* (22 October). Available at: https://schoolsweek.co.uk/we-fear-next-summers-exams-say-lockdown-heads/amp/.

Carr, J. (2021). 'Holding back of exceptionally low attendance data frustrating, say EPI', *Schools Week* (14 January). Available at: https://schoolsweek.co.uk/holding-back-of-exceptionally-low-attendance-data-frustrating-say-epi/amp/.

Central Advisory Council for Education (1963). *Half Our Future: A Report of the Central Advisory Council for Education (England)* [Newsom Report] (London: Her Majesty's Stationery Office). Available at: http://www.educationengland.org.uk/documents/newsom/newsom1963.html.

Children's Commissioner (2020). *Briefing: Tackling the Disadvantage Gap During the Covid-19 Crisis* (22 April). Available at: https://www.childrenscommissioner.gov.uk/report/tackling-the-disadvantage-gap-during-the-covid-19-crisis.

Clark, A. (2003). *Natural-Born Cyborgs: Minds, Technologies, and the Future of Human Intelligence* (Oxford: Oxford University Press).

Claxton, G. (2018). *The Learning Power Approach: Teaching Learners to Teach Themselves* (Carmarthen: Crown House Publishing).

Claxton, G. (2020). 'Knowledge and skills: how you can achieve both in your school', *SecEd* (30 June). Available at: https://www.sec-ed.co.uk/best-practice/knowledge-and-skills-how-you-can-achieve-both-in-your-school-guy-claxton-education.

Claxton, G. and Carlzon, B. (2019). *Powering Up Children: The Learning Power Approach to Primary Teaching* (Carmarthen: Crown House Publishing).

Claxton, G. and Powell, G. (2019). *Powering Up Students: The Learning Power Approach to High School Teaching* (Carmarthen: Crown House Publishing).

Claxton, G., Robinson, J., Macfarlane, R., Powell, G., Goldenberg, G. and Cleary, R. (2020). *Powering Up Your School: The Learning Power Approach to School Leadership* (Carmarthen: Crown House Publishing).

Coughlan, S. (2019). 'PISA tests: UK rises in international school rankings', *BBC News* (3 December). Available at: https://www.bbc.co.uk/news/education-50563833.

Covey, S. M. R. (2006). *The Speed of Trust: The One Thing That Changes Everything* (London: Simon & Schuster).

Cullinane, C. and Montacute, R. (2020). 'COVID-19 and Social Mobility. Impact Brief #1: School Closures' (April). Available at: https://www.suttontrust.com/our-research/covid-19-and-social-mobility-impact-brief.

DeFraites, R. (1999). People, work, leadership, and effective organizations, *The Sentinel*, 21(6): 3–4.

Denning, S. (2007). *The Secret Language of Leadership: How Leaders Inspire Action Through Narrative* (San Francisco, CA: Jossey-Bass).

Department for Education (2017). *Statutory Framework for the Early Years Foundation Stage: Setting the Standards for Learning, Development and Care for Children from Birth to Five.* Ref: DFE-00169-2017. Available at: https://assets.publishing.service.gov.uk/government/uploads/system/uploads/attachment_data/file/596629/EYFS_STATUTORY_FRAMEWORK_2017.pdf.

Department for Education (2020a). 'Attendance in education and early years settings during the coronavirus (COVID-19) outbreak – week 42 2020' (20 October). Available at: https://explore-education-statistics.service.gov.uk/find-statistics/attendance-in-education-and-early-years-settings-during-the-coronavirus-covid-19-outbreak/2020-week-42.

Department for Education (2020b). 'Early years support package to help close Covid language gap' (24 August). Available at: https://www.gov.uk/government/news/early-years-support-package-to-help-close-covid-language-gap.

Dickens, J. (2020a). '100k more laptops for schools – but access is slashed', *Schools Week* (23 October). Available at: https://schoolsweek.co.uk/100k-more-laptops-for-schools-but-access-is-slashed/amp.

Dickens, J. (2020b). '£140m of tuition catch-up cash remains unspent', *Schools Week* (16 October). Available at: https://schoolsweek.co.uk/140-million-dfe-national-tutoring-programme-funding-remains-unspent/amp.

Dickens, J. (2020c). 'Badly targeted £80 per-pupil catch-up cash "unlikely" to stop learning gap widening', *Schools Week* (20 July). Available at: https://schoolsweek.co.uk/badly-targeted-80-per-pupil-catch-up-cash-unlikely-to-prevent-widening-of-learning-gap.

Dickens, J. (2020d). 'The cost of lockdown: attainment gap widens by up to 52% for primary pupils', *Schools Week* (24 July). Available at: https://schoolsweek.co.uk/the-cost-of-lockdown-attainment-gap-widens-by-up-to-52-for-primary-pupils.

Donahoo, D. (2013). 'The evolution of parent-school engagement', *HuffPost* [blog] (18 June). Available at: https://www.huffpost.com/entry/the-evolution-of-parentsc_b_3451576.

Drucker, P. (1995). *Managing in a Time of Great Change* (Oxford: Butterworth Heinemann).

Dweck, C. S. (2006). *Mindset: The New Psychology of Success* (New York: Ballantine).

Edkins, L. (2019). 'How to "poverty proof" your school', *TES* (25 October). Available at: https://www.tes.com/magazine/article/how-poverty-proof-your-school.

Education Endowment Foundation (2018). *The Attainment Gap: 2017.* Available at: https://educationendowmentfoundation.org.uk/public/files/Annual_Reports/EEF_Attainment_Gap_Report_2018_-_print.pdf.

Education Endowment Foundation (2019). *The EEF Guide to the Pupil Premium.* Available at: https://educationendowmentfoundation.org.uk/evidence-summaries/pupil-premium-guide.

Education Endowment Foundation (2020a). *Covid-19 Support Guide for Schools.* Available at: https://educationendowmentfoundation.org.uk/covid-19-resources/national-tutoring-programme/covid-19-support-guide-for-schools.

Education Endowment Foundation (2020b). *The EEF Guide to Supporting School Planning: A Tiered Approach to 2021.* Available at: https://educationendowmentfoundation.org.uk/covid-19-resources/guide-to-supporting-schools-planning.

Education Endowment Foundation (2020c). *Remote Learning, Rapid Evidence Assessment.* Available at: https://educationendowmentfoundation.org.uk/public/files/Publications/

Covid-19_Resources/Remote_learning_evidence_review/Remote_Learning_Rapid_ Evidence_Assessment.pdf.

Elliot Major, L. (2015). 'Creating cultural capital', *Sutton Trust* (18 March). Available at: https:// www.suttontrust.com/news-opinion/all-news-opinion/creating-cultural-capital.

Eyre, D. (2016). *High Performance Learning: How to Become a World Class School* (Abingdon and New York: Routledge).

Farthing, R. (2014). *The Costs of Going to School, from Young People's Perspectives* (London: Child Poverty Action Group). Available at: https://cpag.org.uk/sites/default/files/The%20 Costs%20of%20Going%20to%20School%20FINAL.pdf.

Feinstein, L. (2003). 'Inequality in the early cognitive development of British children in the 1970 cohort', *Economica*, 70(277): 73–97.

Freedman, S. (2021). 'Myths about poverty must be refuted so that parents on benefits will be trusted with £20 and not half a pepper', *The House* (14 January) Available at: https:// www.politicshome.com/thehouse/article/myths-about-poverty-must-be-refuted-so-that- parents-on-benefits-will-be-trusted-with-20-and-not-half-a-pepper.

Friedman, M. (1982). *Capitalism and Freedom* (Chicago: University of Chicago Press).

Gadsby, B. (2017). *Impossible? Social Mobility and the Seemingly Impossible Glass Ceiling* (London: Teach First). Available at: https://www.teachfirst.org.uk/sites/default/ files/2017-08/Teach-First-Impossible-Policy-Report.pdf.

George, M. (2019). 'Exclusive: data reveals poor pupils' Xmas jumper shame', *TES* (31 May). Available at: https://www.tes.com/news/exclusive-data-reveals-poor-pupils-xmas-jumper- shame.

Gibbons, P. (2015). *Scaffolding Language, Scaffolding Learning: Teaching English Language Learners in the Mainstream Classroom*, 2nd edn (Portsmouth, NH: Heinemann).

Gilbert, I. (2007). *The Little Book of Thunks* (Carmarthen: Crown House Publishing).

Goodall, J. (2017a). *Narrowing the Achievement Gap: Parental Engagement with Children's Learning* (Abingdon and New York: Routledge).

Goodall, J. (2017b). *Report on the Pilot of a Toolkit for Parental Engagement: From Project to Process* (Bath: University of Bath). Available at: http://oga4schoolgovernors.org.uk/ wp-content/uploads/2017/11/Report-on-the-Pilot-of-a-Toolkit-for-Parental-Engagement- final_.pdf.

Grenier, J. (2020). 'What makes the biggest difference to a child's success in early learning?' *The Education Exchange*. Available at: https://theeducation.exchange/what-makes-the- biggest-difference-to-a-childs-success-in-early-learning/.

Hallam, S. (2002). *Ability Grouping in Schools: A Literature Review* (Perspectives on Education Policy 13) (London: Institute of Education).

Hallam, S. and Parsons, S. (2013). 'Prevalence of streaming in UK primary schools: evidence from the Millennium Cohort Study', *British Educational Research Journal*, 39(3): 514–544.

Halliday, J. (2020). 'Decade of progress in tackling pupil disadvantage "wiped out"', *The Guardian* (3 June). Available at: https://www.theguardian.com/education/2020/jun/03/ decade-of-progress-tackling-uk-pupil-disadvantage-wiped-out-coronavirus-school- closures.

Hansard (2020). 'Oral answers to questions. Volume 682: Debated on Monday 12 October 2020'. Available at: https://hansard.parliament.uk/commons/2020-10-12/debates/ E37926F4-C4A9-4BC9-9C39-E80DC6C87B10/OralAnswersToQuestions.

Hardy, E. (2020). 'Unlike government, education can talk its way out of a crisis', *Schools Week* (25 October). Available at: https://schoolsweek.co.uk/unlike-government-education-can-talk-its-way-out-of-a-crisis/amp.

Harrison, N. and Waller, R. (2019). 'A lack of aspiration is not the problem', *WONKHE* [blog] (11 January). Available at: https://wonkhe.com/blogs/a-lack-of-aspiration-is-not-the-problem.

Hart, B. and Risley, T. (2003). 'The early catastrophe: the 30 million word gap by age 3', *American Educator* (spring): 4–9. Available at: https://www.aft.org/sites/default/files/periodicals/TheEarlyCatastrophe.pdf.

Hattie, J. (2008). *Visible Learning: A Synthesis of Over 800 Meta-Analyses Relating to Achievement* (Abingdon and New York: Routledge).

Hattie, J. (2012). *Visible Learning for Teachers: Maximizing Impact on Learning* (Abingdon and New York: Routledge).

Hattie, J. (2020). 'Visible learning effect sizes when schools are closed: what matters and what does not', *Corwin Connect* (14 April). Available at: https://corwin-connect.com/2020/04/visible-learning-effect-sizes-when-schools-are-closed-what-matters-and-what-does-not.

Hendry, H. and Nicholson, P. (2020). 'How I identified EYFS transition challenges', *TES* (4 September). Available at: https://www.tes.com/magazine/article/how-i-identified-eyfs-transition-challenges.

Herts for Learning (2014). *Pupil Premium in Hertfordshire: Use and Impact* (Stevenage: Herts for Learning).

Hetherington, G. (2020). '1.6 million households worried about payments over winter as mortgage holiday scheme closes', *Joseph Rowntree Foundation* (31 October) [press release]. Available at: https://www.jrf.org.uk/press/one-point-six-million-households-worried-about-payments-over-winter-mortgage-holiday-scheme-closes.

Hines, B. (1968). *A Kestrel for a Knave* (Harmondsworth: Penguin).

Hobbs, G. and Vignoles, A. (2010). 'Is children's free school meal "eligibility" a good proxy for family income?', *British Educational Research Journal*, 36(4): 673–690. Available at: https://www.researchgate.net/publication/233367573_Is_Children's_Free_School_Meal_Eligibility_a_Good_Proxy_for_Family_Income.

Holt-White, E. (2021). 'Different lockdown, same problems?' *Sutton Trust* (7 January). Available at: https://www.suttontrust.com/news-opinion/all-news-opinion/different-lockdown-same-problems/.

Hurst, N. (2017). 'Students more likely to succeed if teachers have positive perceptions of parents', *PHYSORG* (21 February) [press release]. Available at: https://phys.org/news/2017-02-students-teachers-positive-perceptions-parents.html.

Hutchinson, J., Johnes, R., Sellen, P., Perera, N., Mao, L. and Treadaway, M. (2016). *Education in England: Annual Report 2016*. Available at: https://epi.org.uk/publications-and-research/education-england-annual-report-2016.

Hutchinson, J., Bonetti, S., Crenna-Jennings, W. and Akhal, A. (2019). *Education in England: Annual Report 2019* (London: Education Policy Institute). Available at: https://epi.org.uk/publications-and-research/annual-report-2019/.

Hutchinson, J., Reader, M. and Akhal, A. (2020). *Education in England: Annual Report 2020* (London: Education Policy Institute). Available at: https://epi.org.uk/wp-content/uploads/2020/09/EPI_2020_Annual_Report_.pdf.

Hyman, P. (2020). 'Helping every child find their voice'. In. R. Blatchford (ed.), *The Forgotten Third: Do a Third Have to Fail for Two Thirds to Pass?* (Woodbridge: John Catt Educational), pp. 115–122.

Johnes, R. and Hutchinson, J. (2016). *Widening the Gap? The Impact of the 30-Hour Entitlement on Early Years Education and Childcare* (London: Education Policy Institute). Available at: https://epi.org.uk/wp-content/uploads/2018/01/widening-the-gap-final-epi.pdf.

Kegan, R. and Lahey, L. L. (2016). *An Everyone Culture: Becoming a Deliberately Developmental Organisation* (Boston, MA: Harvard Business Review Press).

Langer, E. (1989). *Mindfulness* (Reading, MA: Da Capo Press).

Lemov, D. (2010). *Teach Like a Champion: 49 Techniques That Put Students on the Path to College* (San Francisco, CA: Jossey-Bass).

Lucas, B. and Claxton, G. (2010). *New Kinds of Smart: How the Science of Learnable Intelligence Is Changing Education* (Maidenhead: Open University Press).

McBeath, A. (2003). *Choice, Accountability, and Performance in the Public Schools: How Edmonton Does It and Why It Works.* Address to the Atlantic Institute for Market Studies, Halifax, Nova Scotia (11 July). Available at: https://www.aims.ca/wp-content/uploads/2016/06/ChoiceAccountabilityandPerformanceEventNotes.pdf.

McGowan, M. (2018). '"Remember to look up at the stars": the best Stephen Hawking quotes', *The Guardian* (14 March). Available at: https://www.theguardian.com/science/2018/mar/14/best-stephen-hawking-quotes-quotations.

Mackesy, C. (2019). *The Boy, the Mole, the Fox and the Horse* (London: Penguin).

Mann, H. (1872). *Thoughts Selected from the Writings of Horace Mann* (Boston: Lee and Shepard, Publishers).

Mannion, J. and Mercer, N. (2016). 'Learning to learn: improving attainment, closing the gap at Key Stage 3', *Curriculum Journal*, 27(2): 246–271. Available at: https://rethinking-ed.org/wp-content/uploads/2016/11/Learning-to-learn-improving-attainment-closing-the-gap-at-Key-Stage-3.pdf.

Mazzoli Smith, L. and Todd, L. (2019). 'Conceptualising poverty as a barrier to learning through "poverty proofing" the school day: the genesis and impacts of stigmatisation', *British Educational Research Journal*, 45(2): 356–371.

Millard, W. and Gaunt, A. (2018). 'Speaking up: the importance of oracy in teaching and learning', *Impact* (May). Available at: https://impact.chartered.college/article/millard-importance-of-oracy-in-teaching-learning.

Ministry of Housing, Communities and Local Government (2021). Statutory Homelessness July to September (Q3) 2020 (Revised): England [experimental statistics release] (28 January). Available at: https://assets.publishing.service.gov.uk/government/uploads/system/uploads/attachment_data/file/957573/Statutory_homelessness_release_Jul-Sep_2020_REVISED.pdf.

Montacute, R. (2020). *Social Mobility and Covid-19: Implications of the Covid-19 Crisis for Educational Inequality* (April). Available at: https://www.suttontrust.com/wp-content/uploads/2020/04/COVID-19-and-Social-Mobility-1.pdf.

Müller, L. and Goldenberg, G. (2020). *Education in Times of Crisis: Teachers' Views on Distance Learning and School Reopening Plans During COVID-19: Analysis of Responses from an Online Survey and Focus Groups* (London: Chartered College of Teaching). Available at: https://my.chartered.college/wp-content/uploads/2020/07/EducationInTimesOfCrisisII_FINAL20200708.pdf.

Munby, S. (2019). *Imperfect Leadership: A Book for Leaders Who Know They Don't Know It All* (Carmarthen: Crown House Publishing).

NASUWT (2014). *The Cost of Education* (Birmingham: NASUWT). Available at: http://www.conservativehome.com/wp-content/uploads/2016/12/Cost-of-Education-2014-BIG-SPEECH-BUBBLE-1.pdf.

Nicholls, D. (2020). 'Urgent action required – addressing disadvantage', *Dan Nicholls* [blog] (5 April). Available at: https://dannicholls1.wordpress.com/2020/04/05/urgent-action-required-addressing-disadvantage.

Office for National Statistics (2020a). Coronavirus and homeschooling in Great Britain: April to June 2020 [statistical release] (22 July). Available at: https://www.ons.gov.uk/peoplepopulationandcommunity/educationandchildcare/articles/coronavirusandhomeschoolingingreatbritain/apriltojune2020.

Office for National Statistics (2020b). Deaths involving COVID-19 by local area and socioeconomic deprivation: deaths occurring between 1 March and 30 June 2020 [statistical release] (24 July). Available at: https://www.ons.gov.uk/peoplepopulationandcommunity/birthsdeathsandmarriages/deaths/bulletins/deathsinvolvingcovid19bylocalareasanddeprivation/deathsoccurringbetween1marchand30june2020.

Office for National Statistics (2021a). Labour market overview, UK: January 2021 [statistical release] (26 January). Available at: https://www.ons.gov.uk/employmentandlabourmarket/peopleinwork/employmentandemployeetypes/bulletins/uklabourmarket/january2021.

Office for National Statistics (2021b). Updated estimates of coronavirus (COVID-19) related deaths by disability status, England: 24 January to 20 November 2020 [statistical release] (11 February). Available at: https://www.ons.gov.uk/peoplepopulationandcommunity/birthsdeathsandmarriages/deaths/articles/coronaviruscovid19relateddeathsbydisabilitystatusenglandandwales/24januaryto20november2020.

Ofsted (2018). Inspection report: Ark Isaac Newton Academy, 2–3 October. Available at: https://files.ofsted.gov.uk/v1/file/50036486.

Ofsted (2019a). *Education Inspection Framework*. REF: 190015 (May). Available at: https://www.gov.uk/government/publications/education-inspection-framework.

Ofsted (2019b). *School Inspection Handbook*. REF: 190017 (November). Available at: https://assets.publishing.service.gov.uk/government/uploads/system/uploads/attachment_data/file/843108/School_inspection_handbook_-_section_5.pdf.

Pierson, R. (2013). 'Every kid needs a champion' [video], *TED.com* (3 May). Available at: https://www.ted.com/talks/rita_pierson_every_kid_needs_a_champion.

Prime Minister's Office and May, T. (2016). Statement from the new Prime Minister Theresa May [speech] (13 July). Available at: https://www.gov.uk/government/speeches/statement-from-the-new-prime-minister-theresa-may.

Public Health England (2020). *Disparities in the Risk and Outcomes of COVID-19* (London: Public Health England). Available at: https://assets.publishing.service.gov.uk/government/uploads/system/uploads/attachment_data/file/908434/Disparities_in_the_risk_and_outcomes_of_COVID_August_2020_update.pdf.

Quigley, A. and Coleman, R. (2020). *Improving Literacy in Secondary Schools: Guidance Report* (London: Education Endowment Foundation). Available at: https://educationendowmentfoundation.org.uk/tools/guidance-reports/improving-literacy-in-secondary-schools.

Quigley, A., Muijs, D. and Stringer, E. (2018). *Metacognition and Self-Regulated Learning: Guidance Report* (London: Education Endowment Foundation). Available at: https://educationendowmentfoundation.org.uk/tools/guidance-reports/metacognition-and-self-regulated-learning.

Rebello Britto, P. (2012). School Readiness: A Conceptual Framework (New York: UNICEF). Available at: https://sites.unicef.org/earlychildhood/files/Child2Child_ConceptualFramework_FINAL(1).pdf.

Reuters (2020). UK jobless claims jump by 856,000 to 2.1 million in April (19 May). Available at: https://www.reuters.com/article/health-coronavirus-britain-economy/uk-jobless-claims-jump-by-856000-to-21-million-in-april-idUKS8N2CU0EA?edition-redirect=uk.

Rice, F., Frederickson, N., Shelton, K., McManus, C., Riglin, L. and Ng-Knight, T. (2018). *Identifying Factors That Predict Successful and Difficult Transitions to Secondary School* (London: Nuffield Foundation). Available at: https://www.nuffieldfoundation.org/sites/default/files/files/STARS_report.pdf.

Robinson, K., with Aronica, L. (2008). *The Element: How Finding Your Passion Changes Everything* (London: Penguin).

Rodda, M., with Hallgarten, J. and Freeman, J. (2013). *Between the Cracks: Exploring In-Year Admissions in Schools in England* (London: RSA Action and Research Centre). Available at: https://www.thersa.org/globalassets/pdfs/reports/education-between-the-cracks-report.pdf.

Rogers, T. (2016). 'Parenting not schools has the biggest impact on student outcomes, so why are teachers blamed for results?', *TES* (15 January). Available at: https://www.tes.com/parenting-not-schools-has-biggest-impact-student-outcomes-so-why-are-teachers-blamed-results.

Rogers, T. (2017). 'It's time we came clean: the pupil premium hasn't worked. And it's unfair too', *TES* (22 April). Available at: https://www.tes.com/news/its-time-we-came-clean-pupil-premium-hasnt-worked-and-its-unfair-too.

Rose, J. (2006). *Independent Review of the Teaching of Early Reading* [Rose Report]. (Nottingham: Department for Education and Skills). Available at: https://dera.ioe.ac.uk/5551/2/report.pdf.

Rosenthal, R. and Jacobson, L. (1968). *Pygmalion in the Classroom: Teacher Expectation and Pupils' Intellectual Development* (New York: Holt, Rinehart & Winston).

Roser, M., Ritchie, H. and Dadonaite, B. (2013). 'Child and infant mortality', *OurWorldInData.org*. Available at: https://ourworldindata.org/child-mortality#.

Rowland, M. (2020). 'Improving outcomes for disadvantaged and vulnerable learners', *Challenge Partners* [blog] (20 April). Available at: https://www.challengepartners.org/news/canaries-down-coalmine-what-next-pupil-premium-strategy.

Schleicher, A. (2019). PISA 2018: Insights and Interpretations (Paris: OECD). Available at: https://www.oecd.org/pisa/PISA%202018%20Insights%20and%20Interpretations%20FINAL%20PDF.pdf.

Seligman, M. (1991). *Learned Optimism: How to Change Your Mind and Your Life* (New York: Random House).

Sharma, R. (2020). UK records 819,000 job losses since start of pandemic with hospitality worst hit sector, *iNews* (15 December). Available at: https://inews.co.uk/news/business/uk-unemployment-record-high-covid-19-pandemic-job-redundancies-795295.

Sharples, J., Albers, B., Fraser, S. and Kime, S. (2018). *Putting Evidence to Work: A School's Guide to Implementation – Guidance Report* (London: Education Endowment

Foundation). Available at: https://educationendowmentfoundation.org.uk/public/files/ Publications/Implementation/EEF_Implementation_Guidance_Report_2019.pdf.

Sobel, D. (2018). *Narrowing the Attainment Gap: A Handbook for Schools* (London: Bloomsbury).

Social Mobility and Child Poverty Commission (2014). *State of the Nation 2014: Social Mobility and Child Poverty in Great Britain*. Available at: https://www.gov.uk/government/ publications/state-of-the-nation-2014-report.

Spencer, S. (2015). *The Cost of the School Day* (Glasgow: Child Poverty Action Group). Available at: https://cpag.org.uk/sites/default/files/CPAG-Scot-Cost-Of-School-Day-Report(Oct15)_0.pdf.

Starkey-Midha, G. (2020). *Building a Fairer Future: Tackling the Attainment Gap in GCSE English and Maths* (London: Teach First). Available at: https://www.teachfirst.org.uk/sites/ default/files/2020-08/GCSE%20report%20-%20Building%20a%20fairer%20future.pdf.

Stewart, K. and Waldfogel, J. (2017). *Closing Gaps Early: The Role of Early Years Policy in Promoting Social Mobility in England* (September) (London: Sutton Trust). Available at: https://www.suttontrust.com/our-research/closing-gaps-early-parenting-policy-childcare.

Sutton Trust (2011). *Improving the Impact of Teachers on Pupil Achievement in the UK – Interim Findings* (September). Available at: https://www.suttontrust.com/our-research/ improving-impact-teachers-pupil-achievement-uk-interim-findings.

Sutton Trust (2012). *Social Mobility and Education Gaps in the Four Major Anglophone Countries: Research Findings for the Social Mobility Summit, London, May 2012*. Available at: https://www.suttontrust.com/our-research/social-mobility-education-gaps-four-major-anglophone-countries-research-findings-social-mobility-summit-london-2012.

Sutton Trust (2020). 'Most parents don't feel confident about teaching their child' (10 April) [press release]. Available at: http://www.suttontrust.com/news-opinion/all-news-opinion/ parent-polling-release.

Sutton Trust (2021). 'Sutton Trust research finds the digital divide has not improved since March', *FE news.co.uk* (12 January) [press release]. Available at: https://www.fenews.co.uk/ press-releases/61482-sutton-trust-research-finds-the-digital-divide-has-not-improved-since-march.

Syed, M. (2010). *Bounce: The Myth of Talent and the Power of Practice* (London: Fourth Estate).

Trussell Trust (2020). 2,600 food parcels provided for children every day in first six months of the pandemic [press release] (12 November). Available at: https://www.trusselltrust.org/ 2020/11/12/2600-food-parcels-provided-for-children-every-day-in-first-six-months-of-the-pandemic/.

van Poortvliet, M., Axford, N. and Lloyd, J. (2018). *Working with Parents to Support Children's Learning: Guidance Report* (London: Education Endowment Foundation). Available at: https://educationendowmentfoundation.org.uk/tools/guidance-reports/working-with-parents-to-support-childrens-learning.

Ward, H. (2018). 'Early years policy set for "car crash" – EEF chief', *TES* (12 June). Available at: https://www.tes.com/news/early-years-policy-set-car-crash-eef-chief.

Webster, R. (2020). 'Beware the intervention trap', *TES* (11 September). Available at: https:// www.tes.com/magazine/article/covid-19-catch-beware-intervention-traps.

Whittaker, F. (2020). 'Attendance gap between local authority areas has widened, new data shows', *Schools Week* (15 December). Available at: https://schoolsweek.co.uk/ attendance-gap-between-local-authority-areas-has-widened-new-data-shows/amp/.

Whittaker, F. and Booth, S. (2020). 'Coronavirus: attainment gap could widen by 75%, DfE official warns', *Schools Week* (16 May). Available at: https://schoolsweek.co.uk/coronavirus-attainment-gap-could-widen-by-75-dfe-official-warns/.

Wiliam, D. (2018). *Creating the Schools Our Children Need: Why What We're Doing Now Won't Help Much (And What We Can Do Instead)* (West Palm Beach, FL: Learning Sciences International).

Wilson, M. (2020). 'The coronavirus will widen the education gap in the UK', *Al Jazeera* (12 April). Available at: https://www.aljazeera.com/opinions/2020/4/12/the-coronavirus-will-widen-the-education-gap-in-the-UK.

Wittgenstein, L. (2001 [1922]). *Tractatus Logico-Philosophicus*, tr. D. F. Pears and B. F. McGuinness (London and New York: Routledge Classics).

Woods, D., Macfarlane, R. and McBeath, D. (2018). *The Nine Pillars of Great Schools* (Woodbridge: John Catt Educational).